Law and Faith in a Sceptical Age

Law and Faith in a Sceptical Age is an analysis of the legal position of religious believers in a dominantly secular society.

Great Britain is a society based upon broadly liberal principles. It claims to recognise the needs of religious believers and to protect them from discrimination. But while its secular ideology pervades public discourse, the vestigial remains of a Christian, Protestant past are seen in things as varied as the structure of public holidays and the continued existence of established churches in both England and Scotland. Religious, Christian values also form the starting point for legal rules relating to matters such as marriage. Active religious communities constitute a very small minority of the population; however, those who belong to them often see their religion as being the most important element of their identity. Yet the world-view of these communities is frequently at odds with both the prevailing liberal, secular climate of Great Britain and its Christian, Anglican past.

This necessarily entails a clash of ideologies that puts in question the secular majority's claim to want to protect religious minorities, the possibility of it being able to sufficiently understand the needs of those minorities and the desirability or practicality of any accommodation between the needs of the various religious communities and the secular mainstream of society.

Law and Faith in a Sceptical Age addresses these issues by raising the question of whether a liberal, secular state can protect religion. Accommodation to different religious traditions forms part of the history of the legal systems of Britain. This book asks whether further accommodation can and should be made.

Anthony Bradney is Professor of Law at Keele University.

Law and Faith in a Sceptical Age

Anthony Bradney

Routledge·Cavendish
Taylor & Francis Group
a GlassHouse book

First published 2009
by Routledge-Cavendish
2 Park Square, Milton Park, Abingdon, Oxon, OX14 4RN

Simultaneously published in the USA and Canada
by Routledge-Cavendish
270 Madison Ave, New York, NY 10016

A GlassHouse Book

Routledge-Cavendish is an imprint of the Taylor & Francis Group,
an informa business

Typeset in Times by
RefineCatch Limited, Bungay, Suffolk
Printed and bound in Great Britain by
TJ International Ltd, Padstow, Cornwall

British Library Cataloguing in Publication Data
A catalogue record for this book is available from the British Library

Library of Congress Cataloging-in-Publication Data
Bradney, Anthony.
  Law and faith in a sceptical age / Anthony Bradney.
    p. cm.
  1. Discrimination—Religious aspects. 2. Discrimination—Law and
  legislation—Great Britain. 3. Religion and law—Great Britain.
  4. Church and state—Great Britain. 5. Religion and law. I. Title.
  II. Title: Law and faith in a skeptical age.
  KD4100.B72 2009
  344.41'096—dc22

                                                              2008035320

ISBN 10: 1-904385-73-7 (hbk)
ISBN 13: 978-1-904385-73-8 (hbk)

ISBN 10: 0-203-88215-6 (ebk)
ISBN 13: 978-0-203-88215-3 (ebk)

Contents

Introduction

The first premise for this book is that in the twenty-first century Great Britain is a largely secular society that is sceptical of organised religion. This is truer for England than it is for Scotland or Wales and it is truer for the cities than it is for rural areas but, at the same time, it is a general truth. Vestigial remnants of a largely Christian, Anglican past are still to be found in things such as the structure of public holidays. Some legal regimes such as family law rest partly on Christian antecedents. Nevertheless, on an everyday basis religion, understood as institutionalised structures, becomes publicly less important with each passing day. A general sense of vague individual spirituality has replaced group worship. Yet, at the same time, significant minority religious communities exist, some but not all linked to ethnic groups and some but not all relating to religions that are comparatively new to this country. For these groups, and for many individuals in these groups, their religion is the most important part of their sense of identity. The triumph of the seventeenth and eighteenth centuries was to arrive at an accommodation between different faith groups and the State that prevented civil strife. The problem for the twenty-first century will be to find a way of giving faith groups a space in which they can flourish while allowing individuals to choose and rechoose how they relate to matters of religious belief. This has to be done in the context of a public discourse that is at best indifferent to matters of faith and sometimes is actively hostile to them. Islamophobia and the aftermath of 9/11 are part of the background to the new concordat that needs to be reached; so are patriarchical, homophobic and other similar attitudes that are to be found in some religions. This book is about the contribution that law and thinking about law can make to this concordat.

The second premise for this book can be put more shortly: Great Britain is a part of a State that claims to be a liberal State. Its history of toleration and accommodation to religions is a manifestation of that liberalism. Personally, I feel that liberal theories have too weak a grasp of the radical nature of human choice (Bradney 1993, ch 2). However, for the purposes of this book I take that liberalism and that history of accommodation, including that legal history, as a given and ask how it should be further developed.

Those who write about law are not infrequently imperialistic in their claims. Law's reach is seen to be long and its power, great. I make no such claims. Law – certainly when we talk about state law – may be a small matter in people's lives, particularly when we think about people of faith. For them, their faith and the law of their faith matters more. Nevertheless, state law does make a contribution to people's lives, whether they wish it to do so or not. This book is about that contribution.

My first book on law and religion was published in 1993. Since then much has changed. Not the least of these changes has been the development of a wide range of literature in the United Kingdom on the intersection of law and religion.[1] Some of it is cited in this book. As is almost inevitable in academic life, I disagree with much of that which has been written. Nevertheless, my thinking on matters relating to law and religion has benefited greatly from that literature, whether I agree with it or not and whether I have cited it or not.

It is becoming the custom for scholars of law and religion as with sociologists of religion to state their own religious affiliation. I am somewhat dubious about the relevance of such affiliations to one's writing. However, since others find it significant, I note that from infancy I have been an atheist. My wife is a Quaker. Perhaps more relevant to this book is the fact I have lived in Leicester since I was 9. During that time I have watched Leicester change from a rather ordinary provincial city into a thriving cosmopolitan centre. Leicester is now a city where, according to the 2001 Census, Christians are in a minority (www.statistics.gov.uk/census/). It has the only Jain Centre in Europe and the largest Diwali festival outside India. Alongside Hindus, Sikhs and Muslims are a diverse range of Christian churches including Orthodox churches, Chinese Christian churches and black churches. Leicester's diversity and the fact that it can successfully accommodate so many faith traditions is one illustration of the phenomenon that this book discusses.

As always, the person who has suffered most in the writing of this book is my wife, Fiona Cownie. As always, this book is for her.

Anthony Bradney
Keele University
June 2008

---

1 One illustration of this growth in the literature in the area is the setting up of the Law and Religion Scholars Network (LARSN). To join the mail-base, email LAW-RELIGION-UK-request@jiscmail.ac.uk.

Chapter 1

Religious communities in a secular society

Introduction

This chapter concerns itself with the religious landscape of contemporary Great Britain. In the twenty-first century Great Britain is a secular society that may be in the process of becoming a cosmopolitan society.[1] Religion has become more and more a private and personal matter that occupies less and less public space.

> [O]ur churches are unpopular, their teachings are ignored by the vast majority of the population, their leaders no longer have the ears of our rulers, their efforts to glorify God are barely noticed, and their beliefs no longer inform the presuppositions of the wider culture.
>
> (Bruce 1995, p 125)[2]

Religiosity, individual religious or spiritual sentiments, still has a place,

1 This book concerns itself with Great Britain. The situation in Northern Ireland is so markedly different in matters relating to religion as to prevent meaningful generalisations that cover both Northern Ireland and Great Britain. What Davie noted in 1994, 'Northern Ireland . . . more like the Irish Republic than mainland Britain – manifests markedly higher levels of religious practice than almost all other European countries', continues to be the case (Davie 1994, p 14). In the 2001 Census, 86 per cent of the Northern Ireland population claimed a religious affiliation, much the highest of any of the constituent parts of the United Kingdom (National Statistics Online, 2007). However, for an argument that the differences between Northern Ireland and the rest of the United Kingdom have been overstated, see Mitchell 2004.
2 There are differences in the situation in Scotland and in England or Wales. However, although these differences are significant when matters of detail are concerned, the general pattern described in this chapter is true for all of Great Britain. On Scotland, see, for example, Voas 2006. On Wales, see, for example, Chambers 2005 and Chambers 2006. There are also other variations within these countries. Thus, for example, Davies, Watkins and Winter's 1991 study of the Church of England in rural England found that '[t]here is a dramatic relationship between rurality and the percentage of the population attending church on a Sunday' with rural benefices, as compared with urban benefices, having a much higher, although still low, level of attendance (Davies, Watkins and Winter 1991, p 211).

albeit usually a limited place, in the lives of the majority of the population, but belief in a religion, a commitment to an identifiable institutional structure with its own tenets and precepts that believers undertake to obey, does not.[3]

Some powerful voices continue to reject the idea that Great Britain is a secular society. Thus, for example, in 2003 the House of Lords Select Committee on Religious Offences observed that:

> religious belief continues to be a significant component, or even determinant, of social values, and plays a major role in the lives of a large number of the population. The United Kingdom is not a secular state.
>
> (Select Committee on Religious Offences 2003, p 38)[4]

It produced no evidence to substantiate its suggestion. Its assertion was perhaps grounded more in the fact that, unusually for Great Britain, many of the Committee were active in a faith rather than in any knowledge of conditions prevailing in society (Select Committee on Religious Offences 2003, p 6).[5] Nevertheless, others still take a similar stance. For Brooke LJ, in his decision in *R (on the application of Begum) v Denbigh High School Governors* ([2005] 1 WLR 3372), a case concerning the legality of a school's decision to forbid the wearing of the jilbab, the idea that Great Britain was not a secular state was an important factor in his argument, enabling him to distinguish the case before him from the European Court of Human Rights (ECHR)

---

3 The controversies that surround secularisation theses are not germane to arguments that are developed here. This book is neither concerned with why Great Britain has become a secular society nor when this happened. Both these questions are much debated by sociologists of religion (see, for example, Brown 2001 and Bruce 1995). More generally, this book is concerned with the situation in Great Britain and does not examine the larger questions of the place of institutionalised religion in the wider world and how 'an exclusive humanism became a live option for large numbers of people, first among elites, and then more generally' (Taylor 2007, p 222) or whether 'advanced societies – in the very nature of their being advanced – are essentially secular in their operation' (Wilson 1982, p 53). Instead, this book is simply concerned with the implications of the fact of secularisation in modern-day Great Britain. On secularisation theory in general, see Swatos, Jr and Christian 1999 and Chambers 2005, ch 2. For a rejection of the secularisation thesis, see Stark 1999.

4 State and society are not the same thing. As I note below, the state structure in Great Britain continues to have significant religious elements, not least because of the establishment of the Church of England. However, the Select Committee do not appear to have made a distinction between state and society and, when using the term state, appear to be referring to the day-to-day lives of the British population.

5 Only one member of the Committee, Baroness Massey, declared herself to have no faith. Of the remaining 11 members, two made declarations that they were ordained, two that held positions as church wardens and one that they had a Papal knighthood (Select Committee on Religious Offences 2003, p 6).

decision in *Sahin v Turkey* (41 EHRR 109) because Turkey is, under its constitution, a secular state.[6]

The notion that, in the twenty-first century, Great Britain is a secular society is not self-evident and needs to be both defended and explained. Great Britain is, after all, not a country like France where a formal separation between state and church is written into the constitutional structures of the State.[7] On the contrary, two Christian churches, the Church of England and the Church of Scotland, have settled constitutional links with the State. The Church of England is 'established according to the laws of this realm under the Queen's majesty'.[8] As Doe notes, the relationship that this creates between Church and State is 'ambiguous', in part because all '[d]octrines of establishment are notoriously difficult to construct' (Doe 1996, p 505; Doe 1998, p 13). Nonetheless, notwithstanding the difficulty of describing this relationship in detail, there clearly is a connection between the Church of England and the State that separates it out from other faiths. Equally the Church of Scotland, while not having the same legal relationship with the State as does the Church of England, does view itself, according to its own web-pages, as 'the national Church in Scotland' (Church of Scotland, nd); for some writers at least the fact that:

> in a variety of ways the Church of Scotland has official recognition and a different status from other churches ... [means that it] meet[s] the requirements of our working definition of 'establishment'.
>
> (Munroe 1996–97, p 645. See, also, Taylor 1957, p 137)

Even in Wales, where the Church of England in Wales was formally disestablished by the Welsh Church Act 1914, the Church 'continues to give the impression that we wish to remain an "established" Church' and, Watkin argues, continues to have vestigial establishment privileges in matters pertaining to marriage and burial (Brown 1993–95, p 20; Watkin 1990–92). Establishment, in various ways, is part of the constitutional structure of Great Britain.[9] More than this, important as the relationships created by various forms of establishment are, religion, institutionalised religion, regularly features in our quotidian lives. Thus, for example, religion runs through the media.[10] 'Thought for the Day', on Radio Four's 'Today' programme, is

---

6 At p 3389.
7 Law of 9th December 1905, Journal Officiel, 11th December 1905, 7205.
8 Canon A1.
9 The position of established churches in Great Britain is explored below in detail in Chapter 3.
10 Ofcom is required to produce reports on religious broadcasting. Matters it must consider include looking to see whether there are 'programmes showing acts of worship and other ceremonies and practices . . .' (s. 264(6)(g) Communications Act 2003). For Ofcom analyses of religious broadcasting, see Ofcom 2005 and Ofcom 2007, pp 92–95.

usually, although not invariably, a religious thought, finding its fount in one of the faiths now active in Great Britain, and is part of the start of many people's day.[11] The 'Daily Service' is the longest running programme on British radio (BBC 2002). 'Songs of Praise' is still broadcast on BBC1 on Sundays.[12] Bishops and Archbishops remain part of the House of Lords and other peers sometimes speak on behalf of religions of which they are a part, sometimes a prominent part.[13] Several million parents send their children to faith schools.[14] The structure of the week still reflects the beliefs of the dominant religion within Great Britain. Although the Sunday Trading Act 1994 repealed the Shops Act 1950, there continues, under the new legislation, to be some restrictions on trading on Sunday.[15] Public bank holidays often, although not invariably, reflect the same Christian religious traditions.[16] Religions in these and many other ways regularly feature in the public life of society. It is thus pertinent to ask in what sense, then, is Great Britain secular?

A secular society

In the 2001 census for Great Britain, 71.8 per cent of those who responded to the question on religious identity described themselves as being Christian

11 How many people take serious note of these broadcasts is another matter. Bruce cites 1987 figures that suggest that only 23 per cent of those who attend a religious meeting place less often than once a month and only 13 per cent of those who never attend a place of religious worship pay attention to a religious programme when it comes on television (Bruce 2002, p 322).

12 The BBC's own figures suggest that 'Songs of Praise' had viewing figures of 3.5 million people in 2003/2004 (Impartiality Review 2004).

13 The Wakeham Report of the future of the House of Lords concluded that the Church of England should continue to be represented in the House of Lords, albeit with 16 rather than 26 representatives, but that there should also be specific representation for Christian churches other than the Church of England and also for other faith groups (Wakeham 2000, ch 15).

14 In England in 2004 there were 1,175,520 FTEs in state maintained faith primary schools; 9,090 FTEs were in non-Christian schools (Statistics of Education 2004, p 48). In the same year there were 511,860 FTEs in state maintained secondary schools of which 6,430 FTEs were in non-Christian schools (Statistics of Education 2004, p 48). The State provided some degree of direct support for 6,311 faith primary schools of which 32 were not Christian and 589 faith secondary schools of which 8 were not Christian (Statistics for Education 2004, p 47). In addition to this there are many schools in the independent sector that are faith based.

15 'Large shops' still have restricted opening hours on a Sunday (Sunday Trading Act 1994 Sched 1 para 2). Although the restrictions are considerably less than those under the 1950 Act, they might still justify Rabbi Jonathan Sacks' negative answer to his own question 'Is Britain yet a post-religious society?' because anyone visiting Britain 'would be struck by the fact that a large number of businesses stopped on Sunday and, asking why, would receive an explanation that could hardly fail to mention Christianity' (Sacks 1990, pp 4 and 5). The law may make businesses stop for less time on Sundays, but stop they still do. Moreover, in many cases they stop, even though the law does not require them to do so.

16 Bank and Financial Dealings Act 1971 Schedule 1.

(National Statistics Online).[17] The next biggest group was those who described themselves, in various ways, as having no faith; however, this group was very much smaller than those who had described themselves as Christian; 8,596,488 as against 41,014,811 people (National Statistics Online). The numbers of people who described themselves as being members of other faiths was smaller but, nevertheless, still numbered several million people.[18] Clearly the vast majority of the population in Great Britain see themselves as being religious in some way. Set against these Census figures, however, is a range of other data. Bruce, for example, notes the declining attendance figures for most of the major Christian churches, the decline in church membership, the decline in Sunday school attendance, the decline in the number of clerics and the decline in the number of baptisms (Bruce 2001). There is no doubt the majority of the British population would claim some slight sense of the numinous and would label that spirituality with a familiar religious title.[19] What is in question is whether this personal spirituality is such as to mean that they are, in any significant sense, part of a particular faith community.

By the end of the twentieth century those attending a religious service in England and Wales each week constituted only one-twelfth of the total population (Voas and Crockett 2005, p 19).[20] This fraction has to be read in the context of the fact that the level of Sunday school attendance fell to 4 per cent of the population in 2000 (Bruce 2001, p 198). When so few people attend places of religious worship or Sunday schools on a regular basis, how can they learn about the details and nuances that divide one faith from another? Still less will they know of the differences that divide even the major groups within a faith, even if they do claim that faith as their own and even if they further claim a particular form of that faith as their own. Without this knowledge, how can they in practice attach themselves to any particular community?[21]

17 For a discussion of the reasons why it was desirable to ask a question about religious affiliation, see Aspinall 2000 and Voas 2007. On the difficulties of measuring religious affiliation, see Gill 1992 and Weller 2001. On the particular problems of the 2001 Census, see Weller 2004.

18 The four largest groups were Muslims (1,588,890), Hindus (558,342), Sikhs (336,179) and Jews (267,373) (National Statistics Online). Non-Christian religious groups are not spread evenly throughout the country (Focus on Ethnicity and Religion 2006, pp 61–67).

19 Smart defines the sense of the numinous as being 'the feeling of awe, dread, mystery and fascination men experience when confronted with what is holy, uncanny, or supernatural' (Smart 1969, p 30). Notions like 'awe' and 'dread' seem to somewhat overstate the religiosity of those in Great Britain who still claim a Christian affiliation but do not attend any place of religious meeting.

20 The major Christian churches continue to report declining attendance figures. See, for example, the provisional figures for the Church of England for 2005 (*Statistics for Mission 2005*).

21 Gill argues that '[i]t is precisely because people are no longer socialised within churches or Sunday schools that they find Christian beliefs, values, and practices strange and implausible' (Gill 2002, p 337). My argument would go further and say 'precisely because people are no longer socialised within churches and Sunday schools *they would* find Christian beliefs, values, and practices strange and implausible *if they knew what they were*'. When they do find out what they are then I would agree with Gill's analysis.

As Davie notes 'belief begins to drift further and further away from Christian orthodoxies as religious practice diminishes' (Davie 1994, p 76).[22] 'Christian', in some vague sense of the word, the majority of British people may be; in reality, in the main, Catholic, Methodist or whatever, they are not. The majority of Christians in Great Britain not only do not subscribe to the particularities of religious communities within their declared faith; they have no way of knowing what those particularities are. Equally, what does the majority's self-ascription as Christian say about the way that they live their lives?

Knott has protested, in the context of a study of ethnic minority religions, about the manner of the way in which religious belief is sometimes described; 'one sometimes gets the feeling that religion is like stamp-collecting or playing squash, a minor hobby' (Knott 1986, p 4). 'Surely', write Ahdar and Leigh, 'religion is special – it is not just a hobby or recreational pursuit' (Ahdar and Leigh 2005, p 91). Plainly this criticism can sometimes be correct; for some people in Britain their religion is of central significance in their lives. For these people their religion is not simply another facet of their lives; it is their lives. Thus, for example, Jacobson describes the ways in which their Muslim faith affects the day-to-day behaviour of her informants, 'young British Pakistanis' living in the London Borough of Waltham Forest, at every level of their lives (Jacobson 1998, pp 48, 129).[23] However, in the case of the great majority of the 71.8 per cent who declared themselves as being Christian in 2001, it is not clear that their religion even reaches the status of being a minor hobby.[24] As long ago as 1991, when considerably more people attended places of religious worship on a regular basis than do today, 'forty per cent of people questioned in a British Social Attitudes Survey said that their religious beliefs made no difference in their lives' (Social Trends 1996, p 225). Even a minor hobby is something that is sometimes consciously practised. In the 2001 Home Office survey on citizenship, only 20 per cent of those people questioned listed religion as being important for their sense

22 Voas and Crockett argue that what characterises believing without belonging in contemporary Britain is nothing more than a 'vague willingness to suppose that "there's something out there" ' (Voas and Crockett 2005, p 24).

23 See, similarly, Gillat-Ray's comment that 'Many young Muslims are looking to their faith as a means of identifying themselves and as a tradition in which they hope to find a sense of belonging' (Gillat-Ray 1998, p 352). The contrast is not, of course, between what is true for Christians and what is true for Muslims. There are observant Christians for whom their Christianity is central to their faith and there are Muslims who disregard or are unaware of the tenets of the Muslim faith.

24 Jacobson's analysis is explicitly of the boundaries that Islam creates for her informants. What is in doubt is whether in the Census, Christianity creates boundaries for most of those who described themselves as Christian in the 2001. As Voas and Crockett note, '[t]he basic problem with evidence of residual religiosity is that it is easy to forget that such beliefs often have little personal, let alone social, significance' (Voas and Crockett 2005, p 14).

of self-identity (O'Beirne 2004, p 18).[25] For such people their religion neither tells them what they should do nor does it prevent them from pursuing anything that they see to be in their interest. It is neither a guide nor a limitation to their behaviour on a day-to-day basis. It is thus not surprising to find that, contrary to Davie's earlier 1994 observation, in contemporary society, even the most major events in people's lives are increasingly secular in their nature (Davie 1994, p 81). Thus, for example, in 1991, 50.7 per cent of marriage ceremonies were religious ceremonies, but by 2004 that percentage had fallen to 32.3 per cent (Marriage, divorce and adoption statistics 2007). Equally the birth of a child is no longer regularly followed by baptism and even funerals, once predominantly religious events, are increasingly secular in nature.[26]

Appiah argues that:

> [e]ach person's individual identity is seen as having two major dimensions. There is a collective dimension, the intersection of their collective identities [such as religion, gender, ethnicity, 'race', sexuality], and there is a personal dimension . . .
>
> (Appiah 1994, p 151)

The arguments above would suggest that only a minority of people who said that they subscribed to a religion when answering the 2001 Census would see that religion as being, in Appiah's sense, part of their identity. Their gender, sexuality and so forth might be an important collective identity for them, but not their religion.

A society of strangers[27]

It is not only church attendance and membership that has declined in recent times. A similar pattern can be seen in other institutions and events that once garnered mass allegiance. Trade unions, for example, no longer attract the numbers that they once did.[28] More than this, no other form of mass allegiance has arisen to take their place. Increasingly we live solitary

---

25 However, there were important variations between different ethnic groups. Religion was the second most important factor for Asians, but only the tenth most important factor for those who were White (O'Beirne 2004, p 19). Equally, there were important variations between different faith groups. For Jews, their religion was the most important factor in their self-identity, but for Christians it only came seventh (O'Beirne 2004, p 20).

26 Thus, for example, the Church of England's own figures suggest a year-on-year drop in both baptisms and funerals between 2001 and 2005 (*Statistics for Mission 2005*, 2007).

27 This section draws in small part on material that I have previously published in a study of the connection between law and violence (Bradney 2006).

28 The late 1970s saw the high point of trade union membership with 58 per cent of employees being trade union members (Machin 2003, p 15). By 2005, only 26.2 per cent of all of those in employment were trade union members (Grainger 2006, p 15).

lives.[29] In 1971, the percentage of one-person households where the house-holder was under the state pension age was 6 per cent; by 2005 that percentage had risen to 15 per cent (Social Trends 2006, p 23). We now live with:

> the new facility of family structures, with many a family's life expectation shorter than individual life expectation of any of its members, with the membership of a particular family lineage turning fast into one of the 'undecidables' of the liquid modern era, and the allegiance to any one of several available kinship networks for a rising tide of individuals into a matter of choice, and a *revocable*, until-further-notice choice . . . (emphasis in original).
>
> (Bauman 2003, p 41)

In modernity we live among strangers. 'Strangers are not a modern invention – but strangers who remain strangers for a long time to come, even in perpetuity, are . . .' (Bauman 2003, p 105).

In a world usually indifferent to me and sometimes hostile, I, like others, live a violent life. Our violence does not take the prosaic form of the physical deed. Instead, it lies in the way in which we treat those people that we meet in our quotidian lives; more precisely it lies in the fact that we rarely treat people as people. 'Act in such a way that you always treat humanity, whether in your own person or the person of any other, never simply as a means, but always at the same time as an end' counsels Kant (Paton 1948, p 32). We do not normally do this.[30] Indeed, if we are to live

---

29   This is not just true in Great Britain. See, for example, Putnam's work in relation to the USA (Putnam 2000). In a detailed study published in 1999, Hall has argued that Putnam's thesis about the decline in civic engagement in the USA does not apply to Great Britain (Hall 1999). However, even Hall notes that 'those who grew up in a more individualistic society and were under the age of 30 in Britain in 1981 and 1990 are more inclined to embrace self-regarding values than those who reached maturity in the earlier collectivist era . . .' (Hall 1999, pp 447–448). Hall's study focuses on 'political activism and associational life' (Hall 1999, p 455) and is thus only tangentially concerned with the points I am raising here. Moreover, Hall accepts that, while his data suggests that there is still a high level of membership of secondary associations in Great Britain, it 'does not tell us much about the *quality* of organizational involvement in Britain . . . organizations may not involve their members in as much face-to-face interaction as their predecessors once did . . .') (emphasis in original) (Hall 1999, p 457).

30   I am not arguing that Kant's argument has lost its ethical power. Bauman concludes his 2003 study *Liquid Love* by arguing that '[t]he unity of the human species that Kant postulated may be, as he suggested, resonant with Nature's intention – but it certainly does not seem to be "historically determined". The continuing uncontrollability of the already global network of mutual dependency and "mutually assured vulnerability" most certainly does not increase the chance of such unity. *This only means, however, that at no other time have the search for common humanity, and the practice that follows such an assumption, been as urgent and imperative as they are now*' (my emphasis) (Bauman 2003, pp 155–156). However, once again, I would want to note that analysis in this chapter is of what we have in Great Britain not what we should want.

the lives that we lead we cannot do this. The violence that we do is to disregard the humanity of those people who we encounter. This is a necessary part of urban life in modernity.[31] 'A person walks the streets of a city and encounters perhaps thousands of people in the course of a day' (Giddens 1990, p 143). In order to manage the magnitude of human contacts that occurs, a magnitude that is itself a necessary feature of our lives because of our reliance on others for all manner of sustenance, the humanity of those meetings must be lost. To treat people as human beings would require of us time that we do not have to give. Contact must be fleeting if it is to be so frequent. We live, and largely want to live, in a society of strangers (Giddens 1991, p 152); our modern world allows nothing else. Even with those who are not strangers our contact is usually limited. '[O]ur souls, our feelings, are indifferent to the great mass of people, not only to those who are unknown to us, the strangers, but also even to those whom we know reasonably well' (Tonnies 1955, p 5). In the main, those around us are merely part of the landscape that we see. They are machines to serve our needs. The only dimension that they have for us is that which matches the use that we make of them. Seen, they are not known. More than that, we do not want to know them, could not afford to know them, except at the cost of our lives. We do not, on an everyday basis, make the existential leap of faith that postulates that those that we see are, like us, human beings.

Classically, Sartre's waiter lived in bad faith because, while at work, he acted as though he were only a waiter (Sartre nd, pp 59–60); he failed to acknowledge his continuing humanity and his agency. For us, however, a waiter is almost invariably just a waiter and not a human being. When we know the waiter as a human being, when we become a 'regular', when we become known, when we allow ourselves to be known, it is a matter to be noted and celebrated precisely because it is so much out of our everyday experience. And we cannot be a 'regular' in too many places because it parcels out too much of the time that we do not have to give. Even when we are a 'regular', we know that the transitory nature of the lives of both the waiter and ourselves makes it likely that we will be known for only a short period. Where we are a 'regular' will usually change. Our tastes change; the location of our homes and our work changes. Businesses that allow for even the possibility of intimacy are far more economically vulnerable than the impersonal giants. Sainsburys will be there next year; the small corner shop may not be; if it is, its ownership may have changed and its character may have altered radically. If it is the same as it once was we may have moved on physically, economically or psychologically.

31 The rhythms of rural life can be different. On the relationship between modernity and urban life, see Kumar 1978.

The capacity to let go of one's past, the confidence to accept fragmenta-
tion: these are the two traits of character which appear . . . among people
truly at home in the new capitalism.

(Sennett 1998, p 63)

With little sense of loss, once known to and knowing someone, we become
strangers again.[32]

Institutionalised religion largely stands in opposition to this society of
strangers. Thus, for example, Christianity counsels that all Christians are
'brothers and sisters in Christ' while in Islam there is the notion of the umma,
the worldwide Islamic community. Bruce has observed that he 'cannot think
of any major variety of Christianity that does not recommend community
participation, where at all possible' (Bruce 2002, p 323). A similar argument
could be made for Islam and many other faiths.[33] It is not just the tenets of
faiths that oppose modern society. The physical buildings of faiths also stand
in opposition. Places of religious worship are often far more than that.
Islamic mosques and Sikh gurdwaras are as much social sites as places
of worship (Badawi 1981, p 24; Cole and Sambhi 1978, p 143). They both
symbolise the communities they serve and also function so as to further
the unity of those communities. Membership of a particular faith group in
principle asserts a bond with fellow believers that cannot see them as
strangers. Moreover, this principled connection through shared faith can also
be accompanied by intense social interaction. In a study of a Quaker Meeting
that I coauthored it was clear that many members of that Meeting regarded
it as much as a social community as a religious community (Bradney and
Cownie 2000, p 121); as with this Quaker Meeting, as I shall show below, so
with many other religious groups in Great Britain.[34] Religions, with their

32 Not all scholars would accept this notion of the society of strangers. Thus, for example,
Parekh argues that 'human beings are culturally embedded in the sense that they are born
into, raised in and deeply shaped by their cultural communities' (Parekh 2006, p 120).
However, the ontological status of these communities, where '[b]elonging to a cultural community . . . admits of much variation and is not homogeneous in nature. Some members
might share all its beliefs and others only a few, and the former might differ in their interpretations of or degrees of allegiance to those' (Parekh 2006, p 148), is somewhat unclear. It
would appear that I can presume no more about the beliefs of a member of my community
than I could about those of a stranger.

33 The situation is, however, more complicated in the case of Hinduism where it can be the case
that '[f]ormal temple attendance is sporadic, with some caste members never going at all,
even though they might consider themselves to be "very religious". Instead, it is in their
homes that people unite in meaningful religious activity' (Michaelson 1987, p 32).

34 Indeed the importance of community membership can continue even where belief is at best
attenuated. In Chambers' study of Christian churches in Swansea he writes of Maestref
Baptist Church where '[o]nly a handful of elderly women and a few new members appear to
have any understanding of the basic elements of the Christian faith, while the remaining

stress on the importance of community membership, are thus at odds with some of the dominant tropes of modern British society, the fragility and friability of human relationships. The fact that this division between religions and society owes nothing necessarily and directly to theology does nothing to dissipate the tension that it creates.

If religions in Great Britain are at odds with the notion of a society of strangers, individual religiosity, on the other hand, where religion is lightly worn, can conform with prevailing social mores.

> Don't let yourself be caught. Avoid embraces that are too tight. Remember, the deeper and denser attachments, commitments, engagement, the greater your risk. Do not confuse the network – a swirl of roads to glide over – with a net: that treacherous implement that feels from the inside like a cage.
>
> (Bauman 2003, pp 58–59)

Religiosity, particularly where that religiosity has 'a stronger emphasis on immanence rather than transcendence, on the God within rather than the God without' (Davie 2002, p 332), can be compatible with the individuality, the doubts about, and disregard of, others noted above. Hunt's work, based on focus group discussions with people who had identified themselves as spiritual or religious in response to a recruitment questionnaire, illustrates both the tension between religions and society and the compatibility that there can between religiosity and society. She observes that:

> [s]piritual people are seen as open-minded, something that is highly prized in our society. By contrast religious people [that is people who are members of institutionalised religions], are often considered narrow-minded; allegedly they only believe what they are taught to believe. In a society where children are encouraged to question from an early age, the idea of believing in a rigid set of doctrines is seen as immature.
>
> (Hunt 2003, p 162)

Her own informants stress the personal nature of their spirituality, '[i]t's like your own spirituality, your feeling about yourself' (Hunt 2003, p 161). Hunt observes that there is a possibility of a future where 'without a shared language, spirituality will continue to be privatised. Individuals will create their own sacred space, but will not know how to share it with others' (Hunt 2003, p 168). For Hunt, with a 'background . . . in theology', this is a 'danger'

---

members (and some deacons) are not only quite open about their lack of knowledge but quite unconcerned about it . . . [T]he core of belief and practice has become progressively devalued and puerilized as belonging has superseded believing' (Chambers 2005, p 148).

(Hunt 2003, pp 160 and 168). Others may see, in this seemingly more easy accommodation between religiosity and modern social mores, a harbinger of the future without the negative evaluation that Hunt adds.

A sceptical society

Postmodernist scholars have delineated arguments for rejecting, on theoretical grounds, the possibility of grand narratives that will complete the Enlightenment project and explain the world (Lyotard 1984). While it is safe to assume that the vast majority of the population are only dimly aware of such arguments, scepticism about explanations and those who have explanations is an important trope in modern secular society. Asad, citing Benjamin, argues that:

> [i]n brief, this world is 'secular' not because scientific knowledge has replaced religious belief (that is, because the 'real' has at last become apparent) but because, on the contrary, it must be lived in uncertainty, without fixed meanings even for the believer, a world in which the real and the imaginary mirror each other.
>
> (Asad 2003, pp 64–65)

Scepticism and mistrust rather than the faith that is central to religion are emblematic of modern life.

> Nothing prevents those reference points and guidelines that seem trustworthy today from being debunked and condemned tomorrow (and retrospectively!) as misleading and corrupt. Allegedly rock-solid companies are unmasked as figments of the accountants' imagination. Whatever is 'good for you' today may be reclassified as poison tomorrow. Apparently firm commitments and solemnly signed agreements may be overturned overnight. And promises, or most of them, seem to be made solely to be broken or denied, counting on the short span of public memory. There seems to be no stable, secure island among the tides.
>
> (Bauman 2005, p 119)

Scepticism about figures of authority and statements of authority are accompanied by a more general social mistrust. Even Hall's contested account of the continual importance of associational membership in Great Britain notes a general decline in social trust (Hall 1999, pp 431–433).[35]

What are important here are both the fact of scepticism and mistrust and

---

35 For doubts about Hall's work, see Davie 2002, pp 330–332.

the pervasive nature of that scepticism and mistrust. The scepticism is a scepticism about all claims of truth-telling. At the same time the scepticism is a scepticism about the very notion of authority. Both may have, probably do have, comparatively shallow intellectual roots; nevertheless, they have a powerful place in the public psyche. Similarly mistrust is deeply rooted in modern society.

Once again these tropes in modern society are generally at odds with religion, but do not necessarily conflict with personal religiosity.

> In the religious expressions of a people ... traditional orientations usually acquired elevated and rhetorical formulation so that men were exhorted to live to do the will of God, or to fulfil the law, or to strive for perfection, or to enhance the life of others. These are all substantive values, and it is possible to give them refined expression by reference to a variety of human virtues.
>
> (Wilson 1982, p 48)

In such 'religious expressions' there was a grand narrative that had to be trusted on the authority of those who put it forward. As between religions, what was, and is, at issue is who or what can be regarded as having authority and who or what should be trusted. The concepts themselves, however, are a bedrock for the edifice of each religion. Thus, for example, the Islamic scholar Zaki Badawi wrote:

> I do not know what postmodernism is except that it is a world without any stable conviction. It celebrates doubt. Now religion is nothing but a stability; it is nothing but certainty and without certainty we have no faith.
>
> (Badawi 1995, p 75)

Personal religiosity can be, however, very different. Yip argues that:

> in late modern society, the organization of religious faith and spiritual identity are characterized, increasingly by privatization and individuation ... The self, not religious authority structures, emerges as the primary determining factor in shaping the expression of the individual's spirituality, whose authenticity rests, not on doctrines, but on personal experience.
>
> (Yip 2003, p 143)

Individual religiosity, where 'personal experience' is the measure of religious truth, can be as capricious and as sceptical as modern secular thought. Again, Hunt's work illustrates the phenomenon. Her informants stress the provisional nature of their beliefs, '[for those who belong to institutionalised religions] [i]t's, this is right and it'll be right for ever, it's a rail track to the horizon. And it's not like that, you know' (Hunt 2003, p 162).

Martin argues of the late 1960s that it was a time where '[e]ach person sought a radical individual essence and self-fulfilment' and that, in this context, '[r]eligion itself became a preference, and one which included all kinds of experimentation' (Martin 2005, p 23). However, Taylor, following Trilling, writing about the politics of recognition, has argued that the importance of 'being in touch with our feelings' as having 'independent and crucial moral significance' has a general significance in modernity (Taylor 1994, pp 28–29). Religiosity as personal preference and religiosity as individual experimentation also then takes on more significance.

A cosmopolitan society?

Secularism runs through contemporary British society. More hesitantly we may also note the increasingly cosmopolitan turn in British society.

Appiah dates the term cosmopolitanism back to 'at least the Cynics of the fourth century BC', who did not accept 'the view that every civilized person belonged to a community among communities' (Appiah 2006, p xiv).[36] Cosmopolitanism is a rejection of the notion of the overwhelming priority of the nation-state, not only in the senses associated with the assertion of patriotism or chauvinism, but also in the sense of seeing the nation as a focus for practical politics.

> The important fact is that the human condition has itself become cosmopolitan . . .
> [I]t has become the defining feature of a new era, the age of reflexive modernity, in which national borders and differences are dissolving and must be renegotiated in accordance with the logic of a 'politics of politics'.
>
> (Beck 2006, p 2)

In part, cosmopolitanism is the acceptance of the interconnectedness of the modern world. '[A] world in which communities are neatly hived off from one another no longer seems a serious option, if it ever was' (Appiah 2006, p xx). However, cosmopolitanism goes beyond the acknowledgement of the necessity of global politics. Beck describes the 'cosmopolitan outlook' as being a:

> [g]lobal sense, a sense of boundarylessness. An everyday, historically alert, reflexive awareness of ambivalences in a milieu of blurring differentiations and cultural contradictions. It reveals not just the 'anguish' but

---

36 As with the notion of a society of strangers not every scholar accepts the notion of cosmopolitanism. See, once again, Parekh 2006, p 124.

also the possibility of shaping one's life and social relations under conditions of cultural mixture. It is simultaneously a sceptical, disillusioned, self-critical outlook.

(Beck 2006, p 3)

Cosmopolitanism thus links in with British society's scepticism about total truths noted above. It is, however, more than scepticism because it also includes a desire to inquire into and seek to understand other ways of living and notions of the good life that are different from those of the culture or community into which you are born.[37]

Cosmopolitanism's acknowledgement of those outside the nation-state also means an acceptance of the idea that:

we have obligations to others, obligations that stretch beyond those to whom we are related by the ties of kith and kin, or even the more formal ties of shared citizenship ... [It also means accepting] that we take seriously the value not just of human life but of particular human lives, which means taking an interest in the practices and beliefs that lend them significance. People are different, the cosmopolitan knows, and there is much to learn from our differences.

(Appiah 2006, p xv)

The imperative in cosmopolitanism is thus 'to bring distant strangers near to us' (Dobson 2006, p 182). Here there may be a conflict with the fact that society largely accepts the previously noted necessity of living with people as strangers.[38] Dobson argues that, at root, cosmopolitanism is concerned with notions of political obligation where '[t]he scope of cosmopolitan obligation is in principle universal; it covers relations between all human beings' (Dobson 2006, p 187). Cosmopolitanism is a call to people 'to recognise that they are members of a common humanity ... an appeal to the mechanism of empathy' (Dobson 2006, p 171). But, as we have seen above, empathy is something that is largely lacking in modern British society. It is thus not surprising to see that, while secularism largely dominates the public life of British society, cosmopolitanism does not yet prevail in the same way.[39] It is, nevertheless, an argument for an approach to politics that has an increasing currency at many levels in society.

The diasporas and migrations occasioned by social and economic changes

37 If, indeed, you accept that, in any strong sense, you were born into a culture or community.

38 Resolved, perhaps, by the idea that 'distant' strangers are no more strangers than our neighbours who are strangers.

39 For this reason Dobson argues for a cosmopolitanism based on an acceptance of global causal responsibility (Dobson 2006). Whatever its intellectual attractions, whether this approach is emotionally any more appealing seems open to doubt.

in the world are one source of modern cosmopolitanism.[40] Beck observes that:

> the average migrant is the embodiment of the blurring of boundaries between nations, states and jurisdictions and of their contradictions. In order to survive, the average migrant must become an acrobat in the manipulation of boundaries (in avoiding, exploiting, drawing, bridging boundaries, etc) and at any moment can fall from the tightrope on which he or she is balanced.
>
> (Beck 2006, p 103)

In his writing Rushdie has regularly referred to the effect that being a migrant has on the perceptions that one has of the world. '[C]ultural displacement [means that I am forced] to accept the provisional nature of all truths, all certainties' (Rushdie 1983, p 77).[41] The cosmopolitan spirit is easily seen in the life of a highly successful author such as Rushdie, the lives of the foreign correspondents described by Hannerz or the footballers from various countries who play for Bayern Munich referred to by Beck (Hannerz 2007; Beck 2006, pp 10–11). However, Rushdie's observations are about migrants in general and not the affluent middle-class in particular. Beck notes that:

> [y]ou don't have to search very long in major urban centres such as New York, London, Rio de Janeiro, Berlin, etc, to find transportation workers, doormen, janitors and cleaners who can successfully communicate in more languages than the graduates of the average German or French high school or American college. The counterpart of the transnationalization of capital, of which there is currently so much talk, is a highly restrictive transnationalization of cheap labour which is for the most part neither understood nor recognized for what it is, namely, the model of experimental cosmopolitanism of the powerless in which the capacity to change perspectives, dialogical imagination and creative handling of cultural contradictions are indispensable survival skills.
>
> (Beck 2006, p 104)

Cosmopolitanism in this sense runs through large parts of urban life in

---

40 This is not to neglect the other source for the cosmopolitan outlook, the intellectual tradition that is briefly referred to by Beck (Beck 2006, pp 1–3). Equally, in looking for the sources of the cosmopolitan spirit, one should not ignore Chambers' remark that '[t]ravel ... and movement invariably bring us up against the limits of our inheritance' (Chambers 1994, p 115). EasyJet and Ryan Air have their own contribution to make to cosmopolitanism.

41 See also Rushdie's comment on his writing *Midnight's Children*, '[t]ime and migration placed a double filter between me and my subject' (Rushdie 1991a, pp 23–24).

modern societies. Thus Chambers writes of rap in the *banlieus populaires* of Paris, where the raps are 'in French, with occasional phrases in English and much in subcultural slang . . . part of a *mélange* that stretches from the Bronx to Brixton, to Barbès, to Brazzaville' and goes on to note the same phenomenon in London and Los Angeles 'where Third Worlds rumble beneath the poverty lines in metropolitan ghettos' (Chambers 1994, p 94).

If migration is one source for the cosmopolitan outlook, Great Britain, with the successive migrations into it that characterised the last half of the twentieth century, and which have continued in the twenty-first century, is an obvious locus for cosmopolitanism. As such British cosmopolitanism becomes, in the first instance, much more an urban than a rural feature. It is the major cities that are heavily populated by first-, second- or third-generation immigrants. However, cosmopolitanism is also a cultural matter seen in the backgrounds and inspirations of novelists, musicians, filmmakers and so forth at both the level of popular and high culture. Through this, cosmopolitanism has the potential to permeate British society more thoroughly than demographic statistics would suggest.

Cosmopolitanism and religions intersect in more complicated ways than is true of the previous tropes noted in modern British society where these have been seen to be mainly inimical to institutionalised religion.

Migration can be seen to be supportive of individual religions in very particular ways. The recent influx of Polish migrants into Great Britain will, for example, be significant for the Catholic Church, given its decline over the past decades.[42] Equally, the Hindu, Muslim, and Sikh communities in Great Britain are largely the creatures of various migrations into the country. Cosmopolitanism adds to this by stressing the value of the newly imported cultures and the new connections with foreign cultures that are the result of the impact of migration. In this sense religions benefit from the cosmopolitan turn in society. However, in other ways, cosmopolitanism provides a challenge to religions.

Beck writes of an 'anti-cosmopolitanism' that exists within societies 'whether understated or vociferous, right- or left-wing, union- or *church-driven*' (emphasis added) (Beck 2006, p 117). Elsewhere he notes, as an example of the 'essentialistic populism' that he sees as being an expression of anti-cosmopolitanism, the formation of a Muslim parliament in Great Britain (Beck 2006, p 115). Similarly, Appiah writes about 'neofundamentalists [of

---

42 There were more immigrants into the United Kingdom from Poland than from any other country in 2005 (Self and Zealey 2007, p 10). This is not the first time that the Catholic Church in Great Britain has experienced an expansion due to immigration into the country. The same phenomenon occurred between 1985 and 1989 (Brierley 1991, p 55). The phenomenon is not limited, among Christian churches, to the Catholic Church. One might also note the effect of West Indian migration into Great Britain on various Christian churches (Brierley 1991, pp 74–77).

Islam], whether violent or not . . . who exemplify the possibility of a kind of universalist ethics that inverts the picture of cosmopolitanism . . . [because it is] [u]niversalism without toleration' (Appiah 2006, p 140).[43] The opposition that these writers see between religions and cosmopolitanism arises from religions' conceptions of themselves as vehicles of truth. Insofar as religions see themselves as proponents of a truth that cannot be questioned they are opposed to cosmopolitanism.[44] Cosmopolitanism sees a value in religions; that does not mean that most religions can accept the values of cosmopolitanism.

Religions and religious communities within a secular society

Thus far we have looked at the decline of religion in British society both in the sense of a decline in numbers believing in religion and in the sense of a decline in the impact that religion has on the mores of society. Nevertheless, religion still persists in British society. Religious belief without belonging to a religion, 'believing without belonging', is perfectly possible and, in Davie's phrase, the 'latent religiosity' that this represents is an important part of the religious landscape of Great Britain (Davie 1994, p 93). However, belonging is a necessary feature for the survival of institutionalised religion.[45] The nature of belonging is, however, in this context elusive and it can take a number of different forms.[46] Thus, for example, membership of a faith is plainly a starting point for belonging. However, what is meant by membership varies from faith to faith. Brierley's study of Christian churches in England notes that '[e]ach denomination defines membership in its own way' (Brierley 1991, p 54). Moreover, even though membership, whatever that connotes, is a form of belonging, it may be a very superficial form. Membership of a religion and participation in that religion are not necessarily the same thing. Figures for attendance at places of religious worship are usually different from figures for membership (see, for example, Brierley 1991, p 57). Membership without attendance normally allows for the survival of a religion in only the most formal of senses.[47] Even attendance may not be sufficient for the survival of a religion in any meaningful sense. Most

---

43 Appiah goes on to note the same phenomenon in both the West's Christian past and contemporary USA (Appiah 2006, p 141).

44 Not all religions do see themselves as offering such a truth. Thus, for example, Quakers have 'no infallible scriptures nor church' (Dandelion 1996, p 165).

45 Believing is not necessary. Belonging without believing may be unprincipled but, so long as there is a profession of faith, it will be sufficient for the survival of a religion.

46 Whether the religion has any legal structure or not is not germane to the issues discussed in this section. For a discussion of the legal issues relating to the organisation of religions, see, Edge 2002, ch 4.

47 Attendance without belonging, although less common, is equally problematic for the survival of a religion.

religions, even if they have a priesthood and a professional bureaucracy, depend on their members for a myriad of support functions. Religions are not simply about worship or attesting the truth of the faith; they are also organisations that depend upon, among other things, both money and work for their continuation. Belonging, and, for some members at least, belonging at quite a deep level of regular involvement, is therefore necessary if the religion is to survive.

Belonging to religions, in all of the senses above, has greatly diminished in Great Britain over the last four or five decades. Brown has observed that:

> quite suddenly in 1963, something very profound ruptured the character of the nation and its people, sending organised Christianity on a downward spiral to the margins of social significance.
>
> (Brown 2001, p 1)[48]

It is this, in part, that makes it is possible to write about the secular nature of contemporary British society. Nevertheless, belonging to a religion, again in all the senses described above, still persists and it also forms part, albeit a small part, of the religious landscape of contemporary Britain.

Chambers' study of Christian churches in Swansea illustrates the varied strengths that belonging has in present-day churches. His description of individual churches in contemporary Swansea includes, among others, Faith Tabernacle, originally established in the early twentieth century, with a then current membership of 8 and an average age of 71, and Webside Evangelical Church, first founded in 1986, with a then current membership of 127 (Chambers 2005, pp 91 and 169).

> Average attendance for Sunday worship [at Webside] is in the order of 354 persons, with 213 adult worshippers and 83 children and young persons up to age of 19 in the morning and 59 worshippers (mostly double attendance) in the evening.
>
> (Chambers 2005, p 169)

Churches differ not just in size but in the range of activities they can engage in. Fifteen per cent of the Webside church joined the church because of its recruitment activities (Chambers 2005, p 170). Faith Tabernacle is theologically committed to the notion of evangelising in the local community but, in practice, the age of the congregation makes this impossible (Chamber 2005,

---

48 Brown also notes that 'the strength of attachment to other religions in Britain, has not, in the main, suffered the collapse that has afflicted the Christian churches' (Brown 2001, p 2). Others have argued that the decline in belonging predates the 1960s (see, for example, Voas and Crockett 2005, p 19).

p 92). The Sunday school at Faith Tabernacle closed in 1984 and the leaders of the congregation, at the time of Chambers' study, regarded closure of the church as inevitable (Chambers 2005, pp 92 and 94). In contrast at the Webside church '[t]he congregation is divided into a cell structure for mid-week activities and there are thirteen housegroups, each of which meets weekly' (Chambers 2005, p 171). The Sunday school has 'five age-banded classes' with other activities including 'a mother and toddlers group, after-school clubs and activities for senior citizens' (Chambers 2005, p 171). The church had seen its membership grow year-on-year. From these two accounts of individual churches it can be seen that the religious landscape of Great Britain is not simply divided between personal religiosity on the one hand and organised, institutional religions on the other. Organised religions themselves are divided in the degree of their bonds and the range of their activities. Those who are members of each church, gurdwara, mosque or temple, thereby assert their separateness from those who are not members. In this sense they claim community with each other and difference and distance from those who are not in the community. However, the depth and degree of that community varies greatly.

The most vibrant examples of belonging to a religion occur where the religion is both a religious resource and also a significant social resource for its members. Yilmaz has argued that '[r]eligious groupings, particularly in the post-modern age, have emerged almost everywhere as a basis of the refusal to assimilate' (Yilmaz 2005, p 50). Where this is so, the assertion of community is very strong. Writing about Muslims in Great Britain, Yilmaz notes that Muslims live '[w]ithin their localized settlements, they live in Britain, but in reality in their own world, over which they have a much larger extent of daily control' (Yilmaz 2005, p 56).[49] Such observations build on a tradition of academic analysis of ethnic minorities in Great Britain. Thus, for example, Khanum describes the household patterns of a 'Bangladeshi village' in Manchester (Khanum 2001). These 'localized settlements', these 'villages', are, to a greater or lesser extent, examples of the semi-autonomous communities that form the basis for anthropological analysis (Moore 1978, ch 2). As the way in which identity has focused has shifted from ethnicity or nationality to religion, so the way in which these communities are characterised has also altered.[50]

Social anthropology's move into urban anthropology has broadened our understanding of the way in which people live in modern society. Within the society of strangers noted above:

---

49 This is a separate phenomenon from communities that have been specifically created for religious purposes. See, for example, Taylor 1987.
50 The change can also be characterised as a change to fluid identities, which shift according to the situation that a person finds themselves in (Knott and Khokher 1993).

the age of contingency *für sich*, of self-conscious contingency, is also the age of community: of the lust for community, search for community, invention of community, imagining community.

(Bauman 1991, p 246)

These are communities in a different sense to the way one might talk of the Catholic community in Great Britain. Instead, these are communities that still experience an intense social interaction that is comparable to the modes of living that existed before modernity; semiautonomous social fields that 'can generate rules and coerce or induce compliance to them' (Moore 1978, p 57). There is no data that would allow us to determine how many such communities there are, or how many people belong to them. Plainly, not everyone who belongs to a religious community will also belong to a religious community in this more specific sense. Speculatively, one might suggest that it is only a minority of those who have membership of an institutionalised religion who also belong to a more specific religious community. Equally speculatively, it would seem, following Yilmaz's observations, that it would be more common for such communities to arise in the case of non-Christian religions. What bonds these communities together, varies. The experience of being an ethnic minority, still more the experience of being an ethnic minority and an immigrant, can, as Yilmaz observes, be one cause. Here, communities provide their members with a degree of protection against a world that is perceived of as being alien and probably hostile. However, this is not the only cause for such communities.

A Quaker Meeting that I studied with a colleague had none of the features noted, thus far, which might make for the creation of a semiautonomous community.[51] None of its members were recent immigrants and the vast majority came from the indigenous population of Great Britain. They were almost universally well educated and had secure employment in relatively well-paid jobs. What provided them with their bond was, in the first place, simply their religion, which gave them a set of mores that were profoundly different from the dominant culture that surrounded them. Quaker principles of simplicity, peace, truth and equality gave them different values to those around them. Meetings provide them with a place to worship but also, and for some more importantly, a place to interact with others who had the same approach to life.[52] A membership of approximately 200 people generated not only a range of committees that were devoted to the work of the Meeting

---

51 The material discussed here is dealt with at greater length in Bradney and Cownie 2000, particularly in ch 6.

52 Although Quakers hold a Meeting for Worship each Sunday there is no obligation to attend that Meeting. In the Meeting that we studied there were some people who rarely if ever attended Meeting for Worship, but were active in Meeting in other ways.

(Finance and Premises committee, Catering committee, Funeral committee, and so forth) but also an Arts Circle, and Art group, two Recorder groups, a group to discuss novels and a host of other similar activities. The Meeting was both a religious community and also a social community.

In the end religion is a matter of individual belief and choice. Some believers would assert that they have no choice but to follow the religion that they do. At the same time they would typically urge others to join them in that religion, thus asserting that others have the power to make a choice that they deny they have personally. In reality, choice being the signature of the human condition, our religion, religiosity or lack of either is our choice, a choice that we continue to make and remake, whether we are conscious of it or not, until we die. In this respect religion is no different from any other facet of our life.[53] However, it would be a mistake to see religions only in these terms. Religion can also be a communal activity where believers draw great strength from the community to which they belong. Equally it would be a mistake to see that form of religion as being something that is only experienced by those who are marginal in society. Religion is marginal in contemporary society but, at the same time, religion and strong religious communities run through society.

The fact that strong religious communities persist is an important factor when considering the relationship between religion, in the broad sense, and the State in contemporary Britain. Personal religiosity can result in a deeply held and even a militant faith. The lives of some hermits attest to this. However, the sceptical and provisional nature of much individual religiosity together with its private nature make it an unlikely source of confrontation with the State. Institutionalised religion is, however, another matter. Tenets of faith that have been given public expression by a religious community combined with both the resources of the community and the sense of solidarity that that community has make it more likely that a religion will perceive itself to be at odds with society over some issue and more likely that it will protest.[54] As I have argued elsewhere, the faith-based vision of the obdurate believer will be a particular problem for the State and for the courts (Bradney 2000). Obdurate believers are more likely to be found in strong religious communities.

Religions as jural communities

One manifestation of religion as a form of community can be a religion being a source of law for its members. This can occur when the religion is a form of

---

53 These arguments about the existential nature of our lives are developed at greater length in Bradney 1993, ch 2.

54 Here the term community can mean either the specific sense of community used in this section or the wider sense in which one talks of the Anglican community or whatever.

community in either the broad sense or in the more specific anthropological sense. Not all religions in Great Britain create law and, where law is created, the law may or may not be important in the lives of believers.[55] The legal systems that emanate from religions either lie alongside State law or, in some cases, are intertwined with it. Such law is law in the full sense of the word. '[T]here are many "legal" orders in society, of which state law is just one . . .' (Tamanaha 2001, p 116). Religion is not the only source for a non-State legal system within a modern society.

> According to the new legal pluralism non-state legal orders range from the interstices within, or areas beyond the reach of state legal systems where custom-based norms and institutions continue to exert social control, to the rule-making and enforcing power of institutions like corporations and universities, to the normative order that exists within small social groups, from unions, to sports leagues, community associations, business associations, clubs, and even the family.
>
> (Tamanaha 2001, p 116)

Great Britain, like all modern States, exists in a situation of legal pluralism.[56] Religion is one source of this pluralism.

Religions and religious communities often acknowledge the existence of their own particular legal systems; this is true, for example, of the Muslim community. However, law can sometimes exist even where the community is not aware of it. Cranmer, in his study of Quakers, notes:

> [w]hen I told the clerk of our Preparative Meeting that I was working on an article on 'Quaker canon law' her immediate response was, 'Oh, we don't have any of *that*'.
>
> (Cranmer 2003, p 176)

Despite this he observes that 'Friends regard "right ordering" of worship and the conduct of business as essential to the Society's life', a conclusion that is consistent with my own coauthored study of a Quaker Meeting, which argued that:

> Quaker law lies in the obligation of continual and all-embracing inclusion in the community that each member of Meeting accepts with regard

---

55 The degree of belonging will, for example, effect how important the religion's law is in the life of the believer.

56 This observation about the nature of modern States, and societies that existed in pre-modern times, has now been made many times. Thus, for example, Sezgin comments, 'Israel is a legally pluralistic society. So is India. And they have both been legally pluralistic throughout their history. This is also true of every human society' (Sezgin 2004, p 101).

to all other members of Meeting and with regard to themselves. Quaker law, where law is understood as mutually binding obligations which are known and accepted within the community, lies in their business method.
(Cranmer 2003, p 178; Bradney and Cownie 2000, p 165)

What we know about the law created by religions that exist in Great Britain varies. In some cases the legal rules have been studied in great detail. This is true, for example, of the canon law systems of both the Anglican and Catholic churches.[57] Islamic law and Jewish law – both systems of law that are applied in many other countries as well as in Great Britain – have also received extensive treatment. However, notwithstanding these doctrinal studies of the details of rules and institutions, how any of these systems are actually applied within Great Britain, the 'law in action' as opposed to the 'law in books' in each case, is far less known. Thus, for example, we know that Islamic sharia courts operate in Great Britain. Khaliq suggests that there are a large number of such courts while Badawi reports the existence of four Sharia Councils (Khaliq 2001–02, p 344; Badawi 1995, p 78). How these courts and Councils operate and what impact the law has on the various Muslim communities within Great Britain is, however, far from clear. A number of studies, including those by Pearl and Menski, Shah, and Yilmaz, have given us some preliminary indications as to how sharia law works in Great Britain, but much research is still left to do (Pearl and Menski 1998, ch 3; Shah 2005, ch 6; Yilmaz 2005, ch 4). In the case of many other religious jural systems we know still less.[58] Nevertheless, notwithstanding our ignorance about detail, it is clear that religions not only persist in contemporary Great Britain, albeit as something that is important only for a diminishing minority, but that religions form an important part of the legal landscape of Great Britain.

Conclusion

Detailing the religious landscape of Great Britain produces a complex picture. It includes vibrant and intense religious communities, widespread low-level individual religiosity and also a rejection of both religion and religiosity. However, while both religion and religiosity continue to exist within Great

---

57 See, for example, Doe 1996. Given that the power of the General Synod of the Church of England to make law derives from Church of England Assembly (Powers) Act 1919, and given the establishment of the Church of England, its law is strictly part of State law, although this is largely unacknowledged in books on English law. (On the legislative power of the Church of England see Doe 1996, ch 3.) No such argument can be made for Catholic canon law. For studies of limited aspects of the legal system of the Church of England, see, Bursell 2007 and Illes 2007. For a study of a limited aspect of the Catholic legal system in Great Britain, see, Read, 1990–92).

58 There is further analysis of these legal systems in Chapter 2 below.

Britain, it is clear that that landscape conforms to the concept of secularization articulated by Wilson:

> a process occurring within the social system . . . that process by which religious thinking, practice and institutions lose social significance and become marginal to the social system.
>
> (Wilson 1988, p 196)

Religion is significant for large numbers of people but those large numbers are a comparatively small minority of the country taken as a whole. Religiosity characterises a much larger number of people, but their religiosity is of little significance to them. The interaction between religion, religiosity and law in Great Britain takes place within this secular context.

Chapter 2

Protecting religiosity, religion and religious communities

Non-coercion in matters of religion

Writing as long ago as 1920, Holdsworth observed that the British State:

> gives an equal measure of protection to all sects, whether religious or anti-religious provided that their tenets do not involve a breach of its laws, civil or criminal. It refuses to favour one more than another; and practically the only coercive authority which it exercises is in respect of those whose methods of propaganda are so coarse and offensive as to bring them within the modern rules of the criminal law relating to blasphemous libel.
>
> (Holdsworth 1920, p 340)

As will be shown in later chapters, in some respects, even in modern-day society, let alone Great Britain at the beginning of the twentieth century, Holdsworth's remarks were somewhat simplistic but his reference to the absence of coercion in matters relating to religion provides a starting point for the contemporary legal treatment of religion in Great Britain. Direct legal coercion with respect to religion in Great Britain largely ended in the nineteenth century with the passage of legislation such as the Roman Catholic Relief Act 1829 and the Religious Disabilities Act 1846.[1] Prior to this the law had privileged the position of Christianity in general and the Church of England and the Church of Scotland in particular. Once the ecclesiastical courts had lost their jurisdiction in the seventeenth century it fell 'to the ordinary Courts to apply the many statutes which penalised the nonconformist, whether Protestant or Roman Catholic' (Holdsworth 1920, p 343). However, as Holdsworth shows, from the Toleration Act 1689 onwards there

---

1 For the history of legal discrimination against Roman Catholics in Scotland see Gill 2000, pp 42–43. Holdsworth's *A History of English Law* charts religious repression at various points in its 17 volumes.

was a slow retreat from this policy of penalising those religions that were not state religions.

There are now very few legislative provisions which either specifically disbar an adherent from a particular religion from a public office, area of employment or suchlike or specifically require them to be a member of a particular religion.[2] Equally, there are very few legal requirements regarding the recitation of particular religious oaths; instead, where oaths have to be administered, people can normally either choose from a variety of oaths or decide to affirm instead.[3] Although it is little discussed in contemporary analyses of Great Britain this lack of direct legal coercion in matters of religion continues to be of import, not least because it was not always the case.[4] Very few would wish to introduce changes that could be regarded as coercive with respect to religion.[5] Noncoercion represents, however, only a comparatively slight concession to believers. Not overtly coercing somebody in law as regards their religion is, as will be shown in this and succeeding chapters in this book, compatible with a wide range of practices – legal and social – that make the lives of believers or some believers more difficult than others.

Religion, law and neutrality

British law has long gone beyond mere noncoercion in matters of religion and has claimed neutrality with respect to religion; thus, for example, dictum such as Scrutton LJ's comment in *Re Carroll* ([1931] 1 KB 317 at p 336) that '[i]t is, I hope, unnecessary to say that the Court is perfectly neutral in matters of religion'. This claim of neutrality is reflective of a broad liberal

---

2 One continuing example of such a provision is the requirement, under the Act of Settlement 1700 and the Accession Declaration Act 1910, that heirs to the throne be Protestant and that the monarch be in communion with the Church of England (on this see Doe 1996, pp 9–10).

3 The Oaths Act 1978 contains both specific provision for oaths for a number of religions to be administered (s 1(1)) and also general provisions for other religions (s 1(3)). Anyone may choose to affirm rather than take an oath (s 5(1)). Auld, in his review of the criminal courts, noted that '[t]oday, I suspect that many, if not most witnesses regard its [the oath's] administration as a quaint court ritual which has little bearing on the evidence they are going to give . . .' and went on to recommend the abolition of the oath (Auld 2001, p 599). For a history of the legal oath see Weinberg 1976, pp 27–30.

4 Not every country follows the practice of noncoercion. Thus, for example, Article 160 of the Malaysian constitution defines a Malay as someone who, inter alia, 'professes the religion of Islam'. The implications of this provision have to be understood in the context of a Malay Muslim milieu where '[a] religious identity . . . is *not* a choice or an achieved status. It is, rather, something ascribed, something in the blood, in nature, hence immutable' (Peletz 2002, p 219).

5 One exception to this might be the suggestion, depending on how it was implemented, that a personal law system be introduced into Great Britain.

proposition that the State should makes no choices in terms of what should be the good in its citizen's lives, instead leaving that choice to the individuals concerned.[6]

> One may say that the law-religion relationship is a natural locus of the liberal neutrality. The idea of a secular liberal state, ie the state which neither gets involved with matters religious nor inhibits in any way religious expression and activities, has been long understood as best encapsulated by the idea of the state's neutrality towards religion.
>
> (Sadurski 1990, p 167)

However, 'neutrality is an ambiguous term' (Ahdar and Leigh 2005, p 87). What is meant by neutrality in the context of the law's relationship with religion, whether the law in Great Britain is in fact neutral with respect to religion and even whether neutrality is possible, are all questions that are open to debate.

'Neutrality' in the context of the State's attitude towards belief and religion can be taken to mean:

> [r]oughly, if questions about value or the good are understood to be rationally irresoluble, matters of merely local and contingent commitment, then principles of justice can only be universally rationally vindicable if they do not presuppose that some particular set of values are correct. Hence the aspiration to derive principles of justice from principles of reason . . . without reference to the good or value.
>
> (Fitzmaurice 1993, pp 52–53)

If this is so then the first potential objection is that neutrality contains within it presuppositions that are not themselves neutral. Waldron notes that '[t]he liberal commitment to allowing individuals to pursue their aims is complemented by an insistence that individuals be reasonable in choosing what aims to pursue' (Waldron 2003, p 21). But what liberalism sees as the necessity to be 'reasonable' is not always seen by others as being an objective or value-free matter. Faith not reason is typically the language of religion. Thus, for example, Ahdar notes that Conservative Christians, 'theologically conservative, usually Protestant, Christians, who adhere to "traditional" moral values', reject the notion that secular liberal states are neutral about the notion of what constitutes the good life, instead siding with postmodernists in believing that 'liberalism is just another ideology reflecting a partisan

---

6 See, for example, Rawls' statement that '. . . the [liberal] state is not to do anything intended to favour or promote any particular comprehensive doctrine rather than another, not to give greater assistance to those who pursue it' (Rawls 1988, p 262).

belief culture' (Ahdar 2001, pp 3 and 113). In a similar fashion, from a Muslim perspective, Yousif argues that '[w]estern rationality is only one world-view amongst many different world-views and should not be the yard-stick by which all other world-views are to be measured' (Yousif 2000, p 32).[7]

The language in which the claims of religions and believers are debated in the liberal State is a resolutely secular language grounded in at least an attempt at rational debate. Those taking part in that debate must offer 'public reasons' for their position.

> To offer fellow citizens 'public reasons' . . . is to undertake two burdens. The first is the requirement that the reasons offered be justificatory: that is, they should be reasons which justify the proposals that they are offered to support . . . Second these reasons should also be candidates for free assent by those citizens who will be bound by the proposal. If an argument could not win the assent of others then it cannot be a public reason.
>
> (Festenstein 1999, p 148)

In this respect at least the secular liberal State is not neutral.[8]

The secular liberal State's attitude towards religion might equally be thought to contain a non-neutral value judgement. Even when it makes special provision for believers, the law never recognises the claims of those believers in their own terms. When, for example, British law grants Sikhs exemption from crash-helmet laws it does so because of arguments such as tolerance. It does not do so because it accepts the intrinsic value of Sikhs' faith claims about the importance of male Sikhs wearing turbans; since it is neutral about the value of religion it cannot accept, on their own terms, the claims of any religion. Thus Sadurski notes that:

> [t]here is no basis, in an ideology of a liberal and secular state, to draw the line between the religiously motivated and other deep moral beliefs, with respect to bearing common burdens and fulfilling societal duties. It does not follow that conscientious objection must necessarily be disallowed,

---

7 The argument that there are rational notions which lie at the heart of liberalism has been made from within liberalism. Thus Canovan argues that '[c]oncealed in the very heart of liberalism . . . are a set of legitimising myths about man and society: myths about human rights, the primacy of individuals, the equality of men (and even of women), the naturalness of freedom, the feasibility of government by consent and the rest' (Canovan 1990, p 13). Similarly, Asad notes the view of radical anthropologists 'who criticize the modern liberal state for pretending to be secular and rational when in fact it was heavily invested in myth and violence' (Asad 2003, p 56).

8 For an argument that, even within a liberal democracy, 'citizens should feel free to support coercive laws on the basis of their religious convictions' (Eberle 2002, p 333) see Eberle 2002, passim.

but rather that it should be measured by the sincerity and intensity of moral reluctance to engage in a certain activity, and not by whether this reluctance has religious rather than secular grounds. The fact that an objector derives his or her moral complaint from participation in an organized and recognized religion may be one of the indicia of judging the sincerity of the claim, but it must not be conclusive evidence nor a prerequisite for recognizing it as valid.

(Sadurski 1990, p 190)

Because of neutrality it follows that religious belief is treated as though it were a deep moral belief.

A second potential objection to the proposition that the liberal State is neutral about individuals' choices of the good life is the very fact that it is individuals who are assumed to be making those choices. This is reflected in the special provisions that the law sometimes makes with respect to religion. These provisions include both things like the general protections for religious belief and against religious discrimination afforded by the Human Rights Act 1998 and particular protections and exemptions in individual pieces of legislation such as the fact that Sikhs do not have to wear crash helmets when riding motor-cycles.[9] It is largely individuals and their freedom of religious belief and from discrimination, not religions, that are protected by such legislation.[10]

Liberalism is neutral about choices about what is the good that are made. It is, however, no more neutral about who can make those choices than it is about the language that can be used to justify those choices. There are communitarian conceptions of the good. The liberal neutral State does not forbid those conceptions. It does, however, require that each individual themselves agree to that conception before it can be applied to them; thus communitarian conceptions of the good have to be validated by individual choice. '[N]eutrality as a policy is never . . . self-justifying: one is always neutral . . . for a reason, and it is obvious that one cannot be neutral about the force of that reason' (Waldron 1989, p 79). A liberal thinks that:

---

9 This was originally provided for by the Motor-Cycle Crash-Helmets (Religious Exemption) Act 1976. This exemption is now to be found in s 16(2) Road Traffic Act 1988. A similar provision applies in the case of the use of safety helmets on construction sites (s 11 Employment Act 1989). For a detailed study of the campaign to gain exemption to the construction site legislation, see Poulter 1998, pp 313–322.

10 There are exceptions to this. Two can be seen in the case of the Human Rights Act 1998. First section 13(1) of the Act says that '[i]f a court's determination of any question arising under this Act might affect the exercise by a religious organisation (itself or its members collectively) of the Convention right to freedom of thought, conscience and religion, it must have particular regard to the importance of that right'. Secondly, more generally, religions may, as institutions, be party to actions under the European Convention on Human Rights. On this, see, Rivers 2001 and Cumper 2000.

the shaping of individual lives by the individuals who are living them is a good thing; and she fears for the results if that process is distorted or usurped by externally applied coercion, even the coercion of *gemeinshaft*. On the basis of *these* concerns and *these* fears, she identifies moral views *of this individualistic sort* as those between which legislative neutrality is required. (emphasis in original).

(Waldron 1989, p 80)

While the liberal State can be neutral about which conception of the good life the individual chooses, it cannot, therefore, be neutral about who does that choosing.

Added to all of the above doubts about conceptual clarity of the notion of the neutrality of the liberal State is the very fact that the State is neutral itself has an impact on people's choice of the good life. It means that:

some conceptions of the good will be more easily pursued than others. Cheap conceptions will be more easily attained than those which make heavy demands upon material resources. Individualist conceptions, which demand no more than one's allotted share of liberty, will be more readily pursuable than those which require the widespread agreement and co-operation of others.

(Jones 1989, p 22)

From all of the above it is clear that even if a State says that it is neutral about an individual's conceptions of the good, not all choices of the good are equally easily made. This, however, does not mean that the State cannot be said to be neutral. The differential impact that the neutral State has on different conceptions of the good does not result from a deliberate attempt to preference one version of the good over another. A State will be neutral if:

the basic structure of liberal society can be set without making qualitative judgements that draw upon a theory of the good, or . . . if such judgements are inescapable, they can nevertheless be sufficiently 'thin' for the liberal state to remain largely, if not comprehensively, neutral between rival conceptions of the good.

(Jones 1989, pp 33–34)

From all of the above it is clear that the law's claimed neutrality towards religion is thus of a restricted form. British law does not usually express a view about the value of a religion. It is, however, clear that some religions are different to others and that those differences are important because they justify special treatment. Moreover, the terms of the debate about the place of religion within society are set by a secular liberalism that does not and cannot view religion through religion's own eyes.

Neutrality and special provision for religions

Upon the face of it the law's claim to neutrality with respect to religion is in conflict with the different kinds of special legal provision that it sometimes makes regarding religion, giving adherents exemptions from what is otherwise the normal legal rule.[11] Here, rather than neutrality, there seems to be a preference for one religion or another. Indeed some writers have argued that the purest form of neutrality involves making no special provisions for religions or making special provisions only in extremely restricted instances (see, for example, Barry 2001, pp 44–50). However, Nozick's observation that no one way of living can satisfy the aspirations of all the individuals within a society, is one that is accepted by most and perhaps all liberal States (Nozick 1974, pp 307–310). Special provisions with respect to religion can be justified on the grounds that they help the State to accommodate the complex variety of views of the good that exist within its borders.[12] Thus, for example, for the vast majority of people within Great Britain, motor-cycle crash-helmets are irrelevant to their view of what the good life is, but for many observant Sikh males wearing a turban is more important than the health and safety advantages of wearing a crash helmet, a view which they hold to deeply. The behaviour they wish to engage in is largely self-regarding. If they do suffer greater injury in a road accident because they are not wearing a crash helmet, it is largely they who suffer.[13] Moreover, the State's interest in such legislation is less strong than its interest, both pragmatic and philosophical, in accommodating the deeply held views of individuals within its borders.

Making a special provision for a particular religion does not necessarily involve affirming the value of that religion, thus conflicting with the notion of neutrality and the basic premises of liberalism. In holding that a bequest for the propagation of the works of Joanna Southcott was a valid religious trust, Sir John Romilly noted that Joanna Southcott 'was, in my opinion, a foolish, ignorant woman' and that her writings contained 'much that, in my

---

11 The law in Great Britain does sometimes make special provision because of individuals' conscientious beliefs rather than their religious beliefs, thus meeting Sadurski's point above. Contemporary examples of this include s 4 of the Abortion Act 1967 and s 38 of the Human Fertilisation and Embryology Act 1990 as well as the fact that the Human Rights Act 1998, through Article 9 of the European Convention on Human Rights, protects 'freedom of thought, conscience and religion'.

12 Weale argues that the notion of equal respect for persons requires that neutrality both be an intentional and negative concept and an intentional and positive concept with the latter meaning that it is sometimes necessary for the State to take steps to protect minorities who are disadvantaged by a general practice (Weale 1985, pp 30–32).

13 The standard argument to the contrary would be to say that those who do not wear crash helmets create extra work for the health services and therefore create extra tax liabilities for the population at large. However, as Barry notes, this is a purely empirical argument, rather than a conceptual objection, and its empirical validity is open to question (Barry 2001, p 47).

opinion, is very foolish'.[14] His task as a judge was merely to see whether or not the trust deed met the appropriate legal tests so as to enable it to create a valid religious trust with all the advantages that stemmed from that.[15] However, while making special provision for a religion does not involve affirming the value of the religion, it does necessarily involve saying there is something in that religion that justifies treating it differently to other religions.[16] To say that Sikhs but not Rastafarians should be exempt from crash helmet legislation is to say that Sikhs are different in some significant way to Rastafarians so as to justify giving them particular protection even though it does not necessarily involve saying that the Sikh way of life is better than the Rastafarian way of life.[17]

Toleration and law

If notions like noncoercion and neutrality form part of the background to the approach that British law takes towards religion, so does the idea of tolerance. Thus Rivers argues that since the Toleration Act 1689 'to the extent that one can generalize about religious liberty in the UK, its history thereafter is one of gradually expanding toleration' (Rivers 2000, p 133).[18] In a similar vein, Lord Scarman observed that '[t]o a lawyer, in a sense, toleration is a non-subject. Toleration is, and has been for a hundred years or more, part and parcel of the English way of life' (Scarman 1987, p 49).

The basic shape of the concept of tolerance is fairly clear:

14 *Thornton v Howe* (1862) 31 Beav 14 at p 18 and p 19.
15 However, some of the tests for legal validity for a religious trust have been concerned with the merits of the religion to which the trust deed relates. Thus, on occasion, British law does say that a religion lacks value and therefore will not be accorded the legal advantages that come from the special provisions relating to religious trusts (see further Bradney 1993, pp 121–124).
16 Equally, if the special provision is as regards all religions, it involves saying there is something of consequence in religions that justifies treating them differently from things that are not religions.
17 One justification for this distinction might be a pragmatic one; that is easier to identify with a reasonable degree of certainty who and who is not a Sikh than it is in the case of Rastafarians. O'Brien and Carter note that '[f]or Rastafari . . . [their religion] is a wholly private affair. As a movement it is, to say the least, non-doctrinal. While the bible is regarded as a sacred and central text within the religion . . . the final interpretation [of it] is very much a subjective and individual matter' (O'Brien and Carter 2002–2003, p 221). Equally, Cashmore observes that 'the Rastafarian movement had no active programme of involvement with other groups in the wider society' (Cashmore 1979, p 172). As such they were less likely to make the kind of political contacts that Sikhs could. It might thus be the case that while the political case for exemption for Sikhs has been made, no such similar case has been made for Rastafarians rather than that the case has been made and rejected for discriminatory reasons. However, simple unjustifiable discrimination as an explanatory factor cannot be ruled out.
18 For a history of the development of tolerance in Great Britain see Rodes Jr 1990–1991, pp 868–875. For an argument that Rodes Jr's account is overly whiggish, see, Bush 1990–1991, pp 883–903.

At the heart of the idea of toleration – what might be characterised as the core concept of toleration – is a deliberate choice not to interfere with the conduct of which one disapproves. Three components of this core conception of toleration can be identified. First there must be some conduct which is disapproved of (or at least disliked). Second, this disapproval must not be acted upon in ways which coercively prevent others from acting in the disapproved manner. Third, this refusal to interfere must be more than mere acquiescence or resignation.

(Horton 1993, pp 3–4)

Toleration by the State arises out of its need to treat individuals within it 'as rational moral agents whose ideas can be discussed and disputed', 'to give serious consideration to their ideas' and to acknowledge 'the deeply held convictions of human beings' (Nicholson 1985, p 165). Tolerance by the State, respect by the State for persons as having goals and purposes on which they can reflect and which gives purpose to their lives, is a prerequisite for those within the State being able to enter into arguments about the nature of the good in their lives and to take action on the basis of those arguments (Weale 1985, pp 26–34).[19] In a climate of tolerance, Nicholson argues that individuals can better assess their own ideas resulting in their development, modification or reinforcement (Nicholson 1985, p 166).

Tolerance towards religion in British law in this sense now takes two forms. It both involves not practising coercion, a form of negative tolerance, but it also takes the form of sometimes doing things to facilitate the religious lives of believers so as not to interfere with their conduct.[20] This is a positive form of tolerance. Because a plurality of lifestyles is accepted in Great Britain, so there is accommodation in the law towards the religious beliefs and practices that are the basis for some of these lifestyles. Thus, when Sidney Bidwell MP first introduced the legislation to exempt Sikhs from wearing crash helmets while riding motorcycles, he invoked the notion of tolerance as part of his argument to justify the need for the legislation.[21]

---

19 Weale argues that both consequentialist and contractarian arguments for toleration do not provide adequate foundations for the concept and instead argues for the notion of equal respect for persons (Weale 1985, pp 19–25). See, similarly, Raz's argument for tolerance based on respect for autonomy (Raz 1988).

20 Not all arguments for tolerance are for both negative and positive tolerance. Thus, for example, Waldron notes that Locke's case for tolerance is solely a negative one arguing for the removal of coercion in matters of religion (Waldron 1988, p 76).

21 Hansard, House of Commons, Standing Committee F, 23rd June 1976, col 6. In his four-page discussion of Sikhs in his 1976 book on race relations Bidwell uses the word tolerance, or a variant thereon, seven times (Bidwell 1976, pp 56–60). Lukes argues that '[l]iberalism was born out of religious conflict and the attempt to tame it by accommodating it within the framework of the nation-state. The case for religious toleration was central to its development . . .' (Lukes 1991, p 17).

The necessity for tolerance towards religions and towards believers, like the notions of noncoercion and neutrality above, is relatively uncontroversial in legal terms. Great Britain is legally committed to protecting freedom of religious belief and practice under Article 18 of the Universal Declaration of Human Rights, Article 18 of the International Covenant on Civil and Political Rights and Article 9 of the European Convention on Human Rights.[22] Nevertheless, the notion of tolerance is not without its difficulties.

Nicholson, in his discussion of toleration, defines toleration as 'the virtue of refraining from exercising one's power to interfere with others' opinion or action although that deviates from one's own view over something important and although one morally disapproves of it' (Nicholson 1985, p 162). This is a narrower definition than that offered by Horton above because 'disapproving' of something does not necessarily mean disapproval on moral grounds. Warnock criticises Nicholson's narrow use of the term toleration, arguing that it has both the strong sense that Nicholson adverts to and also an equally legitimate weak sense where disapproval connotes dislike or distaste (Warnock 1987, pp 125–127).[23] Nevertheless, even if Nicholson's definition of toleration is too narrow, it does serve to highlight one of the inherent problems in the idea of toleration; why should one accept that which one disapproves of if one has the power to stop it; more particularly, how can one morally justify permitting or even facilitating that which one morally disapproves of? One might tolerate something one simply found distasteful, but moral judgements are of a different order of things to matters of taste. '[S]urely what is morally wrong *should not* be put up with, in any circumstances' (Warnock 1987, p 127).[24]

Toleration by the liberal State has a particular character of its own. As was noted above, the liberal State seeks, insofar as is possible, to avoid making judgements about matters of value; these are left to individuals within the state.[25] The State does not tolerate that which it finds morally wrong because,

---

22 See, further, Evans, 1997 and Taylor 2005.
23 Nicholson is not alone, however, in seeing toleration as being a moral matter. See, for example, Raphael 1988, p 142.
24 To put it in Kantian terms '[a] class of action is moral inasmuch as it relates "to a possible making of universal law by its maxims", that is, if the maxim behind it is capable of being universally prescribed to all rational beings' (Hampsher-Monk 1999, p 23).
25 Individuals within the State, including individuals who are powerful within the State, may disapprove of something and even campaign against that thing. However, when they act upon behalf of the State, or when they set out to argue about what the State should do they may decide not to argue that the State should forbid what they disapprove of. In doing so they do not contradict themselves. They disapprove of something but they do not, at least in all cases, think that their moral judgement is so certainly right that it should be substituted, using the mechanism of State power, for the moral judgement of others. If they can persuade others, who behave in a way that they disapprove of, that their moral judgement is in fact right, that is another matter.

insofar as it can do so, it does take a view on that which is morally right for those within it.[26] Moreover, the liberal State is not tolerant of everything. '[T]he virtue of toleration, like any virtue, has its limits' (Raphael 1988, p 137). It is not, for example, tolerant of matters that would result in its own destruction. Equally, it is not tolerant of active attempts to prevent someone pursuing their own conceptions of what it is to live the good life where those conceptions do not infringe on others' attempts to themselves live the good life (Nicholson 1985, p 172).

The fact that the liberal State is not tolerant about everything does not mean that the idea of tolerance in such a context is indefensible or incoherent. The fact that the State is not wholly tolerant does not mean that it is not tolerant at all. If it did it would mean that the notion of tolerance would have little conceptual purchase in most and perhaps all situations. The liberal State is tolerant within limits but, despite the limits, tolerance is still central to the way in which the State goes about its business. Religions benefit from this tolerance.[27]

Beyond tolerance

'The principle of "respecting persons", including respecting them as individuals who hold beliefs, is now widely shared; indeed, it has become fundamental to liberal political culture' (Jones 1994, p 323). However, for some writers, from a variety of different theoretical perspectives, this is not enough. Individual protection for believers, based on the principle of tolerance, is not sufficient. Instead, they would argue, there needs to be an acceptance by the State and by society generally of the good in different cultural groups or forms. Rockefeller, for example, has suggested that:

> [a]t a minimum, the politics and ethics of equal dignity need to be deepened and expanded so that respect for the individual is understood to involve not only respect for the universal human potential in every person but also respect for the intrinsic value of different cultural forms in and through which individuals actualise their humanity and express their unique personalities.
>
> (Rockefeller 1994, p 87)

---

26 Raphael, writing about toleration in general, argues that '[a]cts of which we disapprove but which do not infringe rights may be tolerated despite our belief that they are wrong, and should be tolerated if those who do the acts have deliberately chosen to do them. In the latter event toleration is called for because it shows respect for the ends (the choices) of those who do the acts' (Raphael 1988, p 147).

27 Of course not all religions benefit. For example, a religion that has coercion at the centre of its practices will, at best, only be a limited beneficiary of toleration on the part of the State.

Religions would clearly be beneficiaries of this wider politics of recognition, itself the result of a more general demand that 'we all *recognize* the equal value of different cultures, that we not only let them survive, but acknowledge their *worth*' (Taylor 1994, p 64). From a rather different perspective, but with similar conclusions, Raz has argued that there are three liberal responses to the phenomenon of multiculturalism, toleration, non-discrimination and finally affirmation (Raz 1994, pp 174–175). Raz argues for the superiority of affirmation over either tolerance or non-discrimination on the ground that 'it is in the interest of every person to be fully integrated in a cultural group' because '[o]nly through being socialized in a culture can one tap the options that give life meaning' (Raz 1994, p 177).[28] Once again religions would be among those groups who would benefit from the move from toleration to affirmation.

Prima facie, such arguments might appear to be as uncontroversial as the legal call for the protection of religious belief noted above. After all:

> I can be (indeed, I am!) perfectly friendly with Catholics and Muslims while not always agreeing with them about theology. I have no more reason to resent those who go to Mecca on the hajj than I have to begrudge the choices of those who go to Scotland for golf or to Milan for opera.
>
> (Appiah 2006, p 10)

It would be difficult to find anyone in British society who, no matter what their own beliefs are about religion, is not friendly, in at least a loose sense of the word, with some religious believers. If I am friendly with religious believers, why should I not accord respect to and acknowledge the value of the communities to which these believers sometimes belong? Indeed, if I react to some people in the way that Appiah describes, am 'perfectly friendly' with them, how can I not respect and find value in that which, for them and me, gives them at least part of their identity? How can I not respect and acknowledge the value of their religion? Equally, on this argument, how can believers not value non-believers?

> [F]aith, even for the staunchest believer, is one human possibility among others. I may find it inconceivable that I would abandon my faith, but there are others, including possibly some very close to me, whose very way of living I cannot in all honesty just dismiss as depraved, or blind, or unworthy, who have no belief (at least not in God, or the transcendent).
>
> (Taylor 2007, p 3)

28 I have argued elsewhere that Raz's argument does not reflect the reality of most people's experience in modernity, in that they are not fully socialized into any particular community, but one might accept a weaker argument that promoting the possibility of such socialization is desirable because it is one way of giving life meaning (Bradney 2000, pp 103–104).

Moreover, a philosophical call to value and respect different religions, mirrors a call from many religions themselves who feel that, because of their religion, they are marginalized within mainstream Great Britain.[29] It is not merely them but also their religion, so they believe, that should be respected.

The British tradition of tolerance does not meet the arguments above. Tolerance is not necessarily incompatible with condescension, disdain or even contempt. Indeed, one might be tolerant of another's beliefs and practices precisely because one believes they are so trivial, obviously wrong or irrelevant to contemporary times that they will have only the most negligible impact on the wider society. However, condescension, disdain and contempt are not likely to build an inclusive society where all of its members feel fully valued. The move from tolerance to affirmation can therefore be seen as being politically desirable as well as being philosophically necessary if the varied and divergent religious groups that continue to exist in Great Britain are to be fully part of British society.

Notwithstanding the possible, pragmatic, political merits of arguments for moving from tolerance of individual believers to affirmation of the value of religions, there are, however, substantial conceptual difficulties inherent in a secular State taking this position. The difficulties arise because of the precise nature of what is being suggested. The argument above, whether one looks to Rockefeller, Taylor or Raz, is not simply an argument that there is a value to society in having access to different cultures including religious cultures. One could accept this without believing that all, or even any, of those cultures necessarily had value in themselves because, through Mill's marketplace of ideas, even ideas that are wrong can produce improvements in our thinking (Mill 1972, pp 78–113). Instead, there is a requirement to respect all cultures because all cultures have value; something that we should recognize because otherwise 'the members of the unrecognized cultures will feel deracinated and empty' (Wolf 1994, p 75). One might argue for this on the basis that one could accept that all cultures have value for at least some of their members. Thus Parekh suggests that:

[s]ince every culture gives stability and meaning to human life, holds its members together as a community, displays creative energy, and so on, it deserves respect.

(Parekh 2006, pp 176–177)[30]

---

29 Thus, for example, Joly writes that 'the greatest concern for the Muslims settled in Great Britain is . . . the *de facto* agnosticism and secularism which prevail' (Joly 1995, p 12).

30 There is, however, some complexity and possible ambiguity and contradiction in Parekh's position because he writes that he accepts that many cultures 'are exploitative and oppressive and do not promote their members' well-being' (Parekh 2006, p 348). If the contention is that a culture should be respected no matter how much it exploits, oppresses and fails to promote its members' wellbeing, presumably the concept of respect must have only a minimal content.

However, here again, this does not seem sufficient for the demand that is being made. The demand being made is not contingent on some good coming from the culture; instead *we* should simply value all cultures. But how can we do this? More specifically how can those who are secular respect and value those cultures that are religious?[31]

Appiah is surely right to argue that '[w]e can live together without agreeing on what the values are that make it good to live together; we can agree about what to do in most cases without agreeing why it is right' (Appiah 2006, p 71). Indeed this is the standard condition within modern pluralistic societies (Taylor 1994, p 72). Living together within modern states requires compromises about action. Accommodations towards beliefs and actions that you believe to be wrong in a variety of ways have to be made. However, Appiah is surely equally wrong to argue, using the example of incest, that '[y]ou can agree with an Asente that it's wrong, even if you don't accept his explanation of why [which is religious in nature]' (Appiah 2006, p 69). A moral judgement about what is wrong is not just a conclusion. Judgements about what is wrong include the path by which we arrived at the answer. We could not speak of the quality of a judgement were this not the case. If my judgement is based on rational argument and yours is based on assertion of faith we do not agree about anything that relates to the judgement in anything other than a very superficial sense, even though we might, because of the conclusions that we have arrived at, both campaign for a proposed piece of legislation.[32] We do not have the same formula for making our decision. Compromising about actions that enable us to live together should not lead to us ignoring the fact that, at root, we do not agree with each other. For Appiah, '[c]osmopolitans suppose that all cultures have enough overlap in their vocabulary of values to begin a conversation' (Appiah 2006, p 57). The secular and the religious, however, do not, at root, share the same values; at root there is no overlap. '[I]f we accept that the mystic, the prophet, is sincerely undergoing some sort of transcendent experience, but we cannot believe in a supernatural world, then *what is going on?*' (emphasis in original) (Rushdie 1991b, p 408). Disagreement about the basis of argument and the language in which the argument is to be carried on must impregnate the argument as a whole. Precisely because religion for some people is not 'like stamp-collecting or playing squash, a minor hobby' (Knott 1986, p 4) and precisely because, at least for adherents, 'religion is special – it is not just a hobby or recreational pursuit' (Ahdar and Leigh 2005, p 91) and precisely because for those who are secular religion may be different, but certainly is not special (if special in

---

31 And vice versa.
32 In putting forward this argument it is not necessary to suggest that one way of reaching the conclusion is better than another. It is enough simply to say that they are so radically different as to prevent the possibility of there being true agreement.

any way implies superiority), there are limits to how the secular State can react to it. The choice between the secular worldview and the worldview of religions is not, in Raz's phrase, a choice between a preference for tea and coffee (Raz 1986, pp 328–329); to choose the worldview of religions is to deny the fundamental validity of secularism; to choose the worldview of secularism is to deny the fundamental validity of religions.[33] We can live together, find things of value in each other and, within certain boundaries, respect the right of each other to live in the way that we choose. We cannot go beyond that.[34] 'Religion is a mode of activity deploying its own grammar' (Martin 2005, p 171). Faith has no weight for the secular; rationality has no determinant force for the religious.[35] Each denies the foundational value of that which the other finds foundational.[36] The fact that individuals from the two sides can interact with civility should not disguise the divide that exists.[37]

Even conservative political thought, prefaced on the belief that:

> [r]eligion hath such a superiority above all other things, and that indispensable influence upon all mankind, that it is necessary to our living happy in this world as it is to our being saved in the next; without it man is an abandoned creature, one of the worst beasts Nature hath produced, and fit only for the society of wolves and bears,
>
> (Halifax 1969, p 67)

33 As we saw in Chapter 1 above personal religiosity can, however, haver between the two.

34 Ignatieff argues to the contrary. Because religion is central to the identity of many people and because human reason is limited in what it knows, Ignatieff believes that 'secular rationalist liberals', like himself, should not 'dismiss religion en bloc or . . . dismiss religious belief as a whole' (Ignatieff 2005, p 130). They should not 'characterize all religious opinion as a stubborn or irrational prejudice that any reasonable person would change if they allowed reason to influence their opinions in religious matters' because to do so is disrespectful towards religions (Ignatieff 2005, p 130). Ignatieff further argues for a 'politics of empathy' that would understand the feelings of exclusion that religious minorities, particularly those from immigrant groups, sometimes feel (Ignatieff 2005, p 132). However understanding feelings of exclusion and the attitude one takes towards the basis of religion are separable matters. One can appreciate the feelings of exclusion that religions feel in contemporary society and still dismiss religious belief as per se implausible. This may be disrespectful, but then presumably so is the assertion of religious certainties by believers. That is what divides religions and the secular world.

35 On the relationship between religion and reason, see, Macklem 2000.

36 In the quotidian lives of both many believers and the person who is secular there is, of course, a complex mix of faith and rationality. What divides them, however, is what they ultimately value.

37 A quite separate argument against valuing all cultures equally for themselves is that, in doing so, the things that matter to that culture become unimportant. The truth or otherwise of the beliefs and values of the culture are of no particular significance because all cultures and thus all beliefs and all values are valued. See, Jones 1994, pp 327 and 329. More generally, see, Barry 2001, pp 264–271.

distinguished between a belief in the superiority of religion and a belief in the value of all religions (Halifax 1969, pp 71–72).[38] Notwithstanding the overarching claims above for the benefits of affirming the worth of all communities' contemporary thought, others also see problems when faced with the demands of religious groups. Thus, for example, Habermas, in arguing for the general need to protect 'the integrity of the traditions of forms of life of others', does not wish to extend this protection to 'religious ... interpretations of the world that claim exclusiveness for a privileged way of life' where '[s]uch conceptions lack an awareness of the fallibility of their claims, as well as respect for the "burdens of reason" ' (Habermas 1994, p 133). He is, however, prepared to extend protection to 'the subjectivized "gods and demons" of the modern world' (Habermas 1994, p 133). He argues that this will deny protection only to 'fundamentalist' religion (Habermas 1994, p 132). In reality, however, as we have seen in Chapter 1, most institutionalised religions 'claim exclusiveness for a privileged way of life' and most do not always accept, and do not accept at a foundational level, the necessity for 'respect for the "burdens of reason" '. Some are more strident in their position than others but, at base, they take the same stance. If, as Badawi argues, 'religion is nothing but a stability; it is nothing but certainty and without certainty we have no faith' (Badawi 1995, p 75), then all religion is 'fundamentalist' in Habermas's terms; only personal religiosity will receive the protection that Habermas argues for.[39]

To deny the possibility of a secular State affirming the worth of individual religions, even while accepting the necessity for tolerance and nondiscrimination, is no small matter. '[M]uch of modern social and political life turns on questions of recognition' (Appiah 1994, p 149). To refuse to affirm worth in religions in themselves is to marginalise the place of religions in the public life of society and to do so precisely because they are religions. To counter this Rockefeller argues that:

> [i]t is not possible for secular politics to address fully the religious needs of individuals or groups for a sense of unconditional acceptance. However, any liberal democratic politics committed to the ideals of freedom and

---

38 On the place of religion in conservative political thought, see, Quinton 1978.

39 Badawi's contention that religion is certainty is debatable. For example, universalist Quakers, with their belief that 'a relationship with God can be found through a number of religious paths, and that no one path is necessarily more adept in this than others' (Dandelion 1996, p 369), do not seem to fit this mould. The more limited suggestion that many or even most religions are founded on a bedrock certainty, usually grounded in faith, may be more accurate. Some approaches to philosophy involve a search for certainty. However, even the Cartesian search for apodictic certainty comes with an acknowledgement of the importance of Montaigne's dictum 'doubt everything' in his essay 'Apology for Raimond de Sebonde' (Montaigne 1869, p 476). This contrasts strongly with religious notions like papal infallibility.

equality cannot escape the demand that it create inclusive and sustaining social environments that respect all peoples in their cultural diversity giving them a feeling of belonging to the larger community.

(Rockefeller 1994, p 97)

However, to argue this is to understate that which divides the secular world and the world of religions and to ask of both worlds more than they can possibly give. Toleration, nondiscrimination and even an affirmation of the desirability of having different religions within a State are all possible and perhaps even necessary and desirable, but the secular State could affirm the value of religions for their own sake, only at the expense of a schizophrenic disregard for the nature of its own foundation. As Ahdar puts it, somewhat baldly:

[for the secular state] [t]o acknowledge higher antecedent [religious] rights is simply to revisit the very foundations of liberal democracy and to gainsay the longstanding secular basis to the state. That debate is over, the Enlightenment happened and religion lost.

(Ahdar 2001, p 283)

Personal law systems

Historically in Europe the triumph of tolerance in ending religious strife was to separate religion and the State (Cranston 1987, p 108; Saunders 1997, ch 7). However, that separation happened at a time when it could be assumed that almost everyone had some religious belief (Cranston 1987, p 105). More than this, the range of those beliefs in the countries that were to become Great Britain was – the vast majority – not that great. Tolerance and neutrality towards religions in contemporary Great Britain takes on a different tone when religions are more diverse and no religion benefits from what Ahdar, writing about New Zealand, refers to as 'de facto cultural establishment' (Ahdar 2001, p 275).[40]

'[T]olerance' observes Ahdar, who writes from an evangelical Christian perspective, 'is nothing to be sneezed at . . . Nevertheless, tolerance ought to be seen for what it is' (Ahdar 2000, p 283; Ahdar and Leigh 2005, pp 7–8). Cranston cites TS Eliot as saying:

'the Christian does not want to be tolerated' and goes on to observe that what Eliot meant was that 'the Christian desired something better –

---

40 Legal establishment, which is the subject matter of Chapter 3, is a separate matter from cultural establishment. The secular society described in Chapter 1 is clearly not one wherein any religion can be said to be culturally established.

respect, humour, esteem; to be positively welcome and wanted as a member of society'.

(Cranston 1987, p 101)

There is no reason to think that Christianity is alone among religions in wanting this. Thus, for example, Murad Khurran, then the Director General of the Islamic Foundation, has asked of Muslims in Great Britain:

[s]hould . . . we accept to live as a grudgingly accepted minority sub-culture, always under siege, always struggling to retain the little niche it has been allowed to carve out for itself?

(Murad 1986, p 6)

Many religions seek not simply the right to follow their beliefs and practices but also the assurance of a place that is central in society. Toleration, particularly for those who are assiduous in their faith, may not seem to suffice and yet, as we have seen above, the State itself cannot conceptually go beyond toleration in valuing religions.

In some States personal law systems operate, allowing different faith groups to follow their own traditions in some aspects of their lives while still acceding to the authority of the State in general. Derrett defines personal law as:

the system of rules applicable by any court to an individual in respect of topics covered by that law, determined by reference to the religion which he professes or purports to profess or is presumed to profess . . .

(Derrett 1968, p 39)[41]

As Boyd notes:

[h]istorical research has shown that it was the normal practice, from ancient times through the post-colonial era of the last century, for peoples, whether conquerors or conquered, to continue to live under 'personal laws', based usually on a combination of custom, tradition and religion that defined them as a people.

Moreover, such laws 'continue to be prevalent throughout much of the world

---

41 Hooker offers a slightly different definition: 'Personal laws are law which apply to certain defined classes of people, defined either on racial grounds ("Chinese", "Malay") or upon religious grounds ("Muslim"), or occasionally, upon both ("Hindu")' (Hooker 1976, p 1). Allott distinguishes systems that recognise 'the *Law* of a community' from those which recognise 'the *Law* of a person or class of persons, ie as a "personal law" ' (Allott 1980, p 142).

in one form or another today' (Boyd 2004, p 78).[42] Nevertheless, traditionally there has been relatively little attention paid by legal academics to the idea of creating personal law systems in mainstream Western states despite the fact that, prima facie, they seem to offer a further mechanism beyond the concepts of neutrality and toleration for accommodating the needs that religions perceive themselves as having.[43]

In one important sense personal law systems already exist in Great Britain. We saw in Chapter 1 that some religious groups have generated their own law and their own dispute settling mechanisms that use that law to order the community. These systems can be of great importance for the communities concerned. Thus, for example:

> Muslim law is considered as superior and dominant over English law in the eyes and mind of the Muslim individual and community, and Muslims still follow Muslim law in England through the employment and use of a number of strategies, whatever the official law claims and whether it acknowledges this socio-legal reality or not.
>
> (Yilmaz 2005, p 80)

Notwithstanding the attitude of believers, such systems are however usually, in legal terms, wholly separate from the State's legal system. There are, however, two systems that are anomalous in this respect. The law of the Church of England and the Church's courts which make decisions using that law are part of the British state legal system and the Beth Din's commercial decisions, which are made under Jewish law, are enforceable under the Arbitration Act 1996.[44] State law is also connected to the law of other

---

42 For an examination of the history of personal law systems, see, Vitta 1970, pp 170–187. Galanter and Jayanath argue that 'many countries that maintain such personal law systems are under increasing pressure to abandon these structures . . .' (Galanter and Jayanath 2000, p 105).

43 Thus, for example, Bartholomew observes that the problems of conflict of laws between personal law systems 'have been very little studied in this country, which in view of the fact that it is the centre of a Commonwealth, in many countries of which, several personal laws are applied, is rather surprising' (Bartholomew 1952, p 325). Apart from Derrett, Hooker makes some references to the idea of personal law systems as does Patrick Glenn (Hooker 1975, Patrick Glenn 2004). There is also discussion of personal law in Menski 2000 and Menski 2003 and some references in Shah 2005. There are also studies of particular examples of personal law systems in non-Western countries, some of which are noted below. One striking exception to this general dearth of literature is Shachar 2001.

44 On the Church of England's courts, see Doe 1996, ch 5. On Anglican canon law, generally, see Doe 1998, ch 3. There has been very little written about the Beth Din in Great Britain. It is, however, a court that has existed in Great Britain for a considerable time. Alderman, for example, briefly discusses the politics of the Beth Din in nineteenth century Great Britain (Alderman 1992, pp 148–149). For a very brief account of its work, see, Findlay 1999. On the work of religious courts in Great Britain generally, see, Fleming 2003. For a study of the Beth Din in the US, see Kirsh 1971 and Rabbinical Courts 1970.

religious legal systems within Great Britain in the sense that that law may be recognised as part of the facts before a State court. Thus, for example, in a defamation case, *MacCaba v Lichenstein* [2004] EWHC 1580, Gray J held, at paragraph 16, that 'Jewish law is a factor to be borne in mind' when deciding the case, even though it was not determinant of the issue. More unusually, where parties have entered into a marriage under Jewish religious usages as well as under British law, under s 10(A) of the Matrimonial Causes Act 1973, the courts have a discretion to refuse to issue a decree absolute with respect to a divorce unless the parties have cooperated in ensuring that the marriage will also be dissolved according to those religious usages.[45] Here again the religious divorce in issue has no legal status in the State's eyes, but whether it exists or not is part of the factual background that is relevant to the State's exercise of its legal jurisdiction. From these examples it is clear that personal law systems are thus, in various ways, already part of the legal culture of Great Britain. However, Great Britain does not have officially sanctioned personal law systems of the kind that are found in many other jurisdictions.

Attempts to introduce personal law systems into the British legal system go back at least as far as the 1970s (Yilmaz 2005, p 59). The most publicised attempts have emanated from Muslims. '[T]here are immensely important cultural reasons for this, linked with the nature of Islam as a religion and an all-encompassing ethical/moral and thereby legal order' (Menski 1993, p 256). Nevertheless, the case for a personal law system, although most persistently made in Great Britain by Muslims, is not one that is solely linked to Islam.[46] Those jurisdictions that do have personal law systems apply them to a range of religions.[47]

Yilmaz suggests that the Muslim demand for a personal law system relating to family matters arises because of five main reasons.

---

45 This provision was introduced by the Divorce (Religious Marriages) Act 2002. While the provision applies to marriages in accordance 'with the usages of the Jews' (s 10A (1)(a)(i)), other usages can also be prescribed by the Lord Chancellor after consulting the Lord Chief Justice (s 10A(6)); to date this has not happened. If this is done the courts will be able to deal with divorces consequent on marriages involving these other prescribed usages in the same way (s 10A(1)(a)(ii)). On the need for legislation of this kind, see Freeman 2001.

46 Thus, for example, Berkovits' suggestion that the British State courts should recognise *gets* pronounced by Beth Din, albeit where those *gets* complied with s 1(1) and s 1(2) of the Matrimonial Causes Act 1973 is a proposal for a partial personal law system (Berkovits 1990, pp 135–138). Bartholomew argues that historically for many centuries British State courts did recognise marriages contracted under Jewish law (Bartholomew 1961). Chapter 5 of this book deals with the more limited question of the State recognising matters such as marriages and divorces emanating from religious legal systems at greater length than the discussion here.

47 Thus, for example, Malaysia recognises both Muslim and Hindu Law (Hooker 1976). In Israel, Jews, Muslims, Druzes and Christians have religious courts (Shiloh 1970, p 485). Equally, the systems of personal law that already exist in Great Britain but are not recognised by the State are not limited to Islamic law systems (see, for example, Menski 1987).

First, family values among Muslims as in many oriental cultures are held in very high regard. This is most likely to be so when religious beliefs, legal principles and family relations are closely intertwined, as they are in the Muslim ethos. Second, other aspects of Muslim law have given way to Western-spirited laws in many countries with Muslim majorities, so the Muslim family law has come to seem even more precious. Third, Muslims are familiar with the *millett* system that is of a pluralistic nature and permits family laws within the same jurisdiction. Fourth, many Muslims perceive the issue in terms of religious freedom and claim religious tolerance towards other monotheistic faiths. Fifth, finding themselves surrounded by premarital and extramarital sex and children born out of wedlock, abortion, prostitution, pornography, child abuse, marital breakdowns, neglect of the elderly and public acceptance of homosexuality, many Muslims believe that a sensible method of avoiding such problems would be to operate within a system of Muslim personal law.

(Yilmaz 2001, p 299)[48]

Yilmaz further notes that Muslims are aware of the fact that British governments implemented personal law systems in various countries during colonial times (Yilmaz 2001, p 299).[49]

Poulter has suggested that, in relation to one specific suggestion to bring in a personal law system, '[t]he proposal [for a separate Muslim personal law system] seems to have been rejected out of hand [by the Government] on the ground that the suggested legislation would not be "appropriate" ' (Poulter 1990, p 157). The casual nature of this dismissal is disturbing in itself. We noted above that liberalism argues that there is a need to give 'public reasons' when justifying positions; assertions of faith are not, for these purposes, public reasons but, then, neither are assertions of 'inappropriateness'. An argued rejection on the basis of thought-out reasons is one thing; a pre-emptory rebuff, another. Nevertheless, the nature of this response is wholly in keeping with a general history of official silence in response to suggestions that Islamic family forms, such as potentially polygamous marriages, should be recognised in law (Bradney 1993, pp 43–45). This in itself further exacerbates matters. The combination of academic silence and official indifference does not suggest that the matter is receiving the attention that it deserves.

In 2003, in Ontario, Canada, a new Islamic Institute of Civil Justice was set up with the intention of allowing Muslims to settle disputes with respect to

---

48 Poulter gave a similar list in 1990 (Poulter 1990, pp 147–148).
49 Long before contemporary Muslim claims for an Islamic personal law system in Great Britain Bartholomew noted the 'strange fact that although whenever the English have established courts in India, Africa or Asia, one of the fundamental principles of the administration of justice that has been adopted has been that of a system of multiple personal laws . . . no such principle is admitted in England' (Bartholomew 1961, p 83).

family or inheritance matters. The disputes would be determined according to the principles of the sharia, but would be enforceable in Canadian State courts under the Arbitration Act 1991 (Boyd 2004, p 3). The suggestion that Muslims make use of the Arbitration Act 1991 in this way was not entirely novel with respect to the application of religious laws in Canada. The Jewish Beth Din, known in Ontario as the Beis Din, was already making decisions under Jewish law regarding marriage breakdowns, financial support, property division, child custody and access issues and having them enforced under the Arbitration Act 1991 (Boyd 2004, pp 41 and 55–56).[50] Various Christian groups also used the arbitration system in relation to family disputes, applying their own legal rules to decisions (Boyd 2004, p 56). Nevertheless, the suggestion that Muslims would use the jurisdiction proved to be extremely controversial. As a result of that controversy the Ontario Government asked Marion Boyd, a Canadian politician and former Attorney-General of Ontario to report on the proposals. Boyd's report looked at the relevant legislation in the area and also carried out a wide-ranging consultation into reactions to the Muslim proposals. It concluded that, subject to various recommendations for reforms in the system, it should continue to be possible to use the Arbitration Act in family and inheritance law cases and that the disputes should continue to be able to be determined by religious law (Boyd 2004, p 133). Despite this the Ontario legislature passed the Family Statute Law Amendment Act 2006 which, among other things, amended s 1(1) of the Arbitration Act 1991, so as to ensure that all arbitrations are carried out under 'the law of Ontario or another Canadian jurisdiction', thus preventing not only the proposed Muslim use of the Arbitration Act, but also the use that had previously been made of it by the Beis Din and by Christians.

The objections to the Muslim plans that Boyd notes are instructive when considering a possible personal law system in Great Britain.[51] While some who responded to Boyd's inquiry objected to the general idea of using arbitration in the area of family law, others objected to the use of religious law in the area and some even more specifically to the use of the sharia (Boyd 2004, Section 4). Some argued that it was important that everyone should be subject to the same law, some that the law in this area ought to be secular, some that there were difficulties inherent in deciding what the sharia might hold in particular cases because of the varying schools of Islamic law and some that there were a number of discriminatory or objectionable practices inherent in the sharia. The range of objections that Boyd received are very similar to the

50 According to Boyd, the Beth Din also use the arbitration system in Quebec, although in this State the decisions are merely taken to be advisory (Boyd 2004, p 33).

51 The furore that arose in response to the Archbishop of Canterbury's fairly limited suggestions about the need for further legal accommodation to religious systems is also indicative of the pragmatic, political problems in this area (Williams 2008b). See, further, Bradney forthcoming.

list of possible objections to a Muslim personal law system that Poulter noted in relationship to the suggestion that such a system should be introduced into Great Britain (Poulter 1990, pp 158–159). Many and perhaps all of these objections merit further consideration. Moreover, the experience of other jurisdictions that do have personal law systems does not suggest that they are easy to operate. Pinhas, for example, observes of the Israeli system that:

> we have a system affected with legal schizophrenia, for within it, two different judicial systems – that of religious law (or laws) and that of secular law – are struggling and pulling in opposite directions.
>
> (Pinhas 1990, p 537)[52]

Equally, however, none of the difficulties and objections raised in relation to Canada or in relation to other jurisdictions that have personal law systems are of such overwhelming force as to justify rejecting the notion of a personal law system without that further deeper consideration. There are both counterarguments to the objections and reasons why a mixed system of personal law and State law, even though difficult to operate, might be preferable to a single State system, which is imposed on everyone. Thus, for example, it is clear that the values of family law in Great Britain are, in part, derived from the Christian religion, the law already makes special accommodation for some religions in some instances, any personal law jurisdiction would, if it used an arbitration structure, be voluntary and general statements about the discriminatory nature of Islamic law are, in the light of the varying schools and traditions within Islamic law, contentious if they are said to apply to Islam per se. Moreover, it is important to remember that the choice is not between having a personal law system and not having a personal law system. As we noted above, non-State institutions already exist and already settle disputes. It is, in the present climate of opinion, inconceivable that the State could abolish these non-State institutions. The only choice is about the degree to which the State recognises these systems. In the context of the Canadian system, Emon has argued for the value not just of allowing Muslim bodies to use the arbitration system, but also for the State more widely recognising, promoting and *regulating* the work of Muslim institutions; recognising non-State systems can also be a vehicle for influencing non-State systems:

> By creating and regulating institutions of Muslim civil society, the government will provide an equal playing field for diverse voices in the Muslim community to articulate competing visions of Shari'a values.

---

52 For a similar comment about the 'different – and at times contradictory – philosophies of law, world outlooks and social goals', see Frimer 1990, p 553.

No single Muslim voice will be empowered by the state; rather, the state will provide an equal playing field for all voices to be heard, thereby contributing to debate and dialogue between competing civil society groups.

(Emon 2006, p 354)

In a similar vein Ansari argues that:

[c]ompromise might be possible if the British state were prepared to allow Muslim communities greater legal autonomy and were proactively to encourage the settlement of disputes between Muslims by mediation, conciliation and informal arbitration by local and national Muslim institutions, while, of course, not losing sight of proper consideration of gender-based power imbalances and individual children's welfare.

(Ansari 2004, p 286)

Such arguments contend that personal law systems that are recognised by the State, by creating contact between State and religious groups, give the State the opportunity to influence and perhaps prevent those practices that the State finds most objectionable. More broadly, Shachar has argued for the benefits of personal law systems as:

transformative accommodation. This is a variant that takes the two different locuses of authority – the *nomoi* group and the state – and, instead of viewing their conflict of interests as a problem, considers it as an occasion for encouraging each entity to become more responsive to all its constituents. Through an arrangement of *non*-exclusive competition for the loyalties of those citizens who overlap both jurisdictions, transformative accommodation seeks to adapt the power structures of both *nomoi* group and state in order to accommodate their most vulnerable constituents. Each intersection of jurisdictions provides each authority with an opportunity to increase its accountability and sensitivity to otherwise marginalized group members, since each entity must now 'bid' for these individuals' continued adherence to its sphere of authority rather than take it for granted. (emphasis in original).

(Shachar 2001, p 117)[53]

Personal law systems create significant problems at both the technical and conceptual level. However, if they are voluntary in their nature, they offer considerable advantages to those who find the values of State law deficient in

---

53 One very important element in this argument is the notion of competition that it involves. Shachar argues that '[c]learly delineated and selective "entrance", "exit", and "re-entry" options are thus a crucial component in improving the situation of traditionally vulnerable group members . . .' (Shachar 2001, p 124).

one respect or another.[54] In doing so they allow a person to follow what they see as being their notion of the good life and in this respect are consistent with the principles of liberalism noted above. It is therefore more than unfortunate that the concept has not, to date, been given greater consideration in debates on the relationship between law and religion in Great Britain.

Conclusion

A liberal, secular State will always disappoint some religious communities within its borders; at one level it may always disappoint all religious communities within its borders. The different conceptions of the world which form the foundation of the secular State on the one hand and religious communities on the other, the different languages that they have for talking about the world and the different notions of evidence that they have for sustaining their arguments are so far apart as to make conversation between the two difficult. It may be true that 'all cultures have enough overlap in their vocabulary of values to begin a conversation' (Appiah 2006, p 57). Even if this is not true at a lower level in a multicultural society, and still more in a cosmopolitan society, most cultures may have sufficient knowledge of languages of value that are not their own 'to begin a conversation'. However, because so much separates them, that conversation will be halting. At the deepest level communication will be impossible. More than this, as Asad argues with respect to Muslims:

> [t]he ideology of political representation in liberal democracies makes it difficult if not impossible to represent Muslims as Muslims. Why? Because in theory the citizens who constitute a democratic state belong to a class that is defined only by what is common to all its members and its members only. What is common is the abstract equality of individual citizens to one another, so that each counts as one.
>
> (Asad 2003, p 173)[55]

---

54 Whether such systems would be voluntary in practice has been queried by many writers. Some would argue that the patriarchal nature of some religious communities is such as to so constrain choice for women as to make the voluntary nature of any personal law system questionable. Thus, for example, Stoper, writing generally about potential conflict between women's rights and religious and cultural practices, argues that, even where women accept a disadvantageous social practice, 'the disadvantageous practice should not be allowed unless overwhelming evidence proves that the practice is consented to by all the women involved, out of their own, genuine free choice' (Stoper 2003, pp 218–219). Such caution is important, but there is a difference between urging caution and arguing that women can never genuinely consent to the use of personal law systems. To argue that women can never genuinely consent to such systems, or to practices such as polygamy, runs the risk of equating free choice with choices that are commonly made in Western liberal democracies and of denying the possibility of agency on the part of women who live in traditional religious communities.
55 The argument is not, of course, limited to Muslims.

What matters most for those who are wholly committed to their religion – their religious identity – has little if any significance for the liberal State. Where the State accords particular rights to those who are religious it does so, not because of the fact of their religious identity, but because they are secular citizens. However, the very fact that there will inevitably be some degree of frustration and disappointment on the part of members of religious communities, carries with it significant lessons for the liberal State.

A liberal State can only justify its attitude towards those within its borders who have religious sensibilities if there is an exemplary pursuit of those principles and practices that a liberal State claims lies at its root. The least departure from the principles of noncoercion, neutrality or tolerance or the least failure to give public reasons that justify its attitude towards particular religious practices puts in peril the claims that the State makes for itself. History and tradition that explain departures from principle are, in this context, not the public reasons that the State needs to defend its position. What Great Britain once was in terms of its religious composition or other matters may, in some areas of the law, explain why contemporary legal rules and institutions take the form that they do. However history is not in itself a justification for the present position. Instead, each rule and institution needs to be constantly reappraised in the light of the arguments above. This needs to be done not because of any necessity to respond to complaints from religions of whatever size or place in the history of Great Britain. Instead, the State needs to justify to itself its practices. Even if religions are silent about departures from principle, even if religions are complicit in or argue for departures from principle, a liberal State fails if it cannot persuade itself that it lives up to its own claims.

Chapter 3

The established churches

Introduction

As we noted in Chapter 1 the Church of England is established in law in England while the Church of Scotland is, in the view of most commentators, a church that is established in law in Scotland. The notion of establishment is in itself a complex matter. 'Doctrines of establishment', comments Doe, 'are notoriously difficult to construct' (Doe 1998, p 13). Similarly, Davies asserts that there has never been a universally recognised content to the establishment of the Church of England (Davies 1976, p 15). However, whatever the mysterious concept of establishment means precisely, it must signify a separate and different constitutional status for these churches that sets them apart from other religions within Great Britain. Given the principle of neutrality towards religions noted in Chapter 2, the fact of this establishment thus immediately seems potentially to be of considerable import in the analysis of the relationship between religion and law in Great Britain. This, however, depends upon what establishment means.

On one view, whatever it constitutes, establishment, in the case of Great Britain, is at most of symbolic significance and more probably is a mere anachronism, pointing backwards to past beliefs about the relationship between religion and the State in the same way that talk of sunrise defers to a long dead science. Thus, for example, Holdsworth, writing towards the beginning of the twentieth century, observed that:

> [i]t is true that there is still an Established Church, that the King is still its supreme head and the defender of its faith; that its law is still the King's ecclesiastical law, and an integral part of the law of England. But, like many other parts of the law and constitution of England, these are survivals of an older order, from which all real meaning has departed . . .
>
> (Holdsworth 1920, p 340)

Similarly Bogdanor, writing at the end of the same century, noted that:

[t]he history of the relationship between the Church of England and the State ... is one of progressive attenuation. From having been a virtual department of the state, the Church has become almost, although not quite, one amongst many denominations ...

(Bogdanor 1995, p 228)

Writing much more recently, Asad argues that, 'the constitutional privilege accorded to the Church of England in the British state today is largely a formality' (Asad 2003, p 190). Yet, notwithstanding this unity of scholarship across time, nations and academic disciplines, it remains a fact that establishment for the Church of England brings with it the presence of two of its archbishops and 24 of its bishops in the House of Lords.[1] The Church of Scotland continues to hold itself out as being 'the national Church in Scotland' (Church of Scotland, nd). Establishment in this and other ways is more than ceremony and pageantry. Moreover, not all commentators take the same relaxed view of the reality of establishment as that that is to be found in the quotations above. Thus, for example, Pearce writes that:

the institutions of the Church of England still carry on the public administration of English Christianity which was once unequivocally 'the business of government', and has never unequivocally ceased to be so.

(Pearce 2001, p 470)

Another commentator, Mortensen goes even further.

[I]n England and Scotland, Christianity is the national religion because the established churches are enmeshed in the culture, helped to create it, continue to play a role in defining it and are recognized, even by non-adherents, as being conservators of folkways.

(Mortensen 1998–99, p 512)

From the above it is clear that both what establishment is and what effect it has in Great Britain are contentious questions. This chapter will thus look at what establishment means in Great Britain in the twenty-first century and enquire into whether establishment is compatible with the proper attitude of a liberal democracy towards a religion.

---

1 However, the privileges of establishment can change quickly. Historically the common law offence of blasphemy means that any 'person may, without being liable for prosecution for it, attack Judaism, or Mahomedanism, or even any sect of the Christian Religion (*save the established religion of the country*)' (emphasis added) (*Gathercole's Case* 2 (1938) 2 Lewin 237). Section 79 of the Criminal Justice and Immigration Act 2008 summarily abolished the offence.

The concept of establishment

In 1970, the Church of England's Chadwick Commission report on the relationship between Church and State began with the observation that '[i]t is hard to define what is meant by the term "Church as by law established"' (Chadwick 1970, p 1). Most commentators take the same view. Both what establishment means and in what way the Church of England is established are difficult questions. As Ogilvie notes '[e]stablishment is not and never has been a legal term of art' (Ogilvie 1990, p 195). Examples of establishment vary:

> from formal, *de jure*, to informal, *de facto*, establishments, symbolic in contrast to substantive establishments, and establishments of a generic religion, a collection of faiths (or denominations), or just one faith.
>
> (Ahdar and Leigh 2005, p 79)

One expression of the Church of England's establishment is found in its own canon law, itself part of the British legal system. Canon A7:

> acknowledge[s] that the Queen's excellent Majesty, acting according to the laws of the realm, is the highest power under God in this kingdom, and has supreme authority over all persons in all cases, as well ecclesiastical as civil.

Under Article IV of the Schedule to the Church of Scotland Act 1921 the Church of Scotland:

> receives from Him [Jesus Christ], its Divine King and Head, and from him alone, the right and power subject to no civil authority to legislate, and to adjudicate finally, in all matters of doctrine, worship, government, and discipline in the Church . . .

One thing that establishment thus means is that, at a very basic level, the Christian God, and more than that the particular Christian God of two churches, is written into the constitution of Great Britain. In *Marshall v Graham*, Phillimore J held that '[t]he process of establishment means that the State has accepted the Church as the religious body in its opinion truly teaching the Christian faith' ([1907] 2KB 112 at p 126). Nevertheless, although it is clear that establishment means that there is a close formal link between the Church of England and the Church of Scotland and the State and thus between religion and the State, what exactly that establishment entails and even when it began remains elusive.

As Doe notes, there is no Establishment Act that establishes the link between the Church of England and the State (Doe 1996, p 8). Instead, establishment is the result of an historical process of the passage of statutes and the making of precedents that has bound together the Church of England and the State (Doe 1996, pp 8–9; Edge 2002, pp 129–130).[2] The same is also true of the Church of Scotland (King Murray 1958). The way in which the juridical components of establishment are categorised varies from author to author. Edge, for example, groups the legal characteristics of the establishment of the Church of England into four categories: constitutional law, such as the fact that the monarch must, under the Act of Settlement 1700, be Protestant; civil law, such as the duties of a minister as regards celebrating the marriages of their parishioners; criminal laws, such as the law of blasphemy; and fiscal or property laws, such as special legal rules relating to the ownership of church property (Edge 2002, p 329). As Edge observes, as befits the happenstance of their historical origins, these legal rules collectively do not suggest any 'comprehensive plan' (Edge 2002, p 129). Ahdar and Leigh, on the other hand, conceptualise juridical establishment somewhat differently, seeing its main legal incidents as being in the sovereign as head of State and Supreme Governor of the Church of England, State involvement in church procedures such as the appointment of bishops and the Church's involvement in State processes such as the coronation of a new monarch (Ahdar and Leigh 2005, pp 76–77). The difference between these approaches is a difference between seeing the concept of establishment as being coextensive with a description of the legal relationship between Church and State and seeing the concept as descriptive of that which is central to the legal notion of establishment. Both approaches point to important aspects of establishment. The fact that, under the Act of Supremacy 1558, the sovereign is Supreme Governor of the Church of England and, under the Bill of Rights Act 1688, the Coronation Oath Act 1688, the Act of Settlement 1700 and the Accession Declaration Act 1910, has to be in communion with the Church of England is of constitutional moment. This leads on to the fact that the appointment of bishops is part of the royal prerogative. In practice this part of the prerogative is exercised on the advice of the Prime Minister (Hill 2001, p 113). Whether this itself is of great consequence for the constitution is debatable.[3] However, the fact that there is no legal requirement that the Prime Minister be in communion with the Church of England is plainly of significance to the Church. The historical process of committees, some internal to the Church and some not, with a final shortlist of two candidates that preceded the advice of the Prime Minister reflected, as Hill suggests, 'the delicate balance

2 In relation to the establishment of the Church of England, Laundy argues that 'establishment may be said to date from the time when the Anglo-Saxon kings were first converted to Christianity. In other words, there has never been a time during its existence when the Church of England was not established, except for a brief period under Cromwell' (Laundy 1958, p 445). For a history of early establishment see Rodes Jr 1977.

3 It is not mentioned in constitutional law textbooks.

between the established nature of the Church of England and autonomous self-governance' (Hill 2001, p 113). Equally, legal rules that are consequent upon establishment can have their own importance, whether or not they are central to the notion of establishment. Thus, for example, the relationship between the Church of England and the law of property is unique to it (Doe 1996, ch 15). Most of the legal incidents that are consequent upon establishment are ancient in origin. However, this is not true for all of them. The standing advisory councils on religious education, first created in their present form by the Education Reform Act 1988 and now provided for by the Education Act 1996, must, under s 390 (4)(b) of the 1996 Act, 'except in the case of an area of Wales', have representatives of the Church of England on them. This is quite separate from the provision requiring representatives of Christian denominations and other religions and denominations reflecting the principal religious traditions of an area.[4] Juridical establishment also means more than the fact that the Church of England has separate rights and protections not accorded to other religions. It also means that all citizens have legal rights against the Church as regards marriage, baptism and burial with respect to their parish.[5]

The juridical nature of establishment does not, of itself, exhaust the concept. Ogilvie writes that establishment 'is first and foremost a political word . . . most frequently [used] by church leaders in dealing with state authorities' (Ogilvie 1990, p 195). By the middle of the twentieth century, suggests Chandler, '[t]he essence of the Establishment lay not in its [largely legal] formalities, but in its manners, its informal respects and courtesies' (Chandler 1993, p 921). Hastings similarly suggests that:

> [t]he ease, the informality as well as the formalities of an interlocking relationship at every level between civil and religious authority was what establishment meant. England's secular establishment was riddled with ecclesiastical woodworm in such a cunning and natural way that it displeased almost no one.
>
> (Hastings 1986, p 664)

---

4 Section 390(4)(a) Education Act 1996. Local authorities were given the discretion to set up standing councils under s 29(2) of the Education Act 1944. However, they were not required to do so. Under the 1944 Act, membership of the standing councils, if they were set up, was at the discretion of the local authority (s 29(3) Education Act 1944). The new arrangements for standing councils were brought in as amendments to the Education Reform Act 1988 as it passed through the House of Lords. In introducing the amendments the Bishop of London said that they had the goodwill of the Government and had been agreed with the churches ((1988) Hansard, House of Lords, vol 146 col 415).

5 In *Aston Cantlow and Wilmcote with Billesley Parochial Church Council v Wallbank* [2004] 1 AC 546 at p 557 Lord Nicholls held that parishioners had 'certain rights . . . in respect of marriage and burial services'. For an analysis that casts doubts upon the traditional view of these matters see Doe 1996, pp 358–362.

Doe argues that establishment, in the case of the Church of England, means that the Church of England is the institutional result of a series of legislative acts, that it is treated legally as the State-recognised form of religion, that it has a series of legal rights and duties that do not apply to other religions and that there is a 'fundamental identification of the Church of England with the state' (Doe 1996, p 9). Establishment, on this basis, is a mixture of politics and law. It is about legal rules that pertain directly and peculiarly to the Church of England, but it is also about the place that the Church has in the practical politics of the State. Even here, however, where establishment is examined as a matter of the place of the Church of England in society, the focus of enquiry varies from commentator to commentator. Ahdar and Leigh note the distinction made by some:

> between 'earthed' or 'low' establishment, by which they mean the daily on-the-ground presence of the Church of England in community life, and 'high' establishment – referring to the constitutional apparatus.
>
> (Ahdar and Leigh 2005, p 78)

Thus, for example, Beckford and Gilliat look at the way in which the idea of establishment impinges on the work of Anglican chaplains in prisons and their role in assisting other faiths in prison (Beckford and Gilliat 1998). However, for Davie this notion of the non-juridical side of establishment refers to something at a rather higher level. Establishment, in its non-juridical form:

> evokes the pervasive but nonetheless elusive links existing in certain circles of British society, the nature of which are conveyed in the title of Paxman's book on the subject, *Friends in High Places*.
>
> (Davie 1994, p 139)

The establishment of the Church of England in England is thus a multi-faceted matter that has evolved through history and continues to change (Davie 1994, p 140).

The legal incidents of establishment associated with the Church of Scotland vary somewhat from those associated with the Church of England. The monarch, for example, is the head of the Church of England but not the Church of Scotland (King Murray 1958, p 158).

There is a general view that the degree of establishment of the Church of Scotland is somewhat less than that of the Church of England. When the Chadwick Commission made recommendations for changes to the establishment of the Church of England that, in part, reflected its acknowledgement of the arguments that the Church and State should 'stand further apart', it noted that these recommendations bore 'a distant resemblance to the Scottish establishment' (Chadwick 1970, pp 11, 15–16). Nevertheless, the variation in the legal incidents of establishment between the two Churches is not always to the advantage of the Church of England.

The Church of England has the power to pass Measures – legislative acts of the Church.[6] Parliament gave the Church this power through the passage of the Church of England Assembly (Powers) Act 1919.[7] Any Measure that is properly passed is not merely delegated legislation; rather it:

> enjoys the invulnerability of an Act of Parliament and it is not open to the courts to question *vires* or the procedure by which it was passed, or to do anything to interpret it (per Sir Thomas Bingham in *R v Archbishop of Canterbury, ex parte Williamson*).
>
> (Hill 2001, p 675)[8]

However, the advantage conveyed by this legislative power is somewhat lessened by the fact that a Measure must receive the approval of the Queen in Parliament to be lawful. This approval has not always been forthcoming. Noting the refusal by the House of Lords to allow changes to the Prayer Book in 1927 and 1928 the Chadwick Commission went on to observe that further vetoes would cause a constitutional crisis (Chadwick 1970, pp 15–16).[9] Despite this, the Appointment of Bishops Measure was rejected in 1984 and the Clergy (Ordination) Measure was rejected in 1989, although the latter Measure was later accepted by Parliament in 1990. In addition to the power to reject Measures, Parliament also has the power to, and in practice does, legislate directly and independently for the Church of England.[10] By contrast, the Church of Scotland is much more independent of Parliament. As we saw above, Article IV of the Schedule to the Church of Scotland Act 1921 gives the Church:

> the right and power subject to no civil authority to legislate, and to adjudicate finally, in all matters of doctrine, worship, government, and discipline in the Church. . . .

As with the Church of England, establishment is both a matter of legal incidents and non-juridical matters; thus, when in Scotland, the monarch

---

6   For a discussion of the procedure for passing Measures, see, Doe 1996, pp 57–70.

7   For a discussion of this process, see, Doe 1996, pp 63–66.

8   This case was reported in *The Times* 1st March 1994. It is also set out in full in Hill 2001, pp 672–676.

9   For a discussion for the events surrounding the rejection of these Measures, see, Bell 1935, pp 1325–1360; Machin 2000 and Grimley 2004, ch 4.

10 See, for example, the Church of England Convocations Act 1966.

worships in the Church of Scotland (King Murray 1958, p 161). In both the case of the Church of England and the Church of Scotland:

> [t]he sovereign enjoys a special relationship with the Church of England and the Church of Scotland. Both of these Churches are national churches in that they regard themselves as having a responsibility to bring religion to people in every parish in England and Scotland.
>
> (Bogdanor 1995, p 215)

Kellas notes that the Church of Scotland 'likes to think of itself as the "voice of Scotland" ' and that '[t]he three historic Scottish institutions of the Church, education, and law are to a large extent the basis of the national identity of Scotland' (Kellas 1989, pp 178 and 185).[11]

Wales is the only part of Great Britain where there has been a formal disestablishment of a church.[12] The Welsh Church Act 1914, which was not implemented until 1920, disestablished the Church of England in Wales.[13] The status of the Church in Wales, created as a result of the 1914 Act, is somewhat unclear:

> [I]nsofar as the contemporary institutional Church in Wales was founded in direct consequence of a legislative act of the civil power, and given the notorious difficulties which exist in defining establishment, there is modest judicial support for the view that the Church in Wales is a re-established church. Indeed, three notable vestiges of establishment remain today: the duty of clergy of the Church in Wales to solemnize the marriages of parishioners, the right of parishioners to burial in the churchyard, and the appointment of clergy of the Church in Wales as prison chaplains.
>
> (Doe 2004, p 107)[14]

Establishment thus takes various forms in the different parts of Great Britain with it being comparatively strong in England, rather weaker in Scotland and having only a vestigial form, if any, in Wales.

---

11 The impact that that degree of devolution for Scotland, resulting from the passage of the Scotland Act 1998 and the consequent creation of the Scottish Parliament, has on this is a matter for debate.

12 Northern Ireland is part of the United Kingdom of Great Britain and Northern Ireland. The Irish Church Act 1869 disestablished the Church of Ireland in Ireland.

13 For a brief account of the history of the disestablishment of the Church of England in Wales, see, Taylor 2003, pp 228–231.

14 See, also, Brown 1993–1995, p 20 and Watkin 1990–1992.

The consequences of establishment

Beckford and Gilliat write that:

> [i]t is undeniable that the established Church of England has enjoyed, privileges and advantages to which no other religious organisation has been granted access in the country's history since the late sixteenth century. The fact that establishment has also entailed numerous and, in some cases, onerous responsibilities and constraints on the Church's autonomy does not alter the basic picture of Anglican privilege.
>
> (Beckford and Gilliat 1998, p 205)

The privileges of the Church of England are various and some have already been noted in the passages above on the nature of establishment. The privileges include the less tangible benefits of access to places of political power as well as direct advantages in, for example, the way in which property is held. Weaker forms of establishment in Scotland and Wales bring with it smaller degrees of privilege. Indeed, in Wales, the limited nature of establishment is such that it can be seen to bring with it only burdens without benefits, tangible or otherwise. Taylor notes that there is a sizeable body of opinion within the Church in Wales that would wish to withdraw from the duty to marry and bury all parishioners and put itself on an equal footing with other Christian churches within Wales (Taylor 2003, p 237). Nevertheless, establishment is normally equated with advantage. This privilege does not on first appearances appear to bespeak of the neutrality that is fundamental to the liberal State's attitude towards religion that was noted in Chapter 2.

The consequences of establishment also involve matters that are more related to status than to privilege. Leigh observes that:

> [t]he coronation of a new sovereign plays an important symbolic part in vesting a new monarch with authority . . . and in perpetuating the ill-defined notion of a 'Christian state'. The ceremony is a religious one, modelled on Old Testament accounts of the anointing of the kings of Israel. It includes specifically Christian elements, such as anointing the sovereign with oil and a communion service, and is conducted by the Archbishop of Canterbury in Westminster Cathedral. The Christian, indeed Protestant, character of the existing service is unmistakeable.
>
> (Leigh 2004, p 270)

Establishment is as much about the place of institutionalised religion in society and the State as it is about particular legal rights. Establishment says that '[t]he Church of England remains a significant institution, *of course*, despite the tiny number of regular church-goers' (emphasis supplied) (Cox 1982, p 3). For its supporters, establishment only gives the Church of England those advantages that are 'consonant with its size and its place in what the Chadwick Commission called "the facts and memories of English life" ' (McClean 2003/2004, p 303).[15] However, in twenty-first century Britain, the question that establishment poses is whether those facts still remain facts and whether those memories are distant, nostalgic or even false. The status asserted by establishment, upon which are consequent the legal advantages of establishment, is now the point in issue.

The historical sovereignty of Church and State

In England and in Scotland and even possibly in Wales the State is, at least at one level, not neutral towards religion. It has written a form of Christianity into its constitutional structures. Why this once should have been done is clear. Great Britain was at one time a Christian State and a Christian society; the Church of England was formally 'a virtual department of state' (Bogdanor 1995, p 228). For centuries the Church of England was deeply engaged in the governance of the country, as was the Church of Scotland in Scotland. Indeed, '[i]n the past, Church and State were so closely connected that they could not be conceived as separate entities, each with a separate life' (Davies 1976, p 14). Temporal governance and spiritual governance did indeed go hand-in-hand. The relationship between Church and State was, in Moore's words:

> in the nature of a marriage between the two with the further characteristic of marriage that the two parties retained their individual characteristics, but were regarded for many purposes as one.
>
> (Moore 1967, p 12)

However, at the time of these initial origins, not just Great Britain but Europe was a very different place from present times. It was somewhere where 'spiritual forces impinged on porous agents, [and] in which the social was grounded in the sacred and secular time . . .' (Taylor 2007, p 61). The intellectual milieu was wholly different from today. Individuals, 'porous agents', were not conceived of, did not conceive of themselves, in the way that individuals are now conceived of; religion, spiritual life, the sacred and society all were both differently related and differently thought about to that in the present day. The history of the West is, in part, a history 'of the abolition of the enchanted cosmos, and the eventual creation of a humanist alternative to faith' (Taylor

---

15 Establishment also makes the same case for the Church of Scotland.

2007, p 77). In this history 'porous agents' become 'buffered selves', who are disengaged 'from everything outside the mind', and an 'ethic of freedom and order' arises (Taylor 2007, pp 38 and 300). The buffered self can see 'itself as invulnerable, as master of the meaning of things for it' whereas, for the porous self, 'the very notion that there is a clear boundary, allowing us to define an inner base area, grounded in which we can disengage from the rest, has no sense' (Taylor 2007, p 38). To put the matter much more prosaically than Taylor, the intellectual and social world that was lived in in medieval times and the intellectual and social world that we live in now are far apart.[16] The very notion that establishment needed a justification would, at the time of the origin of establishment for both the Church of England and the Church of Scotland, have seemed strange.[17] However, now these assumptions of the unity of Church and State are 'in large measure, anachronistic' (Medhurst 1999, p 276). Because of this the reason why churches were once established provides an explanation of how we came to be in the situation that we are now in, but not a justification for their continued establishment in this radically altered current era. The historical antecedents of establishment in Great Britain are not unusual. '[A]lmost all the central political institutions of the United Kingdom continue to be marked by arrangements inherited from the age of the confessional state' (Madeley 2003, p 3). However, neither history nor this universality in themselves justify their continuation in contemporary Britain.

A troubled establishment

The arguments for disestablishment in the present era are powerful ones. Nearly four decades ago, in 1970, the Chadwick Commission's report to the Church of England on the relationship between the Church and the State described the National Secular Society's evidence to the Commission:

> [The National Secular Society] recommended legislation to make the coronation no longer a religious ceremony and not performed by an officer of the Church; to abolish prayers, from whatever quarter, at all official, national, civic and legal ceremonies; to remove the bishops from the House of Lords and to allow Anglican clergymen to be Members of Parliament and practise at the bar; to abolish the statutory position of the church courts so that they become simply internal disciplinary

16 Although, as Chapter 1 showed, not everyone has become, or sees themselves as having become, a buffered self.
17 Thus, for example, Bogdanor argues that there was no question of needing to justify the establishment of the Church of England in the sixteenth century (Bogdanor 1995, p 220).

bodies; to abolish the right of Parliament to control the worship of the Church; and to remove the endowments of the Church of England.

(Chadwick 1970, p 10)

These were suggestions, the Commission dryly observed, that '[y]our Commission is not naturally in sympathy with'. But the Commission nevertheless went on immediately to add, '[a]nd yet the reason for alteration is one which we cannot quite reject; for it is the reason of abstract justice' (Chadwick 1970, p 10). If, as the Chadwick Commission suggested, establishment 'hints' at an 'identification' between State and Church in a society where many, even in 1970, did not even profess to be Christian and where most did not participate in institutionalised religion, 'abstract justice', it felt, called for the Church to stand further apart from the State (Chadwick 1970, p 11).

The Church of England, the Church of Scotland and the State have not been united in the coterminous way that they once were for several centuries. As was noted in Chapter 1 the rise and increasing prominence of different denominations, churches and faiths and, even more, the rise of non-belief and individual religiosity changes the religious landscape in significant ways. Thus for example, by the late 1970s, its decline had made the Church of England, in the words of a sympathetic commentator, 'almost a minority community' (Hastings 1986, p 605).

The Church of England has long recognised the fact of its decline and its potential implications. Grimley notes that:

[o]ne of the ways in which the Church of England had mitigated decline in the nineteenth and early twentieth centuries was by creating a moral community which went well beyond those who were within its fold. This community not only comprehended other Protestant denominations, but also those who were not religiously observant.

(Grimley 2004, p 227)

The Church's attempt to speak for a wider community than itself benefited in the nineteenth century from the Christian churches' general success in making 'deference to religious values – and public acknowledgement of the importance of religion – almost universal among the upper and middle classes' (Cox 1982, p 5). The Church's claim for prominence among these churches did not lie in its assertion of the superiority of its theology. Indeed, it could be argued that it is precisely the doctrinal weakness of its theology that aided the Church's cause:

[T]he mainstream of Anglican polity renounced ... the quest for doctrinal orthodoxy as such. The continual trend in Anglican history was not towards a resolution of disputed [theological] questions but toward the development of forms that would enable both sets of disputants to live at peace.

(Rodes Jr 1977, p xii)[18]

Thus Smith writes about the Church's 'provision to the nation of a resource of broad Christianity' (Smith 2003, p 693). The loose orthodoxy of the Church's doctrine arguably made the Church more comfortable in claiming to speak for those whose theology was often rather distant from its own and it also made it easier for those others to accept the Church as their voice.[19] This claim to speak for more than those who are its members remains part of the Church of England's position. In his 1986 book on England and Christianity Hastings writes that:

> Anglican priests retain very widely a sense of responsibility for the whole of our society and all that is in it which goes far beyond what most ministers of other churches feel.
>
> (Hastings 1986, p 664)

Even more recently, in evidence to the Wakeham Commission, the Church of England argued that its bishops in the House of Lords spoke 'not just for the Church of England but for its partners in other Christian churches, and for people of other faiths and none' (Wakeham 2000, p 153).

Attempting to be a voice speaking for religions and for religious values, thus both reflecting and, in part, justifying its position as a national church, has not always been an easy task for either the Church of England or the Church of Scotland. For example, during the Second World War some people had doubts, sometimes very severe doubts, about the possibility of morally justifying the policy of the obliteration bombing of Germany (Chandler 1993). Some of those who had doubts were bishops in the Church of England. A number voiced those concerns, either internally in the Church through diocesan magazines and in the legislative bodies of the Church or more widely in the national press or the House of Lords. At the beginning of the war, one bishop, George Bell, Bishop of Chichester, argued that the Church was not the State's 'spiritual auxiliary' and urged that the churches, including

---

18 See, also, Medhurst's observation that unity, for the Church of England, has been achieved 'through common liturgical practices rather than through a clearly agreed theology' (Medhurst 1999, p 275).

19 This is not say that the Church has been undivided in its approach to its mission. Thus, for example, '[the Liberal Anglican] tradition propounded a moral, organic state which embodied the whole national community. It held that Christianity had an essential role to play in providing common social values for the state, and that this was best accomplished through a national Church' (Grimley 2004, p 25). Although this is an important tradition within the Church in a Church that claims to be both Catholic and Reformed, it is just one tradition.

the Church of England, 'must rise above the clamour to bless and sanctify the war; instead they must transcend their respective nationalities and "strike the universal note" ' (Chandler 1993, p 925). Nevertheless, during the war, both Cosmo Gordon Lang as Archbishop of Canterbury and his successor, William Temple, expressed support for government policy and the impression the Church of England in general gave 'was a consensus of tacit endorsement, with an often acknowledged sense of unhappiness that the ways of the world could be so terrible' (Chandler 1993, p 936). As the then Bishop of Durham, Herbert Henson, had observed before the war, the primacy of the Church of England was not necessarily 'congenial with moral independence' (Chandler 1993, p 946). Similar problems arose over Britain's possession of nuclear weapons. This issue posed a:

> unique moral dilemma which highlighted the difficulties for the established Church of England in reconciling ecclesiastical functions with an informal political role.
>
> (Kirby 1995, p 599)

Many, including some bishops, spoke out against the use of such weapons and 'the churches, ecclesiastical assemblies and reports from the late 1940s on constituted a major forum for public debate on nuclear weapons' (Kirby 1995, p 622). Nevertheless, the Church of England failed to take a stance against Britain's use of such weapons and Geoffrey Fisher, the Archbishop of Canterbury during the late 1940s and 1950s, 'remained steadfast in his support of the state' (Kirby 1995, p 618).[20]

Writing in 1976, Norman argued that:

> [t]he contemporary Church has . . ., in general, attempted to practice the traditional formula about political involvement: that the Church has the duty to define general principles within which human society may be ordered, but the individual applications are best left to the expertise of political leaders.
>
> (Norman 1976, p 457)

However, the difficulties of holding to the position of both speaking for religion and being a national church magnified and changed as the twentieth century progressed. The break-up of the postwar political consensus on social issues, following Margaret Thatcher's election in 1979, caused deep problems for the Church of England. The Church found itself in increasing conflict with the Thatcher administration and the Major government that

---

20 Medhurst argues, more widely, that 'the immediate post-war leadership of the Church tended to be relatively uncritical of governments of either party' (Medhurst 1991, p 247).

followed (Nicholls 1990; Medhurst 1991, p 240; Medhurst 1999, pp 280–288). The worsening tension between Church and State came from two directions in the Church.

> For some, [the challenge to the Thatcher administration] meant little more than standing still and seeking to cling to the old 'middle ground' as that ground appeared to be crumbling. For others, the challenge posed by government policies tended to produce a certain radicalization that in political terms could be construed as a leftward move.
>
> (Medhurst 1991, p 246)

For both groups within the Church the 'general principles' that they variously held to were not ones that the Thatcher administration was disposed to accept. At the same time, however, the Church itself was divided on how far these governments should in fact be criticised (Medhurst 1999, p 283). More generally than this, the present day has seen a division between the laity and the clergy in the Church as to how far the Church should venture into social and political issues (Field 2007). Equally, Medhurst argues that the legislative changes that had occurred in the Church, and especially the creation of the General Synod in 1970, had served to create:

> a new type of specialized ecclesiastical elite whose theological and polit- ical views will not necessarily be representative of the views of the major- ity of those regularly or semi-regularly worshipping at parochial level.
>
> (Medhurst 1991, p 242)

It is thus understandable that, even at a time when Conservative administra- tions secured considerable popular support in elections, the Church failed to endorse the general tenor of government policy. In any event, whatever the reason for the change of approach by the Church, it is not surprising that the result was:

> dismay, if not occasionally bewilderment, on the part of Conservative party leaders who had come to expect a generally supportive attitude from the established Church.
>
> (Medhurst 1991, p 241)

The issue of Scottish nationalism has, on occasion, caused similar problems for the Church of Scotland, creating tensions between its view of its role in representing the voice of religion, on the one side, and its ability to reflect the views of its members, on the other. The Church has long 'reflected and con- tributed to a distinctively Scottish culture and consciousness' (Proctor 1983, p 523). However, its support for the 1979 referendum on devolution, which in fact resulted in the rejection of the idea, led to questions about the Kirk's role 'in the national life of Scotland' and also resulted in some church members turning away from the church (Proctor 1983, pp 540 and 543).[21]

An Erastian church?

It is not just the Church's role as a voice of religion that has proved problematic for the Church of England in its relations with the State. The reverse side of establishment, the involvement of the State in the Church, has historically also caused its problems. Here, however, there is a significant difference between the position of the contemporary Church of England and the contemporary Church of Scotland. As was seen above, following the Church of Scotland Act 1921 the State lost any control that it might previously have possessed over the Church. '[T]he Scottish Kirk is an example of a thing that is rare, if not unique, in Christendom, a Church that is both established and free' (Taylor 1957, p 137). For the Church of England the situation is very different; the State continues to exercise a degree of control over the legislative activities of the Church and to play a role in ecclesiastical appointments, including the appointment of its bishops.[22] Both these matters have at times caused problems for the Church.

The twentieth century saw considerable changes in the legislative powers of the Church of England. Until 1920, Parliament had legislated directly for the Church. However, the nineteenth century had seen a change in the religious character of the House of Commons. A House that had once by law contained only members of the Church of England had, because of legislative changes, become a House that was open to members of any faith or no faith at all (Laughlin 1988, p 32).[23] This put in question the legitimacy of its role in determining what the Church of England did. The Archbishop's Committee on Church and State Report 1916 argued that 'parliament has neither the leisure, fitness or inclination to perform efficiently the function of an ecclesiastical legislature' (Torke 1995–1996, p 413). As a consequence of pressure from the Church, the Church of England Assembly (Powers) Act 1919 was passed, creating the National Assembly of the Church of England with the power to legislate by Measure. In 1969, the Assembly was reconstituted as the General Synod of the Church of England by the Synodical Government Measure 1969 and given the additional power to legislate by Canon.[24]

---

21 Medhurst similarly notes doubts about whether the Church of England's leaders can now be said to speak for their followers (Medhurst 1991, p 247).

22 The Crown appoints, 'Diocesan and Suffragan Bishops, as well as Cathedral Deans, a small number of Cathedral Canons, some 200 parish priests and a number of other post-holders in the Church of England . . .' (Governance 2007, p 25).

23 Prior to the passage of the Roman Catholic Relief Act 1829, it could be argued that the House of Commons was 'a representative Anglican assembly' (Grimley 2004, p 26).

24 On Measures and Canons, see, Hill, 2001, pp 10–11 and 12–13.

Notwithstanding these reforms the Church of England remains under the control of the State. The legislative powers that it has arise because of statute passed by Parliament, which could be amended or repealed by a future statute. Moreover, Measures must, under s 4 of the 1919 Act, be agreed by Parliament before they can have legal effect. Nonetheless, given the fact that the General Synod is a broadly representative body, comprising three Houses – bishops, clergy and laity – the consequences of legislative reform in the twentieth century have been a slow increase in the legislative autonomy of the Church of England (Hill 2001, p 24).

The State's role in the appointment of bishops and archbishops has caused difficulties for the Church, even at times when its relationship with the State has been relatively harmonious. In 1944, when the then Archbishop of Canterbury William Temple, died, 'the nature of the relationship between Church and the State, in its cordial mutuality, its courtesy, its governing wish neither to offend nor to undermine', meant that Church authorities did not recommend George Bell, Bishop of Chichester, as Archbishop nor as Bishop of London when that see became available because of Bell's strong opposition to obliteration bombing and the feeling that that made him unacceptable to Winston Churchill as Prime Minister (Chandler 1993, p 945). The present system for nominating a bishop or archbishop, first established in 1976, involves the Crown Nominations Commission, a body comprised of various representatives of the Church, recommending two names to the Prime Minister (Governance 2007, p 25).[25] However, while it is usual for the Prime Minister to recommend the first name to the monarch, they do not have to do so and may put forward the second name instead or they may decline to put forward either name and may ask for further names to be put forward (Doe 1996, pp 163–164).[26] In 1981, Margaret Thatcher put forward Graham Leonard rather than John Hapgood as Bishop of London; in 1987, she put forward Mark Slater rather than Jim Thompson as Bishop of Birmingham; and in 1990 she put forward George Carey rather than John

25 For the current membership of the Crown Nominations Commission, see www.cofe.anglican.org/about/gensynod/commissions.html/.

26 Under s 18 of the Roman Catholic Relief Act 1829 and s 4 of the Jews Relief Act 1858, it is illegal for Roman Catholics and Jews to give advice to the monarch on offices in the Church of England. Were the Prime Minster to be Jewish or Catholic it would thus be necessary for some other minister to give the advice. Although, on one level, this may seem understandable, because the Church would not wish its senior personnel to be appointed by someone from another faith, the same rules do not exist if the Prime Minister is from some religion other than the Catholic or Jewish faith or has no faith at all. Moreover, both the Prime Minister and the Lord Chancellor, whatever their religion, are, by virtue of their office, Church Commissioners, responsible for a broad range of matters relating to the financing of the Church (Hill 2001, pp 38–42). It is difficult to see how excluding those belonging to some religions from some parts of the workings of the Church can be justified. Because of this, neither the 1829 Act nor the 1858 Act appear to be compatible with the Human Rights Act 1998.

Hapgood as Archbishop of Canterbury (Bogdanor 1995, p 228). In 1999, Tony Blair rejected both candidates who had been put forward as Bishop of Liverpool (Maer 2007, p 5). In 2007, the Government issued a Green Paper that, inter alia, suggested a change to the present procedure with only one name being forwarded to the Prime Minister by the Crown Nominations Commission (Governance 2007, p 26). In response, the consultation paper of the Archbishops of Canterbury and York broadly welcomed what they described as 'a further evolution in the long history of the Church's relationship with the State' (Cantaur and Ebor 2007, p 2).

The gradual loosening of the ties between the Church and the State may seem to be of advantage to the Church. However, they also put in doubt the Church's position as a national church. The State's role in legislating for the Church and in appointing its bishops can be seen to be a price that the Church has historically paid for establishment (Heubel 1965, p 651).

> One consequence ... [of the increase in the Church's powers of self-government] has been to establish a certain distance between parliament and the Church. The Church of England, which has always claimed to serve the nation, far beyond the limits of active worshippers, now excludes much of the nation from effective influence in its affairs.
>
> (Bogdanor 1995, p 225)

A continuing establishment?

Upon the face of it the Church of England's and the Church of Scotland's connection with the State appears to be much the same position in the twenty-first century as it was through the twentieth century. There have been no major legal changes to the nature of establishment, nor are any mooted for the foreseeable future. In its 2007 Green Paper on the governance of the United Kingdom the Labour administration continued to welcome 'the role played by the Church [of England] in national life in a range of spheres' (Governance 2007, p 26). Bogdanor has argued that Parliament is not 'equipped or likely to make' any decision as regards disestablishment (Bogdanor 1995, pp 238–239). The Churches thus appear to be as secure in their establishment as ever they were. No significant challenges to establishment seem to exist. However, this appearance belies reality.

Establishment, as was noted above, is not a purely legal matter. The legal incidents of establishment are part of a wider tapestry that is concerned with the actual relationship of a church and a State. This wider tapestry has shown considerable alterations that reflect the changing place of institutionalised religion in Great Britain described in Chapter 1. Hastings has described the way in which the twentieth century saw a transformation in the State's approach towards the Church of England whereby 'the political establishment no longer bothered very seriously about this section of its former empire' (Hastings 1986, p 606). Illustrative of this phenomenon is the attitude of recent Prime Ministers to the Church. Neither of the autobiographies of Margaret Thatcher or John Major make any significant reference to their dealings with the Church. According to Seldon, George Carey, while Archbishop of Canterbury, saw John Major as Prime Minister every six months (Seldon 2004, p 523). However, although Carey makes reference to these meetings in his memoir and devotes one chapter to the relationship between the Church and government, John Major's autobiography is entirely silent on the matter (Major 1999; Carey 2005). Similarly, Margaret Thatcher's autobiography of her years as Prime Minister makes reference to the Church of England only to regret that its bishops were not better trained (Thatcher 1993, p 31). It is not that recent Prime Ministers have necessarily been un-interested in religion. Religion for Thatcher, for example, seems to have been both an abiding interest and a matter of deep concern (Young 1991, pp 418–422). However, personal faith has not translated into an acceptance of the authority of the Church.[27] In this, Prime Ministers reflect the wider attitude of their parties.

> When the 1984 Conservative party conference . . . gave a standing ova-tion to a turbaned Indian elder who delivered a ferocious attack on the established Church, it said something definitive about the way Church–state relations were changing . . .
>
> (Young 1991, p 425)

The reality of the Churches' role in politics and the wider life of the nation now falls far short of their public perception of their place.[28] Bishop Nazir-Ali, for example, argues that establishment reflects 'the desire of the state and of the people of this country to hear the voice of the church in national affairs' (Nazir-Ali 1997, p 33). There seems little if any evidence to suggest that there is such a desire and in the light of the lack of belief in institutionalised religion noted in Chapter 1, the existence of such a general desire seems implausible. Kutwala (2006) refers to 'the largely absent-minded maintenance of an established Church' while Minkenberg observes that:

---

27 The same is true of Tony Blair (Seldon 2004, p 521). Blair's recent conversion to the Catholic faith does not seem to have come from an alteration in the individual nature of his religiosity, given his well-documented and apparently unchanging attitude towards matters such as abortion and gay rights. Gordon Brown is a member of the Church of Scotland.

28 The private beliefs of members of the Churches may be another matter. In his memoir, George Carey, formerly Archbishop of Canterbury, while still defending the notion of estab-lishment writes about the 'shift from the Church being at the centre of leisure and the community, to a place on the periphery' and, more widely, about 'Europe and North America, where I believe a crisis of faith places traditional Christianity at risk' (Carey 2005, pp 442 and 440).

[w]hatever remains of the privileged position of the Church of England is rooted more in the general public's perception of the positive role of religion in British public life than in specific institutional arrangements guaranteeing political power to the church.

(Minkenberg 2003, p 203)

Medhurst describes a future in which there is a ' "creeping disestablishment" whereby, over a lengthy period, existing arrangements continue to be modified on an incremental basis' (Medhurst 1991, p 256; Kutwala 2006, p 246). As institutionalised religion has ceased to matter in Great Britain so, to the majority of the population, establishment has ceased to matter and the legal incidents of establishment have become increasingly anachronistic. Hastings writes that:

many religious non-Christians – Hindus, Muslims, Sikhs and Jews – as well as many non-Anglican Christians like myself actually prefer some establishment to remain as a public symbol of the importance of religion, of belief in God, of the limits of Caesar's sovereignty.

(Hastings 1997, p 42)

It is precisely the appropriateness of such a symbol that is in question in the liberal, secular society described in Chapter 1. There is now no evidence that the Church of England's and the Church of Scotland's pronouncements carry any more weight in public debate than do statements from any other faith. More than this, faith-based arguments are not part of the currency of public debate. If the established Churches are to convince, their arguments need a secular not a theological basis. It is thus not surprising that the Church of England has increasingly shown a tendency 'to share in coalitions with secular interest groups having parallel or overlapping concerns' (Medhurst 1991, p 259).

At its least, the Church is a subject of nostalgia facing an uncertain future from what appears to be an increasingly marginalized position on the fringes of a society whose main dynamics seem almost wholly secular.

(Torke 1995–1996, pp 444–445)

While establishment, whether of the Church of England or the Church of Scotland, seems to be of marginal importance in the day-to-day politics of Great Britain and equally seems inevitably incapable of continuing in the medium or long-term future, irrespective of the wishes of either Parliament or the Churches, its continued existence in contemporary times still matters in principle. Establishment misspeaks the place of religion in present-day Britain and pretends that the past is the present. Churches speak on behalf of a population that has largely rejected the right of anyone or any institution to speak on their behalf. Christian Churches purport to speak on behalf of a population that, on the whole, no longer knows much of Christ. Establishment for the Church of England means sectional representation in a legislature that otherwise does not have sectional representation. Establishment means not only that the State fails to recognise the reality of its secularity but, by opting for a special connection with just two faith groups, it diminishes the respect it shows both to other faith groups and to those who have no faith.[29] Modood has argued for the continuing importance of establishment because it reflects the fact 'that religion has a place in a secular public culture [and] that religious communities are part of the state' (Modood 1994, p 72). An end to establishment, he goes on to argue, would be seen by minority faiths as 'triumphal secularism' (Modood 1994, p 73).[30] Modood's arguments are accurate, but his conclusions are fallacious. Establishment partially masks the limited place that religions have in the public culture; secularism has triumphed. Religious communities, including the Church of England and the Church of Scotland, are part of society. However, even collectively, they are only a small part of British society and their mores are, in the main, very different from the dominant cultures around them. The question is how to address this fact. Continuing establishment, with its implied suggestion of an elaborate interconnection between religion and state, is merely a way of putting off an attempt to answer this question.

29 Whether other faith groups wish to retain establishment as, for example, Modood suggests, for either political or theological reasons, is not to the point (Modood 1994, p 61). Establishment is contrary to the notion of neutrality; the position that the liberal State espouses in relation to religions. Ahdar and Leigh argue that weak notions of establishment are compatible with the right to religious freedom found in a range of legal jurisdictions at both national and international level (Ahdar and Leigh 2004). Even if this is correct the more important questions are, first, is establishment consistent with religious equality and, secondly, does establishment accurately reflect the position of religions in society.

30 Such arguments, in a rather milder form, also find their place in a series of reports on reform of the House of Lords, which has recommended continuing the representation of the Church of England in the House of Lords, albeit usually in a changed form. Thus, for example, the Wakeham Report argues that the Church of England's 'representation has been acknowledged by leaders of other Christian denominations and faith communities as a voice in Parliament for religion in general' (Wakeham 2000, p 152). The Report goes on to argue that for some members of the Committee 'the presence of the Lords Spiritual is a sign that Governments are in the end accountable not only to those who elect them but also to a higher authority' (Wakeham 2000, p 152). Smith observes that 'in an age accustomed to the idea of the supreme value of democracy, and the idea that power ultimately rests with the people, the justification of the presence of the Lords Spiritual on the basis that they demonstrate accountability to a higher power seems rather strange' (Smith 2003, p 680).

Chapter 4

Incitement to religious hatred

Introduction

Were the Church of England and the Church of Scotland not already established churches in Great Britain, no one would now seek to establish them. It is as much the symbolic impact and the practical difficulties of disestablishment that keep the two churches established as it is any positive desire to see these particular churches given priority in the present day. In this sense establishment represents an old answer to questions about the appropriate relationship between religions and the State – the antiquity of the answer in itself serving to preserve, for the present, the position of the churches. By contrast, the offence of incitement to religious hatred, resulting from the passage of the Racial and Religious Hatred Act 2006, is very new to Great Britain and represents a conscious attempt by the State to deal, in a novel manner, with the problems that some religions see themselves as having.[1] The justification for the offence, if there is any justification, therefore lies in its ability to provide a solution for problems relating to religion rather than in the fact that it is simply part of the established constitutional order. The major questions that the new criminal offence raises are thus: what problems does the offence address, how does it propose to deal with those problems and will the solution be effective?

---

1 The legislation only applies directly to England and Wales (s 3(4) Racial and Religious Hatred Act 2006). However, an opinion by Herbert Kerrigan QC and Neil Addison, obtained by the Christian Institute, argues that legislation of this form will have an impact on Scotland because, for example, Scottish publishers would be criminally liable, under the legislation, if material that they published in Scotland, which was then distributed in England or Wales, broke the provisions of the 2006 Act (Kerrigan and Addison 2005, pp 5–9). Incitement to religious hatred was made an offence in Northern Ireland under the Prevention of Incitement to Hatred (Northern Ireland) Act 1970. Writing in 1998, White states that there have only been two prosecutions for hate crimes in Northern Ireland; one successful, one unsuccessful (White 1998, p 78).

The origins of the legislation

The Racial and Religious Hatred Act 2006 amends the Public Order Act 1986 so as to make it an offence to use threatening words or behaviour, or display any written material that is threatening if a person intends thereby to stir up religious hatred.[2] The legislation is general, applying to all religions, and indeed, since, under s 29A of the 1986 Act, ' "religious hatred" means hatred against a group of persons defined by reference to religious belief or *lack of religious belief*' (emphasis added), covers those with no religious beliefs at all.[3] Despite this it is clear that the origins of the Act lie largely in the particular concerns of Muslim groups within Great Britain.[4]

Historically, the majority view has been that a general offence to protect religious believers is unnecessary in Great Britain because religion does not cause any general public order problems (Robilliard 1981, p 556).[5] However,

2 Section 29B(1) Public Order Act 1986.

3 Addison argues that this wording does not just apply to those who have no religious belief. '[I]ts meaning is in fact more subtle. Lack of religious belief can cover any person other than believers in a particular religion ... Furthermore, the words "lack of religious belief" can mean those who do not share the specific interpretation of religious belief held by a particular person or group' (Addison 2007, p 141).

4 This is not to say that the need for such legislation was not supported by other faith groups. In oral evidence to the House of Lords Select Committee on Religious Offences the Council of Christian and Jews asserted that the 'general view' of faith communities was to support incitement legislation (Select Committee Vol II 2003, p 52). Similarly, Ali quotes a joint statement in support of incitement legislation issued by the Board of Deputies of British Jews, the Churches Commission on Inter-Faith Relations and the Muslim Council of Britain (Ali 2005, pp 47–48). The 2006 Act is not the first time that general legislation has been used to address the problems of a particular group. The conscience clause in the Abortion Act 1967 is general in its terms, but was created largely because of the perceived needs of Roman Catholics (Bradney 1993, p 146).

5 See also the Law Commission's report on religious offences, which argued that blasphemous material was not likely to cause public disorder and, if it did, existing public order offences would be sufficient to deal with the matter (Law Commission 1985, pp 14–16). In addition to general public order offences there are a range of criminal offences, such as s 2 of the Ecclesiastical Courts Jurisdiction Act 1860, which protect specific believers in specific circumstances. However, the proposition that public order did not necessitate general protection for religion has never been a universal view. In *Whitehouse v Lemon*, Lord Scarman began his judgment by stating that 'I think that there is a case for legislation ... to protect the religious beliefs and feelings of non-Christians. The offence belongs to a group of criminal offences designed to safeguard the internal tranquillity of the kingdom. In an increasingly plural society such as that of modern Britain it is necessary not only to respect the differing religious beliefs, feelings and practices of all but also to protect them from scurrility, vilification, ridicule and contempt' ([1979] AC 617 at p 658). The minority in the 1985 Law Commission Report proposed that the common law offence of blasphemy should be replaced by a statute that 'would penalise anyone who published grossly abusive and insulting material relating to religion with the purpose of outraging religious feelings' (Law Commission 1985, p 43). They grounded the need for the offence, however, not, as in Lord Scarman's case, on the need to preserve the 'internal tranquillity' of the country but on the fact, as they saw the matter, that 'people generally share ... respect for reverence' (Law Commission 1985, p 41).

in September 2001, following the 9/11 attacks in New York and Washington, the then Home Secretary, David Blunkett, announced his intention to introduce legislation to make incitement to religious hatred a criminal offence, as part of the Government's response to community tensions resulting from the attacks (Kelly 2005, p 7). While it was sitting between 2002 and 2003 the Select Committee on Religious Offences received evidence from a number of different Muslim groups about a rise in the number of attacks on Muslims following 9/11 (Select Committee Vol III 2003, p 47).[6] Pressure for a new offence also came from outside Great Britain. Thus, for example, the United Nations Committee on the Elimination of Discrimination called for incitement legislation to be introduced because of the consequences of 9/11 (Committee 2003, pp 5–6). Less specific pressure also comes from halting international moves to include religion within the general compass of racism. In April 2007, the Council of the European Union announced that it had reached agreement about a draft Framework Decision on Racism and Xenophobia. The draft provides that European Union States will make intentionally 'publicly inciting to violence or hatred, even by dissemination or distribution of tracts, pictures or other material, directed against a group of persons or a member of such a group defined by reference to race, colour, *religion*, descent or national or ethnic origin' (emphasis added), punishable (Council 2007, p 23). The ambit of this provision is not, however, as wide as it seems. States 'may choose to punish only conduct which is either carried out in a manner likely to disturb public order or which is threatening, abusive or insulting' and '[t]he reference to religion is intended to cover, *at least*, conduct which is a pretext for directing acts against a group of persons or a member of such a group defined by reference to race, colour, descent, or national or ethnic origin' (emphasis added) (Council 2007, p 23).[7] Equally of some significance in this respect is the Council of Europe's European Commission against Racism and Intolerance's 'General policy recommendation no 7 on national legislation to combat racism and racial discrimination' (Recommendation CRI (2003), CRI, Council of Europe, 2003), which includes, in paragraph 1(1)(a), religion in its definition of racism.[8]

The impetus for incitement legislation did not, however, just lie in the specific effects of terrorist attacks in the US or international pressure,

6 Allen and Nielsen's study of Islamophobia in Europe post 9/11 notes a 'significant rise' in the number of attacks on Muslims in the United Kingdom reported after that date (Allen and Nielsen 2002, p 29).
7 At the time of writing this draft had not been published.
8 For an analysis of this provision, see, Howard 2005. Provisions made by the Council of Europe are voluntary and not binding but, as Howard observes, the fact that the Council publishes reports on member States which review the effectiveness of those States' legislation, policies and other measures with respect to matters such as racism does give the Council some power (Howard 2005, p 471).

whether specific or general. There were also more widespread and more longstanding perceptions by Muslims about their relationship with the legal systems of Great Britain that hastened the legislation. In 1997, the Runnymede Trust's Commission on British Muslims and Islamophobia argued the need for the new term 'Islamophobia' because:

> anti-Muslim prejudice has grown so considerably and so rapidly in recent years that a new item in the vocabulary is needed so that it can be identified and acted against.
>
> (Commission 1997, p 4)

One of the reforms suggested by the Commission was the widening of the offence of incitement to racial hatred so as to include religious groups because this:

> would give Muslims equal treatment with Jews and Sikhs, and would give them reassurance that their interests are sufficiently respected to warrant protecting them from religious hatred.
>
> (Commission 1997, p 60)

In 2003, the House of Lords Select Committee on Religious Offences noted that:

> [m]any Muslims . . . believe that the law treats them as second-class citizens of British society due to the combination of a lack of remedy for religious discrimination in civil settings; the absence of powers to prosecute when the group (rather than its individual members) is the target for incitement to hatred, because of its multi-ethnic composition; and *the absence of any proscription of incitement to religious hatred.* (emphasis added)
>
> (Select Committee 2003, p 8)

In 2004, a second report by the Commission on British Muslims and Islamophobia noted that Jews and Sikhs, but not Muslims, were protected by legislation relating to incitement to racial hatred and described this as having 'been a standing insult to Muslims for two decades' (Commission 2004, p 13). The 2006 legislation is thus rooted both in the particular problems for Muslim communities in Great Britain resulting from 9/11, international pressure and in wider complaints by Muslims about their place in British society. In 2005, the Labour Party's election Manifestos for England and for Wales, although not the Manifesto for Scotland, specifically pledged to introduce legislation relating to incitement to religious hatred (Addison 2007, p 139).

From the above it is clear that, on one level, the pressure for incitement legislation resulted simply from a claim for equal treatment by the law.

Muslim groups sought rights that they felt other religious groups already had.[9] However, although this is part of the argument for incitement legislation, it is not the whole argument; equality is part of the case, but so are the specificities of the Muslim situation. Jacobson, in her ethnographic account of Muslim youths, argues that those she observed:

> are set apart from the majority population of Britain not only in terms of their religiously oriented actions, but also on account of the beliefs and values on which these actions are based.
>
> (Jacobson 1998, p 136)

For some the fact of these different beliefs and values forms part of the case for general incitement legislation. Modood, for example, argues that Muslim notions of honour, and in particular notions of honour with respect to their religion, make it imperative that they receive the protection in law that they see as being afforded to other religious groups (Modood 1993, pp 143 and 147).[10] Kunzru writes more widely about communities in which 'offending against religion is viewed as a kind of public violence against the believer' (Kunzru 2005, p 123). Such arguments follow a similar form to more specific claims made by Muslims following the publication of Salman Rushdie's *The Satanic Verses*. At this time some Muslims argued that the law of blasphemy should be extended to Islam on grounds of equality (Qureshi and Khan 1989, p 22). Others, however, argued that the special place that Muhammad has in the Islamic faith was the point at issue (Akhtar 1989, ch 1). Slaughter, in his analysis of the furore that followed publication of *The Satanic Verses*, argues for a need to understand the particular place that notions of honour have in Muslim communities (Slaughter 1993, pp 193–200).[11] Honour, for Muslims, touches on more matters and is much more significant than it is in liberal societies.

9 See, for example, the evidence of the Muslim Council for Religious and Racial Harmony to the House of Lords Select Committee on Religious Offences (Select Committee Vol III 2003, p 62). See, also, Kelly 2005, pp 31–32.

10 Muslims in Great Britain are, of course, a multiethnic group with differences in, among other things, the precise nature of their theological beliefs, their cultural background and, indeed, the degree of their attachment to Islam. Nevertheless, valid generalisations can be made. In the context of the argument here it is, for example, relevant that Muslims in Great Britain see their religion as being the second most important thing in terms of their sense of self-identity while for Christians their religion is only the seventh most important factor (O'Beirne 2004, p 20).

11 On the importance of honour in Muslim communities and on the differences between notions of honour in Muslim communities and liberal democracies, see, Ahmed 2003, pp 56–73.

If the maintenance of one's public image is paramount in an honor society, loss of honor is loss of social existence and shame is almost literally experienced as annihilation.

(Slaughter 1993, p 195)[12]

Thus the case for incitement legislation lies not just in the proposition that it would 'give people of all faiths the same protection' (Labour 2005, p 111). For some Muslims the argument is for a recognition by the State, through its legal system, of the importance that they attach to their own values.[13] The likely success of the incitement legislation thus has to be judged with respect to both these arguments.

The new legislation

In large part the new offence relating to religious hatred is modelled on much older legislation making it an offence to incite racial hatred. However, the new legislation is more tightly drawn than the older legislation. Thus, for example, while in relation to racial hatred, under s 18(1) of the 1986 Act, a 'person who uses threatening, abusive or insulting words or behaviour, or displays any written material which is threatening, abusive or insulting' is guilty of an offence; in relation to religious hatred the offence is limited to using 'threatening words or behaviour, or displays any written material which is threatening'.[14] More than this, in a provision that is intended to ensure that the new offence is compatible with notions of freedom of speech, s 29J of the amended 1986 Act holds that:

[n]othing in this Part shall be read or given effect in a way which prohibits or restricts discussion, criticism or expressions of antipathy, dislike, ridicule, insult or abuse of particular religions or the beliefs or practices of their adherents, or of any other belief system or the beliefs or practices of its adherents, or proselytising or urging adherents of a different religion or belief system to cease practising their religion or belief system.[15]

---

12 Kamali notes that insulting someone can be an offence under sharia law, even if the insulting words were not uttered in public and even if there is no intention to insult (Kamali 1997, pp 177–182).

13 Thus the Commission on British Muslims and Islamophobia argues for a need to recognise 'the politics of difference' (Commission 2004, p 27).

14 Section 29B(1) Public Order Act 1986.

15 The current legislation is the Government's third attempt to introduce an offence of this type (Kelly 2005, pp 37–40). The first attempt involved a much wider offence. 'Incitement was to be by words, behaviour, or material which was "threatening, abusive or insulting". Intention to stir up religious hatred was not necessary. The offence would be committed if the words, behaviour or material were likely to be seen or heard by any person in whom they were likely to stir up such hatred' (Goodall 2007, p 89).

Insulting words are thus part of the offence in relation to incitement to racial hatred, but insulting religions, religious beliefs and religious practices is something that is specifically protected by the 2006 legislation.

The very much more limited ambit of the new legislation as compared with legislation concerned with racial hatred raises the question of what type of behaviour the new offence is intended to prevent. As Goodall notes, prior to the creation of the offence, there were already a wide range of criminal offences:

> which can tackle behaviour displaying religious prejudice. From religiously aggravated abuse and violence to criminal harassment; from the Ecclesiastical Court Jurisdiction Act 1860 to the Malicious Communication Act 1988; from incitement to crime to aggravated breach of the peace, most incidents would have been covered by existing law; usually public order offences.
>
> (Goodall 2007, p 91)[16]

The only behaviour not caught by previous offences that is now prohibited by the new legislation is thus incitement to religious hatred in itself. Where the incitement involves suggestions that, for example, acts of violence should be committed against believers or their property, the incitement would already be caught by previous offences. This raises the question of why theoretically incitement to religious hatred should be a criminal offence. Muslim groups and other faith communities would like there to be such an offence but, in a liberal, secular society, should their wishes be acceded to?

Forbidding hatred

Racial hatred

As was noted above, the crux of specific Muslim complaints about the legal situation prior to the 2006 Act was that they did not receive the same protection afforded to Sikhs and Jews. Sikhs and Jews have been protected by incitement to racial hatred legislation since the passage of the Race Relations Act 1965. The present offence of incitement to racial hatred is to be found in Part 3 of the Public Order Act 1986. Racial hatred is by s 17 of the 1986 Act hatred of 'a group of persons . . . defined by reference to colour, race, nationality (including citizenship) or ethnic or national origins'. Sikhs and Jews, although they are faith groups, are protected by the legislation because they also can claim they have a distinct ethnic origin. In *Mandla v Dowell Lee* [1983] 2 AC 528, itself a case about a Sikh applicant, Lord Fraser held (at p 562) that:

---

16 On this first attempt at legislation, see, Idriss 2002.

[f]or a group to constitute an ethnic group in the sense of the Act of 1976, it must, in my opinion, regard itself, and be regarded by others, as a distinct community by virtue of certain characteristics. Some of these characteristics are essential; others are not essential but one or more of them will commonly be found and will help distinguish the group from the surrounding community. The conditions which appear to me to be essential are these: (1) a long shared history, of which the group is conscious as distinguishing it from other groups, and the memory of which is kept alive; (2) a cultural tradition of its own, including family and social customs and manners, often but not necessarily associated with religious observance. In addition to these two essential characteristics the following characteristics are, in my opinion, relevant: (3) a common geographical origin, or descent from a small number of common ancestors; (4) a common language, not necessarily peculiar to the group; (5) a common literature peculiar to the group; (6) a common religion different from that of neighbouring groups or from the general community surrounding it; (7) being a minority or being oppressed or a dominant group within a larger community, for example a conquered people (say, the inhabitants of England shortly after the Norman conquest) and their conquerors might both be ethnic groups.

A group defined by reference to enough of these characteristics would be capable of including converts, for example, persons who marry into the group, and of excluding apostates. Provided a person who joins the group feels himself or herself to be a member of it, and is accepted by other members, then he is, for the purposes of the Act, a member.

Sikhs, the House of Lords concluded, were a racial group. Following on from *Mandla* in *Seid v Gillette Industries* [1980] IRLR 427, the Employment Appeal Tribunal held that Jews constituted a distinct racial group. Goodall, among others, notes that the question of whether or not Muslims could be a racial group has never been argued out in the higher courts (Goodall 2007, p 93). She cites *Walker v Hussain* [1996] ICR291 as being the only reported case that refers to the issue, although, as she notes, this judgment from the Employment Appeal Tribunal merely asserts that Muslims are not a racial group and does not explore the arguments (Goodall 2007, p 93). Nash and Bakalis refer to the 1998 case of *R v Director of Public Prosecutions ex parte Merton LBC (No 1)* [1998] EWHC Administrative 1009 (Nash and Bakalis 2007, p 351), although in this case the court explicitly refused to rule on the matter. Other writers refer to a variety of low-level, unreported cases that take the same view that Muslims are not an ethnic group. Thus, for example, Addison cites *Tariq v Young* (1989) 2 Equal Opportunities Review 4, a case in an Industrial Tribunal, where it was held 'Muslims are identified by their religion and not by their race or nationality or as being an ethnic group'

(Addison 2007, p 28).[17] Nevertheless, notwithstanding the absence of high-level authority or even sustained argument in any other judicial dicta, there can be little doubt that any claim that Muslims, a multi-ethnic faith group, are a racial group would, on the basis of the *Mandla* test, fail.

Idriss is one of the few commentators to take a contrary view to the majority of commentators, arguing that:

> Muslims form a distinctive community by virtue of certain common characteristics, traditions, beliefs, customs and cultural traits because of their adherence to Islamic scripture. Muslims are monotheists, desist from consuming alcohol and any derivatives from the pig, fast during Ramadan for one lunar month, pray five times a day and read the Holy Quran in Arabic. Moreover, Muslim men sport beards, Muslim women observe Hijab and Muslims speak basic words of Arabic.
>
> (Idriss 2002, pp 910–911)

Dobe and Chhokar make the same point and go on to argue that 'the majority of British Muslims migrated from, India, Pakistan and Bangladesh'. This, they suggest, means that British Muslims do not have the cultural diversity that is true of Muslims taken as a whole (Dobe and Chhokar 2000, pp 375–376). The argument advanced by both Idriss and Dobe and Chhokar involves empirical assertions about the unity of Muslim's cultural practices that some would wish to contest. The Commission on British Muslims and Islamophobia for example, while acknowledging that two-thirds of British Muslims have their background in Bangladesh, India or Pakistan, argue that 'Islam in Britain . . . is a multi-ethnic community' (Commission 2004, p 29).[18] More important than this, however, is the fact that such an approach would be a considerable departure from the position adopted in *Mandla*. Religion and social practices that flow directly from that religion would, in themselves, become an indication of ethnicity. It would not just be Muslims who would benefit from such a change in the court's practices. Christians, taken as a whole, might still not be an ethnic group, even on this more liberal interpretation of ethnicity, but some individual Christian faith communities would, as would other non-Christian faith groups. It does not seem likely that, in the absence of express statutory authority, the courts would readily conflate ethnicity and religion. Individual Muslims may thus be protected by the 1986

---

17 See, similarly, Bradney 1993, p 111.
18 Different cultural or ethnic backgrounds clearly lead to a diverse range of religious practices among British Muslims. For example Küçükcan's study of Turkish Muslims in Britain observes that 'the regular fulfilment of prescribed Islamic practices in the daily lives of young adherents does not seem to be a salient devotional/ritualistic dimension of their religiosity' (Küçükcan 1999, p 158). In this study, 61 per cent of respondents never observed daily prayers and 28 per cent did so only sometimes (Küçükcan 1999, p 158).

Act because, in addition to being Muslims, they also come from some particular ethnic group; Muslims as a whole and Muslims as Muslims, however, fall outside of the legislation. In this Muslims are treated in the same manner as a number of other religions. For precisely the same reasons as in the instance of Muslims, any argument that Christians are a racial group would fail.[19] Equally, it should be noted that neither Rastafarians nor Jehovah's Witnesses have succeeded in claims to be a racial group (Addison 2007, p 28).[20]

The notion that Muslims are not a racial group is not a specifically legal one. It is difficult, notwithstanding the arguments above, to think of any coherent use of the term racial or ethnic group that could be applied to Muslims. The argument brought by Muslims must therefore be not that they are a racial group and should therefore be protected, but that they have analogous claims to those religions that are racial groups and should therefore be protected. In turn, the theoretical claim for the justification for making incitement to religious hatred a criminal offence must be that there is an analogy between why religious hatred should be criminalised and why racial hatred is criminalised.[21]

The notion that there was a need for the crime of incitement to racial hatred was in its time contentious. Two main arguments have been deployed in defence of the legislation. In its 1985 'Review of Public Order' the then Conservative administration argued that the legislation was justified by the need to preserve public order (Review 1985, p 39).[22] The link between inciting racial hatred and the occurrence of public disorder was so close and so inevitable as to make it impossible to divide the two; racial hatred meant violence, therefore it was unnecessary and indeed undesirable to wait for the violence before prosecuting. The second argument justifying the crime of incitement to racial hatred was and is grounded, not in the pragmatics of public safety, but in broader conceptual considerations; thus, for example, Barendt observes:

---

19 Once again there is no high-level authority on this point.
20 This is not so obviously true with all of the other religions that have been held to fail to meet the *Mandla* test. Thus, for example, Rastafarians succeeded in their claim to be a racial group at first instance and lost only by a majority when the case was heard by an Employment Appeal Tribunal. In the Court of Appeal it was held that they were not a racial group because they did not have a long enough shared history (*Crown Suppliers v Dawkins* [2003] ICR 517). This presumably means that at some time point in the future they will have a long enough shared history to constitute a racial group.
21 Werbner narrows the question to one of why Islamophobia – hatred of Muslims – should be made a criminal offence (Werbner 2005, p 5).
22 Cohen, citing *R v Osborne* (1732) W Kel 229, 25 English Reports 584, argues that the notions of a threat to public order and incitement to hatred have been mixed together since the very first origins of the law (Cohen 1971, pp 741–742). For a history of the offence of incitement to hatred, see, Leopold 1977 and Williams 1967, ch 7.

I sometimes think that rather than being designed to lead to prosecution, it's really there to declare some fundamental value; the value being that all people are equal.

(Martino 2007, p 49)

Religious hatred

The argument most frequently advanced with respect to religious hatred focuses on the link between religious hatred and violence. In its 1997 report, the Commission on British Muslims and Islamophobia, in arguing for the need for an offence of incitement to religious hatred, suggested that an incitement offence is needed where there 'is a danger to . . . [the] material and physical interests' of a group (Commission 1997, p 60).[23] Similarly, Modood suggests that 'Muslims will argue . . . that historically vilification of the Prophet and their faith is central to how the West has expressed hatred for them and which has led to violence and expulsion on a large scale' (Modood 1993, p 146). Jeremy argues that the 2006 Act:

serves an important purpose, which is to recognise and give support to groups in society who are afraid for their safety and integrity. Such laws serve to condemn and denounce bias, prejudice and hatred unambiguously, and send a signal to potential offenders that society will punish such conduct severely.

(Jeremy 2007, p 200)

Cumper, in his defence of the 2006 Act notes, among other things, that:

the Home Office, prominent Muslims, the Commission for Racial Equality, and senior Police Officers, all previously identified a link between hateful statements by members of extreme Far Right groups and violence against the Muslim community . . .

(Cumper 2006, p 267)

However, Cumper also argues that one of the reasons why an incitement law was sought was because 'religion . . . has increasingly been seen as a form of self identification for Britain's Muslim communities' (Cumper 2006, p 253). Equally, Nash and Bakalis suggest that '[a]rguably . . . the Act will put all religions on an equal footing' (Nash and Bakalis 2007, p 360). Lord Scarman has argued that the law should protect people's religious beliefs from insult, not just because 'such insults can provoke public disorder – though it is

---

23 Chapter 6 of the Commission's report is devoted to cataloguing and describing the link between racial and religious violence (Commission 1997, ch 6).

important. The true reason is respect for other people's *bona fide* religious beliefs' (quoted in Unsworth 1995, p 674). The arguments for the legislation are thus in part empirical, about the incidence of violence that exists and its link with particular views about religion, and in part conceptual, about the status of believers and 'demands for the increasing recognition of rights for Muslims' (Cumper 2006, p 253).

Religious hatred and violence

Assessing evidence about the level of violence directed against believers, whether Muslim or otherwise, and whether that level of violence has changed, is difficult. Much of the evidence contained in documents such as the two reports from the Commission on British Muslims and Islamophobia is, almost of necessity, anecdotal in its nature (Commission 1997, ch 6; Commission 2004, pp 7 and 31). Some limited official attempts at collecting statistical data have been made (Select Committee 2003, Vol II, p 35). However, it is very likely that such data underreports the degree of violence; what is not clear is by how much violence on account of religion is underreported.[24] Where violence is directed against someone because of their religious beliefs, the criminal acts that are committed, irrespective of the offence of incitement to religious hatred, become, under the Crime and Disorder Act 1998, aggravated offences that attract a higher sentence because of the religious motivation for the violence.[25] In Scotland this has been seen as being sufficient to deal with the problem of religiously motivated violence.[26] We have already seen that there are a range of offences within the criminal law of England and Wales, both specific to the instance of crimes arising out of religious animosity and general, which are relevant to violence that occurs because of religious hatred. The question is thus, does the degree of violence to be found in England and Wales, in itself, justify the creation of the new offence of incitement to

---

24 The occurrence of crime tends to be underreported (see, for example, MacDonald 2002).

25 This change to the law was brought into being by s 39 of the Anti-Terrorism, Crime and Security Act 2001.

26 Under s 74(3) Criminal Justice (Scotland) Act 2003, where offences are aggravated by religious prejudice the court must take this into account when sentencing. In 2002, the Scottish Executive's Cross-Party Working Group on Religious Hatred published a report that rejected the arguments for creating an offence of incitement to religious hatred and instead argued for the notion of statutory aggravation (Cross-Party 2002, p 22). Even prior to the 2003 Act, the law in Scotland in respect to these matters was not the same as the law in England and Wales. Equally, the issues that are important with respect to religious hatred in Scotland are not precisely the same as those in England and Wales. Thus, for example, the Working Party's report devotes some time to discussing the problem of football-related sectarianism, something that has not been seen as being of significance in England and Wales (Cross-Party 2002, pp 10–11). Arguments that are valid in the Scottish context may therefore not be valid in the context of the situation in England and Wales and vice versa.

religious hatred when there are already other provisions of the criminal law that address the matter? One might add to this a question of whether the offence is justified if Muslims or others feel that there has been violence directed against them and feel that the offence will protect them from this.

Religious hatred and equal value

The argument that the legislation is symbolic in its nature, simply emphasising the view that all people are of equal value no matter what their religion in the same way that all people are of equal value no matter what their racial origin, is quite separate from arguments about the relationship between religious hatred and violence. Here, however, the question is whether the argument is valid. It is clearly not the case that everyone agrees that all races are of equal value. In some countries in some eras those who do not take this view have been sufficiently powerful as to introduce regimes that have enforced segregation and apartheid. However, a liberal State takes the view that, since expressions of racial hatred logically and inevitably lead to a belief in some form of apartheid, such views should be eliminated from public discourse.[27] The symbolic argument for the offence of incitement to religious hatred is that the same case can be made with respect to religion and that, because of this, their religious feelings should be protected in law. Thus Jeremy asserts that:

> [w]hilst there has been much disagreement about the scope of legislation designed to prohibit incitement to religious hatred, very few would question the need to control it and to protect its victims from violence and *distress*. (emphasis added)
>
> (Jeremy 2007, p 187)[28]

While violence against believers is, of course, unacceptable, and already a matter dealt with by the criminal law, it is the argument about distress that is more questionable.

There are, of course, some who would argue that hatred of people, whatever form it takes, is, *ipso facto*, wrong. For Quakers, the closest they have to a creedal proposition is the notion that 'there is that of God in every person'. Whatever that means precisely, thinking that there is that of God in every person would mean that hating anyone would become almost perverse in its

---

27 Where words are uttered or material is displayed 'by a person inside a dwelling and are not heard or seen except by other persons in that or another dwelling' no offence of incitement to racial hatred is committed (s 18(2) Public Order Act 1986).

28 Olivier puts the matter even more widely. 'As a matter of education, individuals should be courteous and respect the views of others' (Olivier 2007, p 86).

nature.[29] Quakers are not alone in their views. Jains take a similar position. Dundas, in describing Jain theology, writes of 'the existence of a divine principle, the paramatman, often in fact referred to as "god" ... existing in potential state within all beings' (Dundas 1992, p 94). Similarly, Laidlaw, writing about Jain 'renouncers', the most devout of Jains, observes the importance to them of 'ahimsa, avoiding causing harm to even the tiniest living thing' (Laidlaw 1995, p 1). However, most people in their ordinary lives do not hold to views such as these. Hatred, whether of individuals or groups of people, is widespread and commonplace in Great Britain. Where hatred is based on factual error the hatred itself is indefensible.[30] However, is all religious hatred based on error? Is all religious hatred indefensible?

Religious hatred will usually be an example of collective hatred.[31] There is a literature that treats such hatred as being always based on error. Thus, for example, Glaeser examines the way in which politicians have perpetuated myths about various groups so as to arouse hatred (Glaeser 2005). However, while it might be accurate to argue that collective hatred generally and collective religious hatred in particular is commonly based on erroneous views about, or at the very least a limited understanding of, the group hated, it would seem difficult to argue that this is always the case. A radical feminist might, for example, hate some versions of some religions because of the extremely patriarchal nature of their beliefs and practices and be right in their estimate of those beliefs and practices.[32] Is hatred in such an instance wrong and if it is wrong is it so wrong that it should be made a criminal offence?

Yanay, basing their analysis on the work of the psychoanalyst William Stekel, argues, among other things, that hatred is part of human nature (Yanay 2002, p 54). 'Hatred arises when communication between two groups breaks down, and the gap between their ideas, beliefs, values, and moral standing is unbridgeable' (Yanay 2002, p 56). Stekel had argued that '[a]s there is no one that can live without love, so there is also no being who can live without hate' (Stekel 1953, p 29). However, rather than seeing hatred as simply destructive, he contended that 'hate is the really great motive power of all that happens' (Stekel 1953, p 22). For Stekel '[i]n hate, the sense of

---

29 On the Quaker notion of there being that of God in everyone, see, Dandelion 1996, pp 289–291. This is true for the present day. In the past, as will be seen below, Quakers have been fiercely critical of other faith groups and it is not clear that hatred was absent from their behaviour.

30 The right to hold to the belief may still be defensible. The proposition that Berlin is the capital of France is rationally indefensible. However, most doctrines of free speech are going to uphold my right to believe the proposition and assert it if I so wish.

31 Most examples of religious hatred involve hatred of practices or beliefs, whether supposed or real, that are held by a group of people. However, in principle, religious hatred of just one person because of their beliefs or practices, again whether supposed or real, is possible.

32 It does not follow that they must hate that religion if their estimation of the beliefs and practices is accurate. A Quaker radical feminist would presumably not hate a person even if, for religious or other reasons, they had extremely patriarchal views.

personality is struggling for its right to exist. Hate is a reaction of the ego feeling' (Stekel 1953, p 23). Hatred, on this analysis, is, in an important sense, natural and, in a pluralistic society such as Great Britain, likely and perhaps even inevitable. Some people will hate some other people and, on occasion, those hated may be distressed by the very fact of that hatred even though they do not feel that their safety is endangered.

Hatred, even if it is natural, sometimes causes harm.[33] The distress felt by those who are hated can be just as much harmful as are the consequences of a physical assault.[34] How serious the harm occasioned is will vary from case to case.

> If a black is offended by being called a 'nigger' and you harm me by stepping on my toe, it is probable that the 'offense' may be the more serious thing . . .
>
> (Vandeveer 1979, p 178)

Vandeveer, building on the work of Feinberg, argues for 'limited restraint in certain cases of vicious, ridiculing attacks' because of this harm (Vandeveer 1979, p 192).[35] Hatred may be natural and, as Stekel argues, sometimes useful, but its expression is not therefore always inevitable or even desirable; because of the harm that is sometimes caused by hatred in itself we might argue that it should be legally restricted.

Others base their arguments for legal restraint in the case of religious hatred on different grounds. Thus Williams argues for the need:

> to recall the difference between critique and abuse: it is one thing to say that someone may be deeply and dangerously wrong, even to say it with anger, and another to say or imply that if someone is wrong it is because they are infantile, wilfully blind or perverse. A polemical strategy that refuses from the start to accept that anyone could have *reasons* for thinking differently is a poor basis for civil disagreement (in both the wider and narrower sense of the adjective); it is a way of denying the other a hearing.
>
> (Williams 2008a)[36]

---

33 It does not inevitably cause harm. I may be unaware that you hate me. I may be aware that you hate me but unconcerned by your hatred.

34 Thus Webster, writing about the publication of Salman Rushdie's *The Satanic Verses*, observes that 'in the real political world which we all perforce inhabit, words *do* wound, insults *do* hurt' (Webster 1990, p 129).

35 Feinberg, writing after Vandeveer's works had been published, argues that 'when public conduct causes offense, the fact of that offense is relevant to the permissibility of the conduct in question' (Feinberg 1985, p 26).

36 There is, of course, a certain irony in the leader of a Christian church espousing the importance of civility in religious argument. The moneylenders in the Temple presumably would take a fairly sceptical view of the degree of civility that Christ showed to them (Matthew 21: 12–13).

More than this, Williams argues for the need to understand the realities of the different positions of power that people have in society. Those who feel themselves to be marginalised will experience expressions of hatred in a different and perhaps more damaging way to those who feel themselves to be powerful. He quotes Malik's observation that '[r]eflecting back to agents a distorted or demeaning image of themselves will influence not only the perception of outsiders but it will also impact on the self-understanding of "insiders" ' (Malik 2000, p 137). In such a context expressions of religious hatred can have the effect of silencing the subject of the hatred, making it impossible for them to be heard in their own words. Williams' conclusion is that:

> [t]he grounds for *legal* restraint in respect of language and behaviour offensive to religious believers are pretty clear: the intention to limit or damage a believer's freedom to be visible and audible in the public life of a society is plainly an invasion of what a liberal society ought to be guaranteeing . . .
>
> (Williams 2008a)[37]

In a similar fashion Mookherjee argues that criticism of minority religions, even where that criticism is accurate, 'can harm individuals by deepening negative perceptions in society at large' and also cause social harm to groups by jeopardising toleration (Mookherjee 2007, p 37).[38]

Religious hatred and freedom of speech

Arguments such as those above are specific applications of the more general arguments about the politics of recognition and the need to respect people that we noted in Chapter 2.[39] In this lies their limitation. In the liberal, pluralistic and secular society described in Chapter 1, there will not always be respect for persons and civility may not always be appropriate. Religious hatred, the unbridgeable 'gap between . . . ideas, beliefs, values, and moral standing' that Yanay notes above, will sometimes be the reality of the

---

37 This argument is strongest in the case of minority religions. In looking at the reaction to Australian and New Zealand galleries exhibiting works such as 'Piss Christ' and 'Virgin in a Condom' Mortensen notes the argument that galleries were entitled to do so because 'the Christian predominance [in Australia and New Zealand] gives it a cultural strength that enables Christian belief to absorb shocks that would be more damaging to, say, the smaller Muslim Community' (Mortensen 2000, p 193).

38 Mookherjee's call is for self-restraint in such situations rather than for a legal limitation (Mookherjee 2007, p 30).

39 Malik explicitly draws on the work of people such as Raz and Taylor that were discussed in Chapter 2 (Malik 2000).

situation.[40] Ridiculing a religion that one finds ridiculous can be an appropriate thing to do. Indeed, one might argue that not ridiculing a religion that one finds ridiculous, either where one is silent or where one moderates one's comments on the religion, is wrong in a liberal society because that society is founded on public discourse and the exchange of ideas in that discourse. If those ideas are only a pale reflection of what is truly believed the discourse is thereby fundamentally impoverished.[41]

It is possible to develop this argument further. Hatred is one way of expressing oneself. Expression is not limited to rational discourse. Hyperbole, irony, sarcasm and even insult are all methods of expression. Equally, expression is not limited to words. Pictures and cartoons are, for example, also forms of argument.[42] Each form of expression has its own register; each is, in its own way, valid. Religious hatred, whether expressed through words or in other ways, is part of debate within a plural society. Here again there are echoes of the controversy that surrounded the publication of *The Satanic Verses*. Waldron, in response to those who criticised Rushdie for failing to deal with religion in *The Satanic Verses* with the proper degree of respect, something that he described as 'two-dimensional toleration', argued:

> the demeanour with which religious disputation is to be conducted is itself an issue on which religious views are taken. It is bound up with the fact that faith addresses the deepest issues of truth, value, and knowledge. There is nothing necessarily privileged about the norms of civility that we call moral seriousness . . .
>
> . . . it is fatuous to think that there is a way of running a multicultural society without disturbance or offence.
>
> (Waldron 1993, p 139)

He went on to argue that '[i]f the questions addressed [by material such as Rushdie's book] are as important as they seem, then distress at others' answers is part of the price of addressing them. Sensitivity is not trumps in this game . . .' (Waldron 1993, p 139). Waldron's conclusion was that:

---

40 Indeed, the landscape described in Chapter 1 suggests that in contemporary Great Britain this gap will often be the case. A world of strangers who are sceptical about authority figures breeds division about beliefs of all forms.

41 Thus, for example, Feinberg, in arguing that when deciding offensive behaviour should be made a criminal offence, suggests that there is a need to weigh 'the seriousness of the offense caused to unwilling witnesses against the reasonableness of the offender's conduct' (Feinberg 1985, p 26). Judging the reasonableness of someone's conduct in this context involves, among other things, 'remembering always the social utility of unhampered expression' (Feinberg 1985, p 26).

42 Thus, for example, Nash describes the use that atheists made of cartoons in nineteenth century Great Britain (Nash 1999, ch 4).

we are pushed, then, toward three-dimensional toleration. Persons and peoples must leave one another free to address the deep questions of religion and philosophy the best way they can, with all the resources they have at their disposal. In the modern world, that may mean that the whole kaleidoscope of literary technique – fantasy, irony, poetry, word-play, and the speculative juggling of ideas – is unleashed on what many regard as holy, the good, the immaculate and the indubitable.

(Waldron 1993, p 140)[43]

Said, in a comment on the controversy surrounding *The Satanic Verses*, observed that one reaction by Muslims to *The Satanic Verses* was the 'shock of seeing Islam portrayed irreverently' (Appignanesi and Maitland 1989, p 176); an irreverence that might, in Williams' terminology, be seen as being a lack of civility in Rushdie's manner of dealing with religion (Williams 2008a). Yet it is this very notion of reverence that is doubted, and even found offensive, by some. Thus, for example, Farhi, in the course of an argument that rejects the desirability of all religious institutions, contends that reverence is part of the way in which religious institutions exert what he regards as their malign influence. 'Strategies of obedience, reverence and worship, if they are to be effective, must be structured in such a way as to touch every person within their reach, to take cognizance of their lives, aspirations and concerns' (Farhi 2005, p 95). Reverence, respect, on this argument is a weapon used by religion.[44] Rejecting reverence, rejecting respect for the belief, can be part of the process of rejecting religion.[45] There is nothing new about this. It has long formed part of the process of religious disputation. Davies observes of early Quakers in Great Britain:

---

43 Suggestions that there should be restraint in some form in the way we talk about religion mirror to some extent Lord Coleridge's dictum that 'the mere denial of the truth of Christianity is not enough to constitute the offence of blasphemy'; instead there has to be a 'wilful intention to pervert, insult, and mislead others, by means of licentious and contumelious abuse applied to sacred subjects, or by wilful misrepresentations or wilful sophistry, calculated to mislead the ignorant and unwary is the test of guilt' (*R v Ramsay and Foote* (1883) Cox CC 231 at p 236). This prosecution was in relation to a journal, *The Freethinker*, that used, among other things, both satire and cartoons in its attack on religion (Levy 1995, ch 22; Nash 1999, ch 4). Post argues that 'the purported style/substance distinction proposed by Coleridge cannot withstand close logical scrutiny; in the end the distinction rests not on logic at all, but instead on a specific cultural sense of the "decencies of controversy"' (Post 1988, p 309).

44 Hensher argues that '[i]n the face of organized Christian protests against *Jerry Springer*, those involved were forced to insist that their intentions were serious and respectful. They shouldn't have had to: they should have felt free to say, "We just wanted to take the piss . . ."' (Hensher 2005, p 76).

45 Respect for the right to hold the religious belief including the belief that reverence is necessary is, of course, another matter. As we have seen in Chapter 2, liberalism normally necessitates respect for belief.

[t]he appearance on church doors of scurrilous libels denouncing ministers and the heckling of ministers by Quakers as they passed in the street
. . . appear to have been common. 'Serpent', 'liar', 'deceiver', 'children of
the devil', 'hypocrite', 'dumb dog', 'scarlet coloured beast', 'Babylon's
merchants' and 'sodomites' is a list, but not an exhaustive one, of the
names tossed at the clergy by embattled Friends.

(Davies 2000, p 23)

Quaker language at the time reflected the depth of their disagreement with
the mainstream Christian tradition.

Arguments such as those above derive greater strength from the fact that
they are advanced about something, religious belief and religious practice,
which is a matter of individual choice. Criticism of, and comment about,
religion, however it is put forward, carries with it either an explicit or implicit
suggestion that the believer changes whatever is seen as being wrong. Many
writers reject the notion that religious belief is a matter of choice or, at least,
see it as being a simplistic analysis of what, in fact, is a complex matter (see,
for example, Commission 2004, pp 35–36). Religious belief is for some people
something that is of profound importance.[46] It gives them their most fundamental values and determines how they think about themselves and the world
around them. Equally, for many of these people religious belief is not an
individual matter. Instead, it connects them with fellow believers who, to a
greater or lesser extent, form the community or one of the communities
within which they live. For such people even, what to outsiders seem, slight
changes of belief, minor nuances in faith, have supreme importance.[47]
Challenges to belief are challenges to their values, to the way they live their
lives and to whom they can have social intercourse with. Nonetheless, it does
not fall to many religions, if any, to argue that religious conviction is not
about individual belief. Calls to convert and rules about apostasy equally
testify to religions' acceptance of the notion that belonging to a religion is
something that can change because of the individual will. Changing beliefs
may, at its most extreme, involve losing family and friends; nevertheless,
such changes can be made and some people make them despite the attendant
costs that they have to bear.[48] Hard choices are still choices. In this, religion
differs from race. A call to 'not be black' makes no sense; a call to not
to belong to a particular religion or to no longer accept some precept of a

---

46 We have seen in Chapter 1 that this is not typically the case in contemporary Great Britain
where, for the majority, religious labels are worn very lightly.

47 This is one reason for the process of schism that most religions are familiar with. What to
outsiders seem trivial differences, to insiders become reasons for splitting a church.

48 I have argued elsewhere that the fact that as human beings we are all inevitably involved in
constantly making choices is one part of a starting point that allows for the construction of a
schemata of rights that includes the rights held by religious believers (Bradney 1993, ch 2).

particular faith makes perfect sense. This fact of choice in matters of religion sets a context for debate. Notions of the necessity of respect for faith sets limits on either which choices can be debated or the manner in which that debate can be entered into. This is not to say that civility in debate is not desirable, all other things being equal. As we noted above, hurting other people's feelings does cause real harm. However, most of us are neither pacifists in terms of our actions nor in terms of our words. On occasion, in debate, all other things are not still equal if we have to be civil and, in such instances, instead we will rightly choose to do that which we know will harm other people.

Those who argue about the need to take account of the differences in access to power that people have in society make an important point. Some people have more power to wound and for some people the wounds are of more consequence because of other damage already done to them. Liberals, counsels Ignatieff, need to remember that we do not live in Voltaire's time:

> In contemporary liberal democratic societies, religious communities are either declining enclaves within the majority community or else immigrant communities struggling to find a foothold in their countries of adoption. For these immigrants, it is impossible to disaggregate the disadvantages they encounter by virtue of their race, faith, income and language.
>
> (Ignatieff 2005, pp 131–132)

However, issues about power in society are complex matters. Those who are marginal in terms of the wider society may exercise enormous power within their own families or their own communities. Gurpeet Kaur Bhatti's play, *Behzti*, is about sexual abuse within the Sikh community (Bhatti 2004). Sikhs might well argue that they are relatively marginal within British society and have little access to power. However it was the power of Sikh men, exercised through demonstrations in the Birmingham Repertory Theatre, which led to the production of the play being stopped.[49] Some people, particularly Sikh women, might have a different view about who in this situation was powerful and who was not. They would perhaps see *Behzti* as an argument addressed to the powerful, not the powerless, and to see the circumstances of the play's closure as underscoring who had power within the Sikh community. Edgar notes the argument that:

> the protests against *Behzti* were overwhelmingly male and that the sexual abuse of a young Sikh woman by an older Sikh man struck a chord

---

49 Edgar writes that the play 'was closed after a small group of young Sikh men physically attacked a theatre whose frontage consists almost entirely of glass just before the evening performance of a children's show' (Edgar 2006, p 70).

among young Asian women from all faiths. In this reading, *Behzti* and other Asian plays *are* being sensitive to the feelings of a marginalised and silenced community.

(Edgar 2006, p 73)

On this account, when looking at questions of power, an important question becomes: Who do you define as the community when deciding where power lies? Moreover, in considering issues of power, it would be inaccurate to see commentary on religion in Great Britain as just having audiences in Great Britain. In their comment on *The Satanic Verses*, the Syrian filmmakers Omar Amirallay and Mohammed Mallas write about the fact that 'the message of a few rare voices that are truly free do succeed in penetrating the shadows' (Amirallay and Mallas 1994, pp 35–36). Religions that are marginalised in Great Britain may be dominant in other countries. Things that can be and are said about religion in this country can be heard elsewhere in countries where religions have the power to control and even forbid debate.

Conclusion

Most statutory incitement offences seem to have been a failure, being little prosecuted and raising serious issues for civil liberties when they have been prosecuted.[50] The 2006 Act seems likely to follow this pattern.[51] There is little if any merit in the very notion of incitement to religious hatred. For the reasons given above it is conceptually flawed at its very root. Moreover, as is almost inevitable in a secular liberal democracy, the compromises the Government had to come to in order to secure the passage of its legislation meant that it does little to protect what many believers would wish to protect. The core value of freedom of speech is acknowledged in the legislation. The right to 'ridicule, insult or abuse' is specifically protected by s 29J of the amended Public Order Act 1986. Irrespective of the freedom of speech section in the 1986 Act, if the legislation was indeed intended to protect specific feelings about matters of honour with respect to religion that are found in some Muslim communities, the legislation was always likely to fail. The idea that the courts will turn to the sharia or statements about cultural practices in individual Muslim communities when considering cases is implausible. Instead, in the unlikely events of prosecutions designed to protect Muslim

---

50 See, for example, Williams' discussion of the offence of incitement to mutiny or incitement to disaffection (Williams 1967, pp 177–192).

51 Schedule 16 of the Criminal Justice and Immigration Act 2008 added 'hatred on grounds of sexual orientation' to the Public Order Act 1986 alongside religious hatred. Whether the arguments for this offence are analogous to those for making incitement to racial hatred an offence or whether the offence is conceptually similar to religious hatred lies outside the scope of this book.

feelings, they will turn to traditional precedents and general notions of what causes offence. Even if the courts do turn to the sharia and evidence about cultural practice the width of Islam will mean that the picture will be one that is varied and contradictory.[52]

Rather than being a principled statement about the appropriate place of religion in society the legislation is a poor piece of pragmatic politics.

> The small print identified it as an election-year sop to alienated British Muslims, a sign that their faith was recognized, albeit not actively *liked*, at Number Ten, and if only they could find a way to ignore Iraq, Afghanistan, Belmarsh and Guantanamo, they'd realise they were better off under Labour.
>
> (Kunzru 2005, p 117)

As politics the legislation is a failure because it promised far more than it could deliver, raising expectations that will be unfulfilled. Symbolic legislation may have a place in a legal system, but only if the symbol is clear. By the time the Racial and Religious Hatred Bill became an Act it was entirely unclear what symbol it was representing. Like the establishment of the Church of England and the Church of Scotland, the legislation does not offer a defensible way of treating religions in the legal system of a twenty-first century secular, liberal State.

---

52 Thus, for example, Modood observes that 'the anger over *The Satanic Verses* was not so much a Muslim response as a South Asian response . . . It was not the exploration of religious doubt but the lampooning of the Prophet that provoked the anger. This sensitivity has nothing to do with Qur'anic fundamentalism but with South Asian reverence of Muhammad (deemed by many Muslims, including fundamentalists, to be excessive) . . .' (Modood 2005, p 106).

Chapter 5

Families and laws

Introduction

Upon the face of it the law relating to families in Great Britain seems to be an unpromising area to find a possible accommodation between the needs of different religions and the values of a secular, liberal State. Even the most superficial examination of British family law makes it clear that it is an area of law that is firmly embedded in specific Judeo-Christian traditions. Moreover, in many parts of the law relating to families, these traditions still have a considerable hold. Whether one looks at the almost unchallengeable status of the monogamous marriage as the only appropriate form of State-sanctioned marriage in Great Britain or the particular prohibited degrees of affinity and consanguinity in marriage the religious roots of family law are striking. Academic analysis of family law has long acknowledged the particular religious roots of British family law. Thus, for example, the first, 1974 edition of Cretney's *Principles of Family Law* observes that the law relating to the prohibited degrees of marriage is based on canon law, which was itself based on chapter 18 of the Book of Leviticus (Cretney 1974, p 10). More recent analysis continues to acknowledge the theological roots of this area of law.[1] Diduck and Kaganas argue that:

> [t]he *Hyde v Hyde* definition [of marriage as being monogamous] reveals western roots in church or canon law, and that it continues in force and, in effect . . . reveals the continuing influence of the established Church in English marriage law.
>
> (Diduck and Kaganas 2006, p 39)

Historically the very jurisdiction of family law was a matter for the ecclesiastical courts.[2] This does not seem to be an area of law that is likely to

---

1 See, for example, Lowe and Douglas 2007, p 50.
2 Glendon writes of 'the State's eventual assumption by default after the Reformation in most countries, not only of the tasks of regulating marriage and family matters, but also of

reveal ways in which the wide variety of religious traditions that are characteristic of modern-day Great Britain can find a place within the State's legal system. Equally, if one focuses on what contemporary courts actually do, family law once again does not seem likely to be a fruitful area for enquiry for those interested in reaching an accommodation between religion and law. Notwithstanding the religious antecedents of family law, current legislators and lawyers work in a secular mode. Thus, for example, in *Sheffield City Council v E and S* [2005] 1 FLR 965 at p 1000, Mr Justice Munby notes that:

> marriage . . . [is] a civil institution whose duties and obligations are regulated by the secular courts of an increasingly secular society. For, although we live in a multi-cultural society of many faiths, it must not be forgotten that as a secular judge my concern is with marriage as a civil contract, not a religious vow.[3]

The content of family law statutes is now debated by reference to matters of social policy not religion. Lowe and Douglas's argument that:

> [t]oday, the justification [for the prohibition of marriage on grounds of affinity] must be sought on social and moral grounds (some will have religious objections to certain marriages, but in a pluralist society this must be a matter for the individual's conscience)

illustrates this phenomenon (Lowe and Douglas 2007, p 50).[4]

Here it seems we have an area of law that is founded on a specific theology but where current debate sees law and religion as being quite separate. Closer analysis, however, suggests that the relationship between religion and State law is, and long has been, a more complex matter than might at first be supposed.

Accommodating religion

Variation because of religious belief in what is otherwise a uniform pattern of law is part of the tradition of British family law. As long ago as 1753, Lord Hardwicke's Act, which made the first provision for the necessity of a public

---

that elaborate set of canon law rules which has remained the basis of Western family law systems . . .' (Glendon 1977, pp 2–3).

3 Writing extrajudicially, Mr Justice Munby has observed both that '[o]ne of the paradoxes of our lives is that we live in a society which is at one and the same time becoming both increasingly secular, but also increasingly diverse in religious affiliation' and that '[r]eligion – whatever the particular believer's faith – is no doubt something to be encouraged but it is not the business of government or of the secular courts' (Munby 2005, pp 503 and 504).

4 See, similarly, Cretney, Masson and Bailey-Harris 2002, p 41.

marriage ceremony if a marriage was to be legally recognised by the State, laid down that all marriages had to be in churches of the Church of England.[5] However, an exemption was made for both Jews and Quakers, who were allowed to continue to marry according to their own usages.[6] It is easy to underestimate the importance of these exemptions. To modern eyes, where '[e]verybody knows the fine work done by Quakers' (per Atkinson J in *Newell v Gillingham Corporation* [1941] 1 All ER 552 at p 554), this might seem unremarkable. The ostensible purpose of the 1753 Act was to prevent clandestine marriages.[7] Quakers had begun to develop their own marriage certificates in the 1650s in order to rebut suggestions that they were conducting unlawful or clandestine marriages (Davies 2000, pp 97 and 11). A copy of such a certificate, probably dating from 1685, which had been sent by Quakers to the House of Commons, survives in the Friends' House Library in London. The marriage certificates showed that clandestine marriages, even if they were a problem elsewhere, were not a problem in the case of Quakers. Hardwicke suffered considerable difficulties in securing the passage of the legislation through the House of Commons. He agreed a number of concessions in order to ensure the acceptance of the statute.[8] Quakers kept a close eye on Parliament and had lobbied in relation to previous unsuccessful attempts to legislate in this area (Outhwaite 1995, p 85). When they lobbied in relation to the 1753 Act, granting them exemption did not strike at the principle of the law. It is thus not surprising that they received the exemption that they sought. However, although there is much that can be said in favour of such an analysis, there is also another view that could be taken.

Davies, in his analysis of Quakers between 1655 and 1725, argues that:

> Friends spiritual rebirth lay at the root of hostility they encountered in local society, for it led them to profound beliefs inimical not only to the Church and its ministry but also to a whole range of social behaviour which was officially and popularly sanctioned. Religious conversion led Quakers to defy the norm in matters of church attendance, tithe

---

5 The Act applied only to England and Wales and not to Scotland.

6 This exemption for Jews and Quakers continues to the present day. Under s 26(1)(d) of the Marriage Act 1949, Jews may be married according to Jewish usages. There is a similar but broader provision for Quakers in s 47 of the same Act, which not only permits Quakers to marry according to Quaker usages but also allows, under s 47(2)(b), for the legal marriage of non-Quakers according to Quaker form if a Quaker 'registering officer' certifies that permission for the person to marry has been given.

7 Lemmings argues that, in reality, '[t]he first objective of the marriage bill . . . was to prevent marriages among the children of the social elite which were not sanctioned by their parents or relatives' (Lemmings 1996, p 347).

8 Stone says that Lord Hardwicke secured the passage of the new law 'by the use of rhetoric, logic, cajolery, and behind-the-scenes threats, deals, and lobbying' (Stone 1990, p 121).

payments, community rituals, and civility by action which to Quakers seemed clearly sanctioned by the Gospel, but which was considered extremely provocative at the time.

(Davies 2000, p 11)

We saw in the previous chapter that in their early years, Quakers were verbally aggressive in their dealings with others who were not of their faith. Quakers at this time were a faith group far removed, both in their eyes and in the eyes of those around them, from, and in considerable conflict with, the main-stream traditions and practices of British society. In the 1670s Quakers began to seek greater integration with the larger community (Davies 2000, p 217). However, even this greater integration was a relative matter. Even several centuries later Chadwick argues that '[t]he Friends were more removed by religion from Victorian society than any other group outside the com-munities . . .' (Chadwick 1966, p 421). Differences of belief, manner, speech and dress continued to separate them from those around them. 'In 1835 Friends were still a separated community behind a pale . . .' (Chadwick 1966, p 423). What makes the 1753 exemption noteworthy is that it was given to a faith group who, at the time, were still derided and distrusted by most people in British society.[9]

Accommodation to religious needs has been a feature, albeit a spasmodic feature, of the development of family law in the centuries since Lord Hardwicke's Act. Thus, for example, when the Board of Deputies refused to recognise the marriages of the West London Synagogue, s 22 of the Marriage and Registration Act 1856 was introduced to give the Synagogue the same powers as the Board of Deputies (Henriques 1909, pp 38–39).[10] In 1958, the Marriage Acts Amendments Act was introduced to make it easier for Roman Catholic Chapels to register as places of public religious worship (Bradney 1993, p 41). Facilitating needs generated by religious belief remains part of the continuing development of British family law. In 2001, the Divorce (Religious Marriages) Bill was introduced into the House of Com-mons with the support 'of all Synagogue bodies in Anglo-Jewry, as well as the Chief Rabbi, the Board of Deputies and the Jewish Marriage Council'. The intention of the legislation was to help in cases where Jewish husbands refuse to give their wives who have been divorced under civil law, religious divorces.

---

9 Similar observations could be made with respect to the exemption for Jews. Having been expelled from England in 1290, Jews were only formally readmitted during Cromwell's era in the mid-seventeenth century (Katz 1982). Although the legal position of Jews was gradually easing at the time of the 1753 Act their place in society was still uncertain. A statute passed at the same time as Lord Hardwicke's Act that provided for the naturalisation of Jews had to be repealed in the following year because of popular unrest (Holdsworth 1938, p 82). (On the relationship between Jewish marriages and English law, see, Henriques 1909.)

10 See similarly the Marriages (Secretaries of Synagogues) Act 1959.

When this happens the wife, under Jewish law, is much more severely disadvantaged than the husband. She, for example, cannot remarry within the Jewish faith and any children from a subsequent union would be regarded as mamzerim (in approximate terms as being illegitimate) while the husband could remarry and his subsequent children would not be regarded as mamzerim (Freeman 2001, p 371). Passage of the Bill gave the courts the power, under s 10A of the Matrimonial Causes Act 1973, to refuse to issue a decree absolute after the decree nisi until a declaration had been given that the necessary steps to dissolve the marriage in its religious form had been taken.[11]

The long history of using State law to facilitate the lives of believers in relation to matters pertaining to their family practices raises two questions. First, what more, if anything, can be done by the law in this regard? Secondly, what limitations in principle, if any, are there to what a liberal secular State should do with regard to this area?

Law and policy

Initially the law relating to families in Great Britain seems to be deeply embedded in matters of value and policy. The theological and indeed ecclesiastical roots of the law have been noted above. Protracted policy debates lie behind the legislation in many areas of the contemporary law relating to families in Great Britain. Nevertheless, notwithstanding the policy imperatives that lie behind many legal rules about the treatment of families, in the twenty-first century there are now many areas of this law that in fact have little by way of any policy element. It is logical to turn first to these areas in order to explore the possibilities of accommodation to religious need.

Matters of inheritance

Testate succession is a matter that, under English law, is now largely for the testator. Under the present law testators may leave their property in any

---

11 Not all commentators believe that legislation of this type will prove to be effective (see, for example, Freeman 2001). In practice similar problems can occur in the case of Islamic marriages in Great Britain, although there is some argument about whether Islamic law holds that a husband's consent to divorce is necessary (Carroll 1997). The newly amended Matrimonial Causes Act 1973 applies both to marriages according to the 'usages of the Jews', under s 10A(1)(a)(i) and marriages according to 'other prescribed religious usages', under s 10A(1)(a)(ii). During the passage of the Bill it was noted that the measures could potentially apply to Muslim marriages although 'there has been no pressure so far for similar provisions' (Mr Andrew Dismore MP, Hansard, Standing committee D, 7th November 2001). To date the Lord Chancellor has not used the power in the Act, under s 10A(6) to create other prescribed religious usages. Section 15 of the Family Law (Scotland) Act asp 2 2006 makes similar provision to the 2002 Act for Scotland.

way that they wish, subject only to the possibility of challenge under the Inheritance (Provision for Family and Dependants) Act 1975.[12] Some faith traditions contain rules as to succession. Thus, for example, within Islamic law there are a number of different approaches to the appropriate rules of succession (Pearl and Menski 1998, pp 448–478). The freedom that English law accords to testators makes it easy in English law to accommodate different religious traditions. Testators need only to make wills that comply with the dictates of their faith and these, whatever their content, will be enforced by the State courts, not because of the imperatives of the faith, but because they are wills validly made according to English law. In the late 1970s, a Sharia Council arranged for a will to be drawn up that would allow testators to leave their property in an appropriate Islamic manner (Badawi 1995, pp 79–80).[13] Some may find the rules of succession of one faith group or another strange or even, on social policy grounds, undesirable. This, however, is not a reason why English law should not recognise and enforce them when a valid will reflects them. 'Courts continue to say that a person has the right to make an unjust will, an unreasonable will or even a cruel will' (cited in Dainow 1940, p 337).

There are limitations to the accommodation to faith that can be made by the use of a will. First, if a member of a faith, either by choice or inadvertently, does not make such a will those who would have benefited under the rules of the faith will only be able to mount a legal challenge if they can invoke the provisions of the Inheritance (Provision for Family and Dependants) Act 1975. Some may be able to do so, but this will not be because English law takes cognisance of the rules of their faith but because, coincidentally, they have some claim under the purely secular provisions of the Act. The number who will be able to make such a challenge will be very limited because the only potential applicants under the 1975 Act are spouses and some other dependants who, under the terms of the Act, were inadequately provided for by the deceased's will. Secondly, where a will in a form that is appropriate to a faith has been drawn up, those who benefit under the will may have their expectations unfulfilled because of a legitimate challenge under the 1975 Act. The fact that a will meets the dictates of a faith will not be an argument that will, in itself, succeed in any proceedings under the Act. Nevertheless, these limitations notwithstanding, the law in this area offers considerable flexibility in the face of religious needs.

---

12 The only exceptions to this are the very limited number of testamentary conditions to a gift that have been ruled void because they are repugnant, impossible to perform, contrary to public policy or were made *in terrem* (Sherin *et al.* 2002, pp 347–357).
13 Badawi notes that the Council agreed to pay the solicitor's fee for the first 100 applicants who wanted to use the will; only 17 people came forward (Badawi 1995, p 80).

In Scotland testamentary freedom is more limited than it is in England and Wales.

> A distinctive and salutary rule of Scots law which dates from the earliest times is that which prohibits a husband (and latterly a wife) from disinheriting his (or her) spouse, and a parent from disinheriting his children, by guaranteeing to the surviving spouse or children certain 'legal rights' in the estate of the deceased.
>
> (Cooper 1991, p 79)[14]

This makes accommodation to different faiths more difficult under Scots law than it is under the law in England and Wales. Depending upon the precise rules to be found in the faith, perfect accommodation may not be possible. Nevertheless, even under Scottish law, there is some degree of testamentary freedom and a combination of such freedom as there is and the fixed rules of Scottish law will allow for succession, enforceable within the Scottish courts, which can approximate to the rules of a faith.

Divorce

Unlike the law of marriage, where, as is shown below, there are some attempts to accommodate the needs of different faith groups, the law of divorce is an area where both English and Scottish law is uncompromising. Under s 44(1) of the Family Law Act 1986, religious divorces obtained in the United Kingdom have no validity under State law.[15] The fact of a religious divorce might be something that is noted in a legal action, but it will never be regarded as being legally valid (see, for example, *Maples (formerly Melamud v Maples* [1988] Fam 14). What is not clear is why, in the twenty-first century, this is so.

Divorce in both England and Wales and Scotland was once surrounded by a welter of policy considerations and moral judgments that began with the essential judgment that divorce was wrong and, in most instances, unacceptable. Until 1857, divorce was available only by Act of Parliament (Holdsworth 1965, pp 205–206).[16] The history of divorce law is a history of a gradual increase in the number and range of policy arguments that are accepted as making divorce in particular cases acceptable (Cretney 2003, Part II). Such

---

14 For a detailed examination of these rules, see, Walker 1983, ch 7.2.
15 In private international law '[a]t common law, English courts were originally very reluctant to recognise the effectiveness and validity of extra-judicial divorces; but attitudes have changed and it has come to be accepted that they should normally if the general jurisdictional criteria for recognition have been established' (North and Fawcett 1999, pp 798–799).
16 Prior to 1857 the ecclesiastical courts exercised a jurisdiction over matrimonial disputes (Kiralfy 1957, pp 289–297).

has been the success of these arguments that divorce itself is now, in the main, a registration process.[17] Writing in the 1990s, Schuz observed that:

> [u]nder the 'special procedure' ... there is no judicial hearing and only minimal scrutiny of petitioner's allegations ... Thus, it is difficult to see what procedural safeguards are avoided by obtaining an extra-judicial divorce providing that there is adequate proof of the divorce.
>
> (Schuz 1996, p 143)

Schuz goes on to note that:

> [w]here the parties agree, they can obtain a divorce after two years' separation. Where there is no agreement, in many cases it will be possible to satisfy the behaviour fact, if there is no adultery. Thus, in practice, the present law allows most spouses to get divorced virtually at will.
>
> (Schuz 1996, p 143)

Even where there is no agreement, no adultery, no desertion and nothing that will satisfy the behaviour condition of s 1(2)(b) of the Matrimonial Causes Act 1973, the Act, under s 1(2)(e), allows for divorce after five years of separation where just one party wants the divorce. The policy imperative that now lies behind the law is that if one person wants a divorce they should get that divorce in virtually any circumstances. In these circumstances it is unclear why all religious divorces should not be regarded as being legally valid by the State courts.[18] Some non-believers may sometimes regard the grounds for such divorces as being unjust or even immoral. However, the reasons that a person may have for seeking a legal divorce under the Matrimonial Causes Act 1973 may be regarded by others as being immoral or unjust; that will affect neither the outcome of the divorce action nor the validity of the divorce. The reason why someone wants a divorce no longer matters to the State in its own legal system. Providing one party to a marriage

---

17 'The actual process of the pronouncement of the decree has become reduced to a very brief ceremony of a purely formal character in which decrees are listed together in batches for a collective mention in open court before a judge who speaks (or nods) his assent' per Waite LJ in *Pounds v Pounds* [1991] 1 FLR 775 at p 778. This is true only for the divorce itself. The ancillary matters, issues relating to property, maintenance or children, are another matter. Divorce law in England and divorce law in Scotland differ in detail. For example, following the amendments in the Family Law (Scotland) Act 2006, a divorce in Scotland can now be obtained after two years' separation, even where only one party wants the divorce (s 1(2)(e) Divorce (Scotland) Act 1976). However, the differences in detail do not have any impact on the matters of principle that are discussed here.

18 In the case of Jewish divorce Berkovits argues that there is a particular contradiction in the present position in English law in the fact that the State both approves and recognises Jewish marriages, but does neither for Jewish divorces (Berkovits 1990, p 138).

wants a divorce, it therefore seems irrelevant what mechanism they use to achieve it.

There is, as Schuz argues, no policy reason why the relevant authorities of a religious group ought not to be able to apply for a licence to issue divorces that would then be legally binding within the State's courts (Schuz 1996, p 147).[19] Such an approach would both allow for the maximum possible accommodation to the needs of religious groups while also fulfilling the State's need for the public registration of divorces. An accommodation such as this might not go far enough for some religions. They might, for example, want total sovereignty over marriages entered into, using the institutions of their faith, by their believers. They might want to insist that only they could decide whether or not someone could be divorced. However, given the priority that liberalism accords to individual rights, a secular State would necessarily regard this as going beyond what the State could accept in terms of its own decision as to who it recognised as being divorced.[20] In general terms there is no good policy reason why the State should not recognise religious divorces, even if it continues to offer an alternative purely secular mechanism for those who wish to use it.

There is, as in the case of inheritance above, a limit to the law's ability to easily accommodate religious needs. There are situations where the courts will refuse to grant the decree absolute that will finally dissolve a marriage. The effects of the Divorce (Religious Marriages) Act 2002 have already been noted above. More widely, where the divorce is based on five years' separation, under s 5 of the Matrimonial Causes Act 1973, where the respondent shows that grave financial or other hardship will result from the dissolution of the marriage if the court thinks it wrong in all the circumstances to dissolve the marriage, then it should dismiss the divorce petition. Freeman notes that grave financial hardship has rarely been invoked and that there has been no case where grave other form of hardship has successfully been pleaded in a reported case (Freeman 1995, p 555). Even more obscurely, where divorces are based on either two years' separation or five years' separation, under s 10 of the 1973 Act, a divorce can be delayed while a court assures itself that reasonable financial provision either need not be made or has been made. Notwithstanding the fact that these provisions are very rarely used, they do form part of what little policy basis there is in the current English law relating

19 Such a stay would not prevent any ensuing divorce having validity within the rules of the religion concerned, but it would mean that like present-day religious divorces, it would not be recognised, at least until the difficulty had been remedied, as being legally valid by the State.

20 It is necessary to emphasise that the arguments here apply only to the question of divorce itself. The ancillary matters, the distribution of property, maintenance and the custody of children, are entirely separate matters that need separate consideration. What the State recognises here is simply the fact of divorce and thus the right to marry again under the State's legal system.

to the grant of a divorce. Because of this there is an argument that if religious divorces were to be recognised by the State, there would need to be a proviso allowing the State's courts to refuse recognition in circumstances covered by either s 5 or s 10 of the 1973 Act. If this were to happen it is probable that it would be successfully invoked as infrequently as is currently the case in English State law.

The celebration of marriages

Policy is mainly an absent feature in the law relating to testate succession and divorce. By contrast a variety of policy considerations have been and are something that is relevant to law relating to the celebration of marriage in both England and Wales and Scotland. However, what those policy arguments are and whether or not they are now capable of rational justification are other matters. As we saw above, Lord Hardwicke's Act laid down that, with the exception of marriages by Jews and Quakers, if marriages were to be recognised by the State, they had to be held in a Church of England church. However, the period from Lord Hardwicke's Act onwards is one that, in English law, has shown a gradual increase in the number of religious groups who can celebrate a marriage that will be recognised by the State according to the traditions of their faith.[21] The liberalisation of this law has had an impact not just on Christian churches, but also on religions that are much newer to Great Britain. Thus, for example, according to a written answer in the House of Commons in 2008, out of the 785 mosques certified as places of religious worship 152 are registered as places for the celebration of marriage with 36 having registered 'authorised persons' before whom a marriage has to be celebrated if a registrar is not present (Hansard, 29th February 2008 col 1985w).[22] Nevertheless, it remains the case that some religious groups will find the process of applying for registration of their places of religious worship problematic.

Registration of somewhere as a place of public religious worship is not a straightforward matter.[23] The courts' interpretation of the phrase 'public worship' requires that, in Lord Morris's words 'the worship is in a place which is open to all properly disposed persons who wish to be present' or, in Lord Pearce's view, it requires:

---

21 Any religion may celebrate a religion in any manner that they choose, providing the celebration is not in breach of the criminal law. However, if the celebration is not recognised by the State, that purely religious marriage will not itself be recognised by the State (*R v Bham* [1966] 1 QB 159).

22 See, further, s 44(2)(b) Marriage Act 1949 and the Marriage (Authorised Persons) Regulations 1952 (SI 1952/1869).

23 The equivalent area of law in Scotland is to be found in the Marriage (Prescription of Religious Bodies) (Scotland) Regulations SI 1977/1670.

the admission of those members of the public who are reasonably suitable, who come in reverence, not mockery, and who are prepared to behave in reasonable conformity with the requirements of the religion they are *visiting*. (emphasis added)
(*Church of Jesus-Christ of Latter-Day Saints v Henning: Valuation Officer* [1964] AC 420 at p 435 and p 437)[24]

A requirement to accept all 'properly disposed persons', still more a requirement to accept 'visitors', may create difficulties for any religion that sees worship as something for a congregation of believers. However, it is unclear how wide this requirement in fact is. In one judgment the court held that 'a place is none the less a place of religious worship because the public who are invited to that place are a particular section of the public, such as either children or men or women' (per Maugham J in *Stradling v Higgins* [1932] 1 Ch 143 at p 151). Even where a religion is willing to let members of the public attend its acts of worship, this is not enough for there to be a valid registration. 'A building on private property must somehow declare itself open to the public . . .' (per Stephenson LJ in *Broxtowe Borough Council v Birch* [1983] 1 WLR 314 at p 326). Either there needs to be a notice indicating that it is open for public worship or the architecture of the building itself must make this plain. Equally, the fact a building is registered under the 1855 Act does not mean that there has been a valid registration. In *Henning* the House of Lords held that a Mormon Temple that had been registered under the 1855 Act was not in fact a place of public religious worship because it was necessary to get permission from a Mormon bishop to worship there.

The Marriage Act 1994, which allows for marriages to be celebrated in a much wider range of venues that have obtained a licence under the Act and have thus become approved premises, seems to provide a way forward for faiths that have difficulties with registering their buildings as places of public religious worship. However, a series of provisions in statutes and regulations make it impossible for any religion to use the 1994 Act. First, s 46B, inserted into the Marriage Act 1949 by the 1994 Act, stipulates that no religious service shall be used in a marriage on approved premises. The Marriages and Partnerships (Approved Premises) Regulations 2005 states, in Schedule 2 paragraph 11, that '[a]ny proceedings conducted on approved premises shall not be religious in nature' and then goes on to detail the ways in which they cannot be religious. Paragraph 8 of the same schedule states that approved premises 'must be regularly available to the public [for the purpose of the solemnisation of marriage and/or the registration of civil partnerships]'. Section 6(1) of the Civil Partnership Act 2004 states that approved premises

---

24 This decision was affirmed recently in *Gallagher v Church of Jesus Christ of Latter-day Saints* [2006] EWCA Civ 1598.

must not be religious premises.[25] It is clear that there is no intention to allow religious ceremonies in approved premises.

The reasons for the policy objections to having religious marriage ceremonies in approved premises or for further widening the range of religions that can combine both a religious marriage ceremony and one that is recognised by the State are obscure. Cretney suggests:

> the [1994] Act was carefully drafted so as to be restricted to *civil* marriage ... In this way conflict with the Church of England (and perhaps other religious bodies) was avoided ...
>
> (Cretney 2003, p 31)

If this is so, it is difficult to see what legitimate objection there could be, whether from religions that are already able to conduct a marriage ceremony that has State recognition or from any other source, to any religion conducting a marriage according to its own usages, and that marriage ceremony regarded as being legally valid by the State, providing those usages were not in conflict with the criminal law and providing that they complied with certain minimal conditions as to the marriage being publicly registered.[26] Marriage ceremonies are already conducted in a wide range of venues, using a wide range of procedures, many of which, following the 1994 Act, are personal to the parties concerned. Allowing all religions to register their marriages and have them regarded as being legally valid by the State further widens that range of venues and procedures that are recognised by the State but involves no change of principle.

Marriage

The question of who should be married raises questions that are separate from who should be allowed to conduct the ceremony of marriage. Here, policy matters are to the fore. The State holds to principles about matters such as the age of parties to marriage, the need for individual consent, the degrees of consanguinity and affinity and the number of parties that there can be to a

---

25 'The Registrar General's Guidance to Authorities for the Approval of Premises as Venues for Civil Marriages and Civil Partnerships', issued in 2001, suggests, in paragraph 6, that 'premises in which a religious group meets occasionally might be suitable [for registration] if the other criteria [for approval] are met'.

26 Again, it is necessary to note the restricted terms of this argument. What is being debated here is what marriage ceremonies should be regarded as being legally valid by the State. The question as to who the State should allow to marry, or to be more precise, which marriage relationships the State should recognise, is a completely separate matter. Thus the State already recognises marriages in mosques, albeit with restrictive conditions that make it difficult for mosques legally to get the necessary certification, without recognising polygamous marriages.

marriage. In some instances these principles come into conflict with the traditions of some faiths.

Some problems that religions have with the State's approach to who may be married cannot be resolved by any accommodation by the liberal secular State. As has been seen in Chapter 2, such a State gives a priority to individual rights and because of this, individual consent to marriage is a non-negotiable minimum for the State legally recognising a marriage relationship.[27] From this it also follows that some kind of age restrictions on those who may give such consent will follow. There must be some minimum age before which a person cannot be thought to have sufficient understanding as to be able to give consent to marriage.[28] Both these restrictions on who can marry will inevitably bring the law into conflict with any religion that does not accord priority to individual rights; both, however, are things about which the secular liberal State is simply not neutral.[29] Nonetheless, not all of the present legal rules about who can marry lie so close to the centre of the liberal stance. In other areas there is a possibility of accommodation.

The most obvious conflict between the present rules as to who may marry and the traditions of some religions lies in the prohibition, under s 11(d) of the Matrimonial Causes Act 1973, on polygamous marriages by those domiciled in the United Kingdom.[30]

27 The importance of free and genuine consent in marriage has recently been re-emphasised by the Forced Marriage (Civil Protection) Act 2007 in England and Wales. However, on occasion, attention to religious sensibilities seems to have constrained the courts when they considered what might amount to duress that would vitiate consent to a marriage. See, further, Bradney 1984, p 279.
28 There will be, and have been, detailed arguments about what this age should be. These arguments, however, turn on matters pertaining to biology and social development rather than points of principle. In some circumstances there will be a conflict between age restrictions that are set by the State and those that are to be found in faith traditions. Dane, for example, notes that under Jewish law a girl reaches adulthood at the age of 12 (Dane 2001, p 398). In such instances when the age restrictions of a faith tradition give an individual rights at an earlier age, since the issue turns on whether a person can be said to be competent to make decisions for themselves, the liberal State will be unable to accommodate religious tradition and will insist on its own restrictions applying. If the case were the reverse and the State regarded somebody as a competent adult but the religion saw them as still being a child, the autonomy of the individual would prevail. The liberal State cannot make someone act as an adult if they still wish to behave as a child.
29 The impact that such restrictions have varies not simply according to the religion that one is considering but according to the way in which that religion is practised. Thus, for example, Khaliq observes that forced marriage is a practice that is 'considered acceptable and in some cases obligatory by some Muslims and simultaneously repugnant to Islam by others' (Khaliq 2001/2002, p 333).
30 In private international law, polygamous marriages are now recognised for a wide variety of purposes (Collins 2006, pp 850–857). This, in itself, raises a difficulty in defending domestic law's disregard of polygamous marriages. While the position in private international law might be justified by the need to recognise the practical problems which arise because there

> Polygamy, which is the most common form of marriage in past and present human society, can be simultaneous (in which more than one spouse is simultaneously present), or successive (in which the spouses are married one after the other). It is of course only simultaneous polygamy which is prohibited by the laws with which we are here concerned.
>
> (Glendon 1977, p 38)[31]

Historically simultaneous polygamous marriages were banned in Great Britain because 'marriage, as understood in Christendom, may . . . be defined as the voluntary union for life of one man and one woman . . .' (*Hyde v Hyde* (1865–69) 1 P & D 130 at p 133).[32] However, such an argument has no force in a modern liberal secular State. As we saw in Chapter 1, Great Britain is no longer a part of Christendom in the way that it once was. The prohibition of polygamy must therefore be justified by reference to secular, rational arguments rather than an allusion to a Christian past.[33]

To date only very limited attempts have been made to justify the law's attitude towards polygamy in Great Britain.[34] In their joint working paper on polygamous marriages the Law Commission and the Scottish Law Commission simply asserted that Great Britain was a pluralistic but not a polygamous society (Law Commission 1982, paras 5.5 and 6.48). The reality is, however, that a small minority in society do in fact practise polygamy and would like

are in fact people living in this country who have previously contracted a polygamous marriage, much the same range of problems arise when people have contracted a combination of legal and religious marriages in this country, which in fact amount to a polygamous situation (Shah 2005, pp 118–121).

31 Although polygamous marriages are legally prohibited it seems clear that some people do in fact enter into polygamous marriages in Great Britain using a combination of State law and religious law (Pearl and Menski 1998, pp 273–278; Yilmaz 2002, pp 348–349; Shah 2005, pp 118–119).

32 In fact the practice of polygamy is part, albeit a dissenting part, of the Christian tradition. See, Cairncross 1974.

33 Shah suggests that the UK Government has persuaded the European Commission that immigration rules that discriminated against polygamous wives were not in contravention of the UK's human rights obligations because of the need to protect a marriage system that is 'underpinned by Christian norms' (Shah 2005, p 117). However, whatever success such an argument might have in official circles, it remains the case that such arguments lack conceptual coherence in the context of a liberal, secular State.

34 Some commentators appear to think that it is necessary to show that there is a case for recognising polygamous marriages rather than providing a justification for the State not recognising them. Thus, for example, Poulter has written that '[p]olygamy in England today does not possess any objective or reasonable justification' (Poulter 1998, p 228). However, this seems inappropriate in a liberal State. If some people freely to decide to pursue a polygamous marriage as a life choice the State then needs to justify why it not only does not facilitate that choice but, instead, actively makes its pursuit more difficult by, for example, denying such individuals the State benefits that would be available to those in monogamous marriages.

that practice to be officially recognised. Poulter may be correct in suggesting that the majority of white opinion would find the idea of official recognition of polygamous relationships unacceptable (Poulter 1986, p 58). However, the question is whether such opposition can be justified by being grounded in any theoretical position that is defensible. One possibility lies in rights discourse. Faith traditions that permit polygamous marriage almost largely permit it only for men; they are in this, inherently discriminatory in their nature. Hamilton has argued that this in itself, given the United Kingdom's international law obligations to promote the equality of the sexes, would justify not recognising polygamous marriages celebrated in Great Britain (Hamilton 1995, pp 72–73).[35] However, since the law, under s 12(c) of the Matrimonial Causes Act 1973, independently requires consent to marriage, this argument involves enforcing equality on women, even where they do not want it. Hamilton's argument appears to be that women should not be allowed to marry in a polygamous fashion, even when they wish to do so. Great Britain increasingly gives official recognition to a wider and wider range of familial forms, accepting both that people's sexuality and need for intimacy can find expression in many different ways.[36] What is it about polygamy that means that a woman could never freely and genuinely consent to such a relationship?

Hassouneh-Phillips' study of polygamous relationships among American Muslims may give an answer to this question or, at least, suggest a direction in which that answer should be sought. Her study concludes that:

> [e]xperiences of polygamy in this sample of American Muslim women were intertwined with abuse. All women reported feeling that they were treated unfairly in comparison with other wives, and all women perceived this as emotional abuse . . . on the part of their husbands.
>
> (Hassouneh-Phillips 2001, p 746)

The reason for rejecting State recognition of polygamous relationships, it could be argued, is that empirically those relationships are always or nearly always abusive in their nature.[37] Care has to be taken with this argument. Hassouneh-Phillips had only 17 women in her sample (Hassouneh-Phillips 2001, p 738). She herself states that:

> research comparing the prevalence, frequency, and severity of intimate partner abuse in polygamous versus monogamous marriages is needed to

35 See, also, Poulter 1998, p 216.
36 See, for example, the Civil Partnership Act 2004.
37 This seems broadly to be Okin's argument in her 1999 essay 'Is Multiculturalism Bad for Women?' (Okin 1999).

ascertain whether polygamy itself is a risk factor for abuse of women in families.

(Hassouneh-Phillips 2001, p 746)

Justifying the State's current attitude towards polygamous marriages involves showing that there is something particularly oppressive about them.[38] There are those who argue that all marriage relationships are to some degree oppressive for women (Mitchell 1971, p 114). Honiq, among others, has criticised 'the easy judgement that either institution [of polygamy or monogamy] is better or worse as such' (Honiq 1999, p 38).[39] However, it might be possible to show that in a country such as Great Britain, where there are very high levels of expectation of individual fulfilment from relationships and where such expectations percolate into even those communities that have not historically had them, polygamous marriages in practice almost invariably and almost inevitably fail to meet the emotional needs of the female participants.[40] The difficulty of establishing such an argument should not be underestimated. There are very high rates of divorce for monogamous marriages in Great Britain. Even where monogamous marriages do not end in divorce, not all of them consist of happy or even harmonious relationships. Showing that emotional abuse is a factor in polygamous marriages in a way that it is not in monogamous marriages is no small matter. Yet the fact remains that, even if such work could be done, it has not been done to date. The State's attitude towards polygamy rests in part on its religious history and in part on a generalised distrust of traditions that are not common in Great Britain; neither of these things constitutes the public reasons that liberalism demands as a defence of the various stances that the State takes. In these circumstances it is not clear why the State should not accommodate those believers who would wish to see their polygamous marriages accorded State recognition.

The content of the prohibited degrees of relationship for those marrying in Great Britain, which prevent some relatives marrying each other, also creates

---

38 Studies such as that by D'Onofrio, that seek to show that individual polygamous communities are oppressive towards women and/or children, cannot provide the evidence for a general argument that polygamy must be oppressive so far as women or children are concerned (D'Onofrio 2005).

39 Omariba and Boyle, in their discussion of the literature, note that there are both positive and negative assessments of the impact of polygamous practices on women (Omariba and Boyle 2007, p 530).

40 Such a conclusion would be consistent with the views of some people in faith traditions that have recognised polygamy. Sura IV, verse 3 of the Koran, for example, requires that under Islamic law the husband treat all of his wives equally. This requirement is something that some Islamic scholars and communities believe no man can achieve. They therefore hold that Islam does not permit polygamy (Pearl and Menski 1998, pp 238–241).

problems for some religions;[41] like the prohibition on polygamy, it has, as was noted at the beginning of this chapter, a clear historical explanation in the religious traditions that were once prevalent in the country. However, as Glendon observes, if one looks for a secular justification, '[t]here is no ready explanation of the basis for current legal regulation of marriages between persons related in various ways' (Glendon 1977, p 42). The possible policy arguments for such regulation broadly lie in two directions, 'ensuring the integrity of the family as well as promoting biological well-being' (Stone 1960, p 539). In both instances the merits of the arguments are more questionable than might at first be thought.

The first argument in favour of some form of prohibited degree of relationship is that, in the case of some examples of consanguinity, there is a greater likelihood of birth defects in any children born to such a union. There are a number of difficulties that have to be dealt with by those putting forward such an argument. First the argument about the heightened possibility of birth defects is usually put only with reference to marriage and consanguinity. However, there are a number of conditions, such as cystic fibrosis, where, if the parents are carriers of the condition, children born to the union will have a significantly higher chance of themselves suffering from the condition (Welsh and Smith 1995). If there is a concern with birth defects because of consanguinity, surely it would be logical to require appropriate medical tests for everybody before marriage so as to see that their children would not have the same level of risk of defect as those born to unions within the degrees of consanguinity?[42] Why is consanguinity special? Secondly, there is the need to show that there is in fact significant extra risk associated with consanguinity. While some studies have sought to show this, the matter is not straightforward. Bittles notes that estimates of the degree of effect on the health of children born to such relationships are very variable with the later ones suggesting a much lower level of risk than early ones (Bittles 2001, p 91). Equally, even if the risk does exist, does the degree of *risk* justify the *certainty* of not permitting a legal marriage? Next, if the current law is to be justified, then the risk has to be shown to relate to the particular relationships that are currently prohibited. Here again the matter is not straightforward. Bittles' observation about the US, 'it is difficult to discern any coherent rationale in the legislation on consanguinity', applies more widely (Bittles 2001, p 91). Great Britain does not, for example, prohibit first cousin marriage despite the

---

41 The most obvious difficulty is the prohibition on marriages between uncles and nieces that are legal under Jewish law (Dane 2001, p 400). There are also prohibited degrees of relationship with respect to civil partnerships (see s 3(1)(d) Civil Partnership Act 2004).

42 As long ago as 1875, Alfred Huth argued against prohibiting marriages where there was consanguinity between the partners precisely because there was no general prohibition on marriage where the progeny might suffer from birth defects (Kuper 2002, pp 173–174). For a more recent deployment of a similar argument, although with respect to the crime of incest, see, Bailey and McCabe 1979, p 758.

very close genetic relationship that this involves. Moreover, all of these arguments are about the possible risks of having children, not marrying. The State law of Wisconsin restricts first cousin marriages to couples in which one or both of the partners are infertile or the woman is over the age of 55 (Bittles 2001, p 91). Finally, even if all these points can be attended to, arguments about possible birth defects only justify the rules relating to consanguinity, not those relating to affinity.[43]

A second type of argument used to justify the prohibited degrees of relationship relates to the supposed social effects that the possibility of such marriages pose. Thus, for example, Lowe and Douglas refer to the 'tensions within the family' that could be created if marriage between affines was possible (Low and Douglas 2007, p 50). Whether such an argument has significant strength in twenty-first century Great Britain is questionable. British society was once far more rigid in its structure than it currently is. Social rules about how people were to live their lives were more dominant and concern with individual self-fulfilment less prominent. Now, the law makes much greater attempts to facilitate people's search for individual happiness than it once did. In this context restricting the range of relationships that the law will recognise is no longer so obviously defensible as it once was. The harm resultant from birth defects, if it can be shown to exist, is concrete in its nature. The social consequences of marriages within the degrees of affinity are more nebulous. In Bauman's liquid world, where even family relationships are 'revocable', Stone's concept of the 'integrity of the family circle' seems somewhat outmoded (Stone 1960, p 539; Bauman 2003, p 41).[44] The effect of the State recognising marriages by affines seems likely to be negligible.[45]

When analysing the supposed justifications for the prohibited degrees of relationship the concern is that Lowe and Douglas's comment on consanguinity, 'most people view the idea of sexual intercourse (and therefore marriage) between, say, father and daughter or brother and sister with abhorrence' (Lowe and Douglas 2007, p 50), might be the more general justification for all of the prohibited degrees of relationship. It is not the actual relationships that are the problem; it is the abhorrence at the thought of such

---

43 Strictly, they also only justify prohibiting the birth of children rather than marriage itself. However, one might argue that pragmatically in this area the State can hope to superintend marriage, but not the birth of children.

44 The second half of the nineteenth century and the first few years of the twentieth century saw tortuous and protracted debates before the final passage of the Deceased Wife's Sister Marriage Act 1907 (Anderson 1982). It seems unlikely that recognising marriages between affines would create such controversy in the present day.

45 Bradley notes that most States in the US have abolished all prohibitions on marriages between affines while Scherpe states that such prohibitions were abolished in Germany in 1998 'without controversy' (Bradley 2003, p 130; Scherpe 2006, p 34).

relationships that lies at the root of the legislation. The problem with this is that 'abhorrence', however widespread it is, provides, at best, a very weak reason for a liberal State legislating in a particular manner. If the abhorrence might lead to public order problems then that might justify the State taking action. Even here, however, the argument has to be treated with considerable caution. There was considerable, if not universal, abhorrence in so far as homosexuality was concerned when male homosexuality was legalised in 1967 (Moran 1996, ch 3). The dominant view then was that attitude was not thought to justify the continuing criminalisation of such homosexuality.[46] A strong case needs to be made to justify the restriction on individual freedom that the prohibited degrees of relationship represent.[47] It is far from clear that this case has in fact been made. The change that needs to be made to the current law to accommodate religious needs is relatively limited; recognising marriages between uncles and nieces, which are permitted under Jewish law, is one example (Dane 2001, p 400). Legislating for a much more limited set of prohibited degrees of relationship would both accommodate the needs of some religions in Great Britain and also more properly reflect the rather weak arguments that are made for such prohibitions.

Children and religion

Historically, in matters pertaining to children, the British courts have been keen to assert the neutrality that we noted in Chapter 2 as being one of the keystones to liberalism. Thus, in one custody case, Scrutton LJ observed that 'the Court is perfectly impartial in matters of religion' in *Re Carroll* [1931] KB 317 at p 336 while, in a much later case, Scarman LJ continues the same refrain with his statement that '[i]t is not for this court . . . to pass any judgement on the [religious] beliefs of the mother or the [religious] beliefs of the father' in *Re T (Minors) (Custody: Religious Upbringing)* (1981) 2 FLR 239 at p 245. Religious belief in itself, it would seem, is normally irrelevant to how the courts treat a child.[48] In fact, however, the courts' attitude towards the

---

46 Some did argue that majority distaste would justify not changing the law. See, for example, Devlin 1965, p 17. Their arguments, however, did not prevail.

47 In *B and L v United Kingdom* Application No 36536/02 the European Court of Human Rights unanimously found that the prohibition on father-in-laws marrying daughter-in-laws was in breach of Article 12 of the European Convention. In response, the Government introduced the Marriage Act 1949 (Remedial) Order 2007 SI 2007/438. This abolishes s 1(4) to s 1(8)(5) of the Marriage Act 1949 and thus makes such marriages legal. In Scotland, the change was implemented by the Family Law (Scotland) Act 2006. While not all prohibitions on marriages between affines might be found to be in breach of Article 12, this European Court of Human Rights decision further undermines the credibility of the legislation in relation to marriages between those with the prohibited degrees of relationship.

48 There are exceptions. In *Re B and G* [1985] FLR 134 Latey J described the Church of Scientology as 'immoral and socially obnoxious' and 'corrupt, sinister and dangerous'. The

issue of religious belief and children has always been a lot more complex than the simple assertion of neutrality would seem to suggest. Two areas of law, disputes between parents about the custody, care and control of their children and the law's attitude towards medical treatment of children, illustrate the difficulties the courts have in accommodating religious differences.

Religious beliefs in themselves might be irrelevant to court decisions about children, but the social practices that can stem from belief and the reactions that belief may prompt in others have certainly been relevant to court decisions about the custody, care and control of children. Thus, for example, in a custody dispute over three children between a father, who was a member of the Exclusive Brethren, and a mother who had left the same sect, despite the fact that the father had actual custody of the children for six years since the parents' separation, the father lost custody because of what the court referred to as the 'harsh limitations' of Brethren life and the fact the Brethren taught the children to see themselves as 'different and separate from the rest of children' (*Hewison v Hewison* (1977) 7 Fam Law 207).[49] The court's attitude in *Hewison* mirrors the nineteenth century case, *Re Besant* ((1879) 11ChD 508 at p 513), where Jessel MR argued that Besant should lose custody of her daughter, not because she was an atheist, but because of the impact that being an atheist had on her social position and thus on her daughter. Religion in court decisions about children has mattered; difference in itself is seen as being harmful to the child's best interests.[50] However, the last quarter of the twentieth century saw the courts' attitude towards religion and religious practice in relation to children become rather more nuanced.

In *Re H* (1981) 2 FLR 253 a Jehovah's Witness mother was allowed to retain custody of her child when she agreed to give undertakings that her child would take a full part in school activities, not go witnessing with her and be allowed to celebrate his birthday, Easter and Christmas. A comparable approach was taken in the Scottish case of *McKechnie v McKechnie* (1990)

father had had custody of his children for the five years that preceded the case. Latey J gave the father's membership of the Church as the reason for giving the mother custody of the children.

49 The importance of practices consequent upon religious belief in this case is shown by the fact that a study of 855 custody cases, published in the same year that *Hewison* was decided, showed the status quo as to the custody of the child was altered in only 7 cases (Eekelaar and Clive 1977, p 74). For a similar decision to *Hewison* that describes the Brethren's doctrine of separation, where members are placed incommunicado as a disciplinary matter, as 'odious' see *Re C, The Times* 1st January 1964. The courts also treated other religions in the same way; see, for example, the decision on *Buckley v Buckley* (1973) 3 Fam Law 106, which involved a Jehovah's Witness mother.

50 It is only the difference and distance that can come from religion, which is seen as being dangerous. The literature does not, for example, discuss rural isolation in the same terms.

SLT 75. Similar undertakings were also given in *Re T* above.[51] In a 1995 decision, *Re ST (A Minor)*, the court was faced with a mother who belonged to The Family, a group who practised communal living and had been accused of child sexual abuse.[52] The grandmother sought to take care and control of her grandson away from the mother. In his judgment Ward LJ rejected the grandmother's claim, but subjected both leading members of The Family and the mother to a number of requirements, including some relating to the child's education and another that the mother state that she put the interests of her son before her commitment to The Family.[53]

Care needs to be taken so that the new attitudes of the courts are not overemphasised. While parents from minority religions that have mores that separate them from mainstream society no longer regularly lose custody of their children because of the social practices that stem from their religion, living differently continues to be seen as being largely harmful to a child.[54] Although Scarman LJ, as he then was, argued that, in relation to the Jehovah's Witness way of life:

> it was not necessarily wrong or contrary to the welfare of children, that they should be brought up in a narrower sphere of life and subject to stricter religious discipline than that enjoyed by most people

in *Re T (Minors) (Custody: Religious Upbringing)* (1981) 2 FLR 239 at p 245, the court's actions in attaching conditions to the custody order belie such sentiments. The courts are not comfortable with strong religious beliefs. In *Re ST (A Minor)* Ward LJ noted that the mother's:

> closing words to me were to plead with me not to denigrate the Law of Love [The Family's central tenet of faith]. It was an extraordinary observation from her. I would have expected her to plead with me not to remove her son ... But NT did not. It was as if the integrity of the Law

---

51 For recent affirmation by the Court of Appeal that it is legitimate to attach a condition forbidding a child going witnessing, see *In the Matter of S (A Child)* [2007] EWCA Civ 267.

52 This case is unreported and is not available on the electronic databases. A transcript of the court's judgment was given to me by members of The Family. The judgment is more fully analysed in Bradney 2000, pp 96–98.

53 There is a striking contrast between the court's treatment of The Family in this case and the treatment of Scientology in *Re B and G* noted above. The two religions are comparable in the sense that, for a variety of reasons, they arouse considerable public hostility. However, in *Re ST* the court heard evidence from several expert witnesses about the reality of life in The Family. No such evidence seems to have been heard in *Re B and G*. To what degree the difference in outcome in the two cases is related to the difference in evidence is a moot point.

54 This is so even where the child itself favours the different way of life. In *Re R (A Minor)* [1993] 2 FLR 163, the court asks of an Exclusive Brethren child 'whether his holding a [separatist] view is in itself in this child's best interests'.

of Love was more important to her than S [her son]. Where is her sense of priorities?

Ward LJ's observation takes on particular significance, given the care he took before coming to judgment and the detailed argument that is found in his judgment.[55] While there can be no doubt about the sensitivity of his judgment, he is unable to empathise with a person whose religion is central to her identity. Court decisions in this area may now allow parents from minority faiths that are outside the mainstream to bring up their children but they do not allow them to bring up those children within their faith.[56]

Religion does not matter in the majority of custody cases in the way that it once did (Lowe and Douglas 2007, p 591). This is scarcely surprising given the religious landscape that we saw in Chapter 1. Religion does not matter in Great Britain in the way that it once did. However, where strong religious beliefs are to be found, then often they do continue to matter in such cases. The essential principle applied in the nineteenth century in *Re Besant* continues to be applied in the present day, even though its application is carried out in a much more sophisticated manner. Those who hold to religious opinions that are contrary to the mainstream traditions of the day continue to be disadvantaged in any dispute over the custody of their children.

Cases that involve potential medical treatment for children also illustrate the problems that the courts have when looking at the role of religious belief. It is well-established law that:

> the state has a duty towards . . . [a] child and will not let her die for her parents' beliefs. Her welfare is paramount and welfare invariably equates with the maintenance of meaningful life.
>
> (Bridge 2002, p 269)

In pursuit of this duty, as in child custody cases, the courts have emphasised that religion is irrelevant to their decisions. Thus Montgomery, in an essay

55 In his judgment he says that he took one year for consideration of the case before giving judgment in the case. His judgment amounts to some 278 A4 pages.

56 The courts have sometimes argued that what is at issue in disputes about custody is not a question about faith but a question about the fact that in such disputes the two contending parents have different faiths. Thus, for example, Ormrod LJ quotes with approval a first instance judge's comment that '[w]hat it really boils down to is not a matter of the faith of the Jehovah's Witness being wrong or right . . . it is a matter of the custodial parent holding one set of views and the non-custodial parent holding a conflicting set of views and the conflict causing damage to the child' (*Wright v Wright* (1981) 2 FLR 276 at pp 277–278). Conflict in parenting may clearly be bad for a child. However, conflict could be avoided as easily by the views of the parent from the minority religion being accommodated. There does not appear to be a reported case where this has happened.

on healthcare law, quotes Lord Donaldson as saying, in *Re W* [1992] 2 FCR 885 at p 903:

> I personally regard religious or other beliefs which bar any medical treatment or treatment of particular kinds as irrational, but that does not make minors who hold those beliefs any less *Gillick* competent [to make decisions about medical treatment].

However, Montgomery immediately goes on to comment that '[n]evertheless a close examination of the case law suggests that the judiciary has found it more difficult to act upon this neutral stance than to express it' (Montgomery 2000, pp 168–169).

The jurisprudence of healthcare law is replete with examples of court decisions that reject children's attempts to reject medical treatment, particularly when it relates to matters of life and death.[57] The arguments that the courts use in relationship to the children's objection to medical treatment vary from case to case. However, the court's judgment in *Re P (Medical Treatment)* [2003] EWHC 2327 at para 11–12 shows the essence of the court's concern. The case was about a Jehovah's Witness child aged 16 years and 10 months who objected to blood transfusions. The court ruled that:

> [t]o overrule the wishes of John seems to me to be an order that I should be (as indeed I am) reluctant to make . . .
>
> Nonetheless, looking at the interests of John in the widest possible sense – medical, religious, social whatever these may be – my decision is that John's best interests will be met if I make an order in the terms sought by the NHS Trust [that would allow the use of blood transfusions].

In this case, as in *Re ST (A Minor)* above, the court is unable to come to terms with the attitude of the person before the court. For the court, John's religious interests are part of the bundle of his interests; for John, as with the mother in *Re ST*, religion comes first and determines everything else. In *Re W* [1992] Fam 64 at p 88, Balcombe LJ quotes with approval Ward J's observation in the unreported case of *Re E* that 'this court . . . should be very slow to allow an infant to martyr himself'. However it seems unlikely that E would have seen his death as martyrdom.[58] Attitudes to death are in part cultural

---

57 See, for example, *Re S* [1994] 2 FLR 1065, *Re L* [1998] 2 FLR 810 and *Re P* [2004] 2 FLR 1117.

58 In *Re P* [2003] EWHC 2327 at para 8, Mr Justice Johnson says that E did in fact die when he reached the age of majority and was able to insist on his views about medical treatment being respected.

and sometimes that culture is a religious culture.[59] The courts treat death as simply an end, but for many religions there is a continuity between life, death and that which comes thereafter. Put simply, but not simplistically, if what John does now puts in jeopardy what happens to him after death, how can it be in his interests to do it? If we do not accept his views on this jeopardy, how can we say that our views about a religious belief do not enter into our judgement? In practice, the court's approach is dominated 'by a secular humanist world view' (Montgomery 2000, p 161).[60]

Conclusion

The law relating to families in Great Britain shows that it is possible for a secular State to do much to accommodate the needs of religions without breaching any of its own fundamental principles. Such accommodation has already been made in part, but there is much more that could be done with what in truth are relatively minor concessions on points of principle. However, this area of law also shows the difficulty that there is in transcending the limits of what the good life might be. Recognising that *Gillick* competent children might legitimately wish to refuse medical treatment and in doing so put their lives at risk, that individuals might wish to enter into marriage relationships that we regard as strange and even distasteful and trusting the good faith of a wider and wider range of religions so as to allow them to register marriages would be all part of a deeper and more determined effort by the liberal State to accommodate religious differences where its central principles are not put into question.

59 See, for example, Edwards 2007.
60 A view, moreover, that is contradicted by the law. Death is a legitimate choice since the Suicide Act 1961.

Chapter 6

Education

Introduction

The law relating to families in Great Britain includes instances where there has been a successful attempt to accommodate religious differences as well as areas where a lot more could be done without any dramatic break with established legal and political principles. The law relating to education in Great Britain is similar to the law relating to families in that it does contain examples of relatively successful attempts to accommodate religious differences. However, it also contains one example of a complete failure to understand the way in which the place of religion in society has changed in what once might have been a Christian country but is now a largely secular society. It is to that example that we will first turn.

The churches and State education

The Christian churches, largely although not entirely, the Church of England, Dissenters and the Roman Catholic Church, have historically had a close association with primary and secondary education in Great Britain.[1] Primary and secondary education on any large scale mainly grew out of the work of these churches in the nineteenth century.[2] However, even early in the nineteenth century, the State took an interest in education. Limited public State funding was first made available for such education in 1833 (Murphy 1971, p 16) and by 1840 the State had 'established two fundamental principles – the right to promote the extension and improvement of elementary education, and the right to inspect its secular efficiency' (Cruickshank 1963, pp 3–4). The Education Act of 1870 further deepened the State's involvement in

---

1 For a history of the relationship between the churches and schools see Cruickshank 1963 and Murphy 1971.
2 Gardner argues that the impact of what he terms 'working class private schools' has been underestimated because of both difficulties in getting information about their operation and a bias against such institutions in the academic literature (Gardner 1984).

elementary and secondary education. It established Board schools that were State-run (Murphy 1971, ch 4). Nevertheless, even by the twentieth century, the influence of the churches in education remained strong. Although the first few decades of the twentieth century saw a decline in the number of church schools, by the 1940s in England and Wales '[h]alf of the schools in the country were still church schools' (Cruickshank 1963, p 158). However, by that time both the Church of England and the Roman Catholic Church had begun to experience considerable financial difficulties in maintaining their schools. In Scotland, following the Education (Scotland) Act 1918, the churches had been allowed to transfer schools into the State sector while still scrutinising the religious convictions of teachers that were appointed to their schools and controlling religious instruction in those schools. However, in England and Wales the first major reform of the education system did not occur until the Education Act 1944.

The 1944 Act created a new concordat with respect to education.[3] This included new provisions with respect to the treatment of religion in schools that had State funding. Among other things, under s 25(1)(2), it provided for compulsory religious instruction and worship in all schools that received State funding, although, under s 24(4), parents could withdraw their children from such instruction and worship on grounds of conscience if they so wished. In s 15(2) the Act also created a system of voluntary-aided schools that would receive partial State funding, but still be under denominational control. The system that was thus created was not an expressly Christian system. While there had to be religious instruction the religion in which there had to be instruction was not specified. Equally, the fact that schools could be denominational was not, in terms, limited to Christian denominations.

The absence of any explicit reference to Christianity in the 1944 Act is not without significance. It was not only Christian faith groups who had sponsored schools in the nineteenth century. The Jewish community also had its own schools.[4] Limited State funding for these schools had first been given in 1853, only two decades after funding was made available for Christian schools (Alderman 1989, p 19).[5] Like the Christian schools, following the 1944 Act, some of these Jewish schools were to be absorbed into the State

3 On the passage of the 1944 Act, see, Wallace 1981; Simon 1986; and Batteson 1999. On the particular position of the Roman Catholic Church at the time of the 1944 Act, see, Elliott 2004.
4 The first Talmud Torah school, focusing on religious education, was established in 1770. The first 'modern Jewish school', including secular education, was established in 1811 (Cohen 1950, p 53).
5 Alderman notes that the provision of specifically Jewish education in the nineteenth century was not limited to those schools that were formally Jewish. Some Board schools became Jewish, appointing Jewish teachers, celebrating Jewish holy days and closing early on Fridays in the winter so as to allow the observance of the sabbath, simply because the vast predominance of their pupils were Jewish (Alderman 1989, p 17).

system as voluntary-aided schools. However, these schools constituted only a very small percentage of the total number of faith schools in the State system. According to Keiner, even by the 1960s, there were less than 10 State-funded Jewish schools (Keiner 1996).[6] Thus, although in strict terms the 1944 Act resulted in a multi-faith State system, the system was in fact overwhelmingly Christian. Moreover, although the 1944 Act made no explicit mention of Christianity when it referred to religious instruction and worship, the Government publicly stated that the expectation was that religious instruction and worship should in fact be Christian in its nature.[7]

How successful the 1944 Act ever was in introducing Christian religious instruction and worship into primary and secondary schools is open to question. In the early years of its implementation there were shortages of specialist teachers who had the knowledge that was necessary to provide instruction (Copley 1997, pp 55–56). Equally, the Act had not made it clear how much time was to be devoted to worship and instruction. For both these reasons it is thus not surprising to find that schools devoted very different amounts of time to such matters (Copley 1997, pp 53–54). Even where syllabuses had been agreed these were not always used in practice (Copley 1997, pp 54–55). It is thus not clear that the 1944 Act ever succeeded in making the changes that were intended by its progenitors. What is clear is that the decades after the 1944 Act saw large-scale changes in the approach that the majority of teachers took to the place of religion in the school.[8] By 1985, the Swann Committee report 'Education for All', on the education of ethnic minority children, was arguing that a 'major task in preparing *all* pupils for life . . . must . . . be to enhance their understanding of a variety of religious beliefs and practices' (Swann 1985, p 466). This could only be done, the Committee argued, by a phenomenological approach to religion that involved an attempt to understand religions through an empathetic experience of them (Swann 1985, p 474).[9] Studying religion involved the study of religion rather than an induction into a religion. In arguing this, the Committee thought it was doing no more than authorising what in fact had already become the generally accepted practice in schools (Swann 1985, p 471). Religious instruction had become religious education and Christianity was no longer the only religion that was studied (Copley 1997, pp 121–126).

6 Keiner says that by 1996 there were 25 such schools with some more being planned at that time. One of these 25 schools was in Scotland, the rest all being in England and Wales (Keiner 1996).
7 See, for example, the statement by the Earl of Selbourne in the House of Lords (Hansard, House of Lords, vol 132, col 336, 21st June 1944).
8 For a history of religious education after the 1944 Act, see, Copley 1997.
9 On the phenomenological approach to religious education, see, Cox 1983, pp 25–27 and Barnes 2006, pp 398–401.

The 'Fact' of Christianity

The passage of the Education Reform Act 1988 brought with it an attempt to overturn the changes in religious education in State schools that had developed from 1944 onwards and instead 'secure the centrality of Christian education in religious education'.[10] The provisions in the Act that relate to religious education and worship were introduced as a series of backbench amendments in the House of Lords. As a number of different writers have observed, the amendments that were passed into legislation were themselves a political compromise between various individuals and groups who wanted to change the nature of religious education and worship in State schools – the eventual result not going as far in 'Christianising' education and worship as some wished (Alves 1991; Copley 1997, pp 137–146).[11] The central changes introduced by the 1988 Act were that collective worship, which had to be undertaken on a daily basis, was now to be 'wholly or mainly of a broadly Christian character' and that religious education, which had to be given to all pupils, had to reflect 'the fact that the religious traditions in Great Britain are in the main Christian'.[12]

Not all the changes brought in by the 1988 Act were contrary to educational thinking at the time. The Act did, for example, for the first time recognise in law that what schools were engaged in was not religious *instruction*, which was the term used in the 1944 Act, but religious *education*. Secondly, the Act also required the other main faiths in Great Britain to be taken into account in religious education (Skinner 1990, p 167; Rose 2006, p 186). The Act also continued and indeed extended the tradition of allowing parents to withdraw their children from both religious education and acts of collective worship.[13] However, the main thrust of these provisions was clearly intentionally contrary to the prevailing educational orthodoxy at the time.[14] The question was

---

10 Bishop of London, Hansard, House of Lords, vol 498 col 638, 2nd June 1988. The 1988 Act applies to England and Wales. In Scotland section 8 of the Education (Scotland) Act 1980 merely 'permits religious observance to be practised and instruction in religion to be given' without specifying any particulars. On religious education in Scotland, see, Gray 1999.

11 Hull argues that the compromises that resulted in the provisions were themselves a source of the ambiguities in the legislation (Hull 1996). The debate in Hansard regarding the provisions certainly underlies the difficulty of reaching any clear view of a single legislative intent with respect to the provisions (see, further, Bradney 1996, pp 129–133).

12 These provisions are now to be found in Schedule 20 paragraph 3(2) of the School Standards and Framework Act 1998 and s 375(3) of the Education Act 1996.

13 This tradition was first begun on a voluntary basis in some church schools in the 1820s (Louden 2004, pp 278–279). It first achieved statutory form in the Education Act 1870 (Murphy 1971, p 57).

14 Isaac sees the provisions as part of a broader political movement. She writes that 'this Christian supersessionism in schools can be seen as part of a new right attempt to instil what are seen as traditional moral values into children' (Isaac 1990, p 222). See, similarly, Skinner's comment that '[t]he cynic might be tempted to say that the real purpose of specifying

how were they to be interpreted? What was meant by 'broadly Christian' and how, indeed, did one define 'Christian'?

Few if any of the teachers who were the subject of the 1988 Act were in a position, by virtue of their own knowledge or training, to interpret the Act themselves. Instead, they had to rely on others to tell them what the new legislation did and did not permit. Hull, then Professor of Education at the University of Birmingham and an influential figure within religious education, argued for a liberal interpretation of the 1988 Act that would permit the continuance of many of the practices of the past.[15] In relation to worship, for example, Hull suggested that:

[a]ll that is necessary to constitute a broadly Christian act of worship is that the broad traditions (note the plural) of Christian belief shall be reflected. We are not told that these traditions of Christian belief shall be affirmed, presented, acknowledged, proclaimed, made the basis of worship or any other of the dozens of similar expressions which might with clarity have been used. School worship is merely to reflect them. This is a distant and muted expression. . . .

(Hull 1989a, p 120)[16]

A 1989 survey of Religious Education advisers to Local Education Authorities showed both a lack of consensus and confusion as to the implications of the 1988 Act. Thus, for example:

[s]ome advisers considered that the ERA reference (s.8) to the need for every new A[greed] S[yllabus] to '*reflect the fact that the religious*

Christianity in the Act has more to do with re-establishing some form of civic religion for ideological purposes than helping to develop children's religious understanding – part of the new nationalism which identifies Christianity with English culture and tradition' (Skinner 1990, p 168). Barnes has argued, more widely, that 'some critics of modern British religious education clearly harbour desires to reintroduce Christian nurture in State schools and to revive (misguided and inappropriate) links between Christianity and British citizenship' (Barnes 2006, p 397).

15 Hull had, prior to the legislation, published widely on religious education and had been editor of the British Journal of Religious Education since 1976.
16 See, also, Hull 1989b. Liberal interpretations of the provisions continue to be offered to the present day. Thus, for example, Marshall-Taylor answers the question, '[c]an these Collective Worship ideas, based on [the Jewish] Purim, be "broadly Christian"?', in the affirmative by arguing that, '[a]part from the fact the story is in the Hebrew part of the Christian biblical canon, the themes which emerge from it . . . are at the heart of the teachings of Jesus, who directed his followers to maintain the ancient Jewish precept to "love your neighbour as yourself". In fact these are unifying principles common to most belief systems, religious and non-religious. Unquestionably, they can be said to be "broadly Christian"' (Marshall-Taylor 2002, p 209).

traditions in Great Britain are in the main Christian', was, however, exactly what was meant (ie. The emphasis was on '*reflect the fact*') and not that the AS or RE should be '*in the main Christian*'.

(Taylor 1989, p 23)

Taylor comments that interpretations were 'subject to a range of, often subtle, distinctions, reflecting both the advisers' own philosophy of RE and the LEA context for RE' (Taylor 1989, p 23).[17] A circular issued by the Department of Education, Circular 3/89, was widely thought to have done little to clarify the terms of the Act.[18] In *R v Secretary of State for Education ex parte R and D* [1994] ELR 495 at p 502 the courts made their sole ruling on the 1988 provisions, holding that worship which 'reflected Christian sentiments' complied with the 1988 Act even if '[t]here was nothing in them which was explicitly Christian'.[19] In 1991, the Department of Education and Science sent out a letter stating that religious education syllabuses should not be based solely on Christianity and should include material on all of the principal religions in Great Britain.[20] In 1994, the Qualifications and Curriculum Authority published 'the non-statutory framework for religious education' which both set out the legal requirements as to religious education and suggested what should be included in the curriculum (Qualifications and Curriculum Authority 2004). While the framework emphasised the need for schools to meet their legal obligations as to religious education it said nothing specific about the amount of time that had to be devoted to the study of Christianity. It did, however, say that the religious education curriculum ought to include Christianity and 'the other principal religions represented in Great Britain (here regarded as Buddhism, Hinduism, Islam, Judaism and Sikhism)' and also recommended that there should

17 See, further, Thompson 2004, pp 116–120.
18 See, for example, the editorial comment in 'Education' at (1989) 173 *Education* 80. Hull wrote that it 'was little more than a summary of the legislation and Religious Education and Collective Worship' (Hull 1995, p 243). However, one recent commentator, herself a supporter of the aims of the religious education and worship provisions, describes the 1989 circular as 'a model of clarity and prescription . . .' (Thompson 2004, p 114).
19 In 1990, Skinner suggested that '[t]he debate [over the correct interpretation of the 1988 Act] will continue and the precise meaning of the Act may not become clear until it is tested in law' (Skinner 1990, p 170). With the exception of this case such clarification has in fact not been forthcoming. The 1988 Act did provide a mechanism under s 23 by which parents could complain about various educational matters including the provision that was made for religious education and collective worship. However, this mechanism is essentially a matter for resolving individual complaints and therefore does little if anything to clarify a general understanding of the law. For a survey of the early working of this complaints procedure, see, Harris 1993a and for further comment, see, Harris 1993b.
20 Thompson 2004, p 120. Thompson says that this letter was based upon legal advice that was itself based on John Hull's book on the 1988 Act *The Act Unpacked*.

be an opportunity to study 'other religious traditions such as the Bahá'í faith, Jainism and Zoroastrianism' as well as secularist philosophies (Qualifications and Curriculum Authority 2004, p 12). Finally, also in 1994, the Department for Education issued Circular 1/94, which gave further guidance on the interpretation of the Act. In relation to religious education this said, among other things, that:

> the relative content in the syllabus devoted to Christianity should predominate. The syllabus as a whole must include all the principal religions represented in this country. In this context the precise balance between Christianity and other religions should take account both of the national and the local position. In considering this, account should be taken of the local school population and the wishes of local parents, with a view to minimising the number who might exercise the right of withdrawal from RE lessons.
>
> (Circular 1994, para 35)

In relation to collective worship the circular said that 'whatever the decision on individual acts of worship, the majority of acts of worship over a term must be wholly or mainly of a Christian character' but that '[p]rovided that, taken as a whole, an act of worship which is broadly Christian reflects the traditions of Christian belief, it need not contain only Christian material' (Circular 1994, paras 62 and 63).

The addition of layer upon layer of advice, interpretation and comment in itself hindered clarification of what the religious education and collective worship provisions actually meant with not only the content but the status of the various different pronouncements being in doubt. Thus, for example, Rose, in his study of the centralising tendencies in religious education, queries whether some Ofsted inspectors properly appreciated the legal status of the non-statutory framework (Rose 2006, p 192).[21] In addition to the genuine confusion caused by the existence of these various layers of advice, they may also have given practitioners, whether teachers or advisers, a greater scope to act creatively in their interpretation of the legislation because there were so many sources that might be used to legitimate the individual approach that was taken.

From its inception the religious education and collective worship provisions of the 1988 Act proved difficult to implement. Both Ofsted reports and academic surveys consistently showed that the Act was not being universally or even generally obeyed. Thus, for example, in 2001 Watson's

---

21 The court's ruling in *R v Secretary of State for Education ex parte R and D* does not appear to have added to this confusion since it does not seem to have figured in any of the further debate about the meaning of the legislation.

study of Ofsted reports noted that 'most' Norfolk secondary schools were in breach of their duty to provide a daily act of collective worship for their pupils and half were in breach of their obligation to provide religious education (Watson 2001, p 208).[22] Although there was some improvement over time, post-primary education continued to show significant noncompliance with the 1988 Act. In 2007, the Religious Education Council of England and Wales noted that 'non-compliance persists in about 35% of schools at key stage 4 [and] [o]nly about 20% of schools with sixth forms comply with legal requirements for students 16–19, with little evidence of improvement' (Religious Education Council 2007, pp 4–5).[23]

While the 1988 Act changed – however unclearly – the legal context for religious education and collective worship in schools, it does not seem to have greatly changed the attitudes of teachers towards these things. Thus, for example, Marshall-Taylor writes that:

> [m]any of those who lead it [collective worship] see it as important and worthwhile, but, for some, it is a chore which they would rather do without. Some teachers would go further and, particularly in community schools, see it as counter-productive, even destructive for spiritual development. For some it is an inappropriate activity, given the diversity of belief positions – religious and non-religious – which are represented in any school community.
>
> (Marshall-Taylor 2002, p 201)[24]

Hull has described 'the rise of a mature and independent religious education profession' whose 'secularity is ... the cornerstone of the rationale for the existence of religious education as a required subject in the state schools' (Hull 2003).[25] For Hull, religious education specialist teachers have become one theological profession, 'supported by a number of independent professional organisations', while 'the ministry or priesthood' is a quite separate theological profession; the role of the first profession, again for Hull, is

---

22 In 1995, Bocking had observed that 'RE is still in poor shape' citing both non-observance of the law, resources available to religious education and the qualifications of religious education teachers (Bocking 1995, p 233). On Ofsted findings, see, further, Copley 1997, pp 172–175.

23 Hayward observes that '[c]ontrary to those voices which periodically regret the passing of Christianity's place in religious education, so far as may be judged from agreed syllabuses, their fears are unfounded' (Hayward 2006, pp 156–157). However, whether those syllabuses are delivered to pupils and whether the proportion of the time devoted to Christianity would suit the proponents of the original provisions are different matters.

24 See, similarly, Bocking's comment that '[t]he instinct of some RE professionals is to disown school worship altogether' (Bocking 1995, p 233).

25 On the process of professionalization of religious education, see, also, Copley 1997, pp 126–127.

to study and teach about the second (Hull 2003).[26] This professionalisation of religious education teachers has, perhaps, made the continuing
attachment to the orthodoxy of education that was established before the
1988 Act that prevails in universities and schools easier to maintain.[27] This
in turn has set the terms for the reception of Circular 1/94 in particular
and other interpretations of the religious education and collective worship
provisions in general. Thus, for example, Bocking comments, as regards
Circular 1/94:

> [w]hy would *professional* teachers of RE, or head teachers interested in
> promoting corporate values in their school, want to spend their time
> designing Kafkaesque acts of worship which are broadly Christian yet
> different from real worship, are not distinctive of any denomination but
> include non-Christian elements and which give a special status to Jesus
> Christ yet are designed to be acceptable to non-Christian families?
> (emphasis added)
>
> (Bocking 1995, p 235)[28]

Similarly, Cheetham observes that:

> [i]n order to produce what in their view constituted a satisfactory
> assembly the teachers turned the activity labelled 'collective worship' in
> directions other than traditional theistic worship (despite the clear inten-
> tion of the government in DFE Circular 1/94).
>
> (Cheetham 2000, p 76)

In 1993, Hart had suggested that:

---

26 The Religious Education Council of England and Wales noted that 'RE has more non-
   specialists teaching than any other established subject in the curriculum' (Religious Education Council 2007, p 5). This does not necessarily contradict Hull's argument. While such
   teachers are less likely to benefit from both the general advantages of professionalisation and
   the specific support of professional associations that Hull notes, it is also arguable that,
   because of their relative lack of expertise, they are more likely to be led in what they do by
   those of their colleagues who are specialists and who are professionalised.
27 One end of this orthodoxy being that religious education should not be a compulsory subject
   (White 2004).
28 The Circular has also been criticised by those who support the original 1988 provisions. Thus,
   for example, Thompson writes that 'RE operates in a very confused situation. It is an extra-
   ordinary thing that the very opposite of what was intended by Parliament has in fact not only
   come to pass, but has gained strength from the [1988] legislation ... How many teachers
   today know the real intention of the law?' (Thompson 2004, p 123). As noted above, the idea
   that there was any consistent Parliamentary intention lying behind the provisions is questionable. Whether teachers want to know about the legislative intent or, if it exists and was
   explained to them, would regard it as being more important than what they take to be
   appropriate on the basis of their professional expertise, is also debatable.

> [c]ontroversies in religious education occur when there is a mismatch
> between what is provided and what is expected by the community.
> Community and parental pressure will play a highly significant role in
> implementation of the [1988] legislation.
>
> (Hart 1993, p 16)

In fact the latter part of this comment proved not to be correct. Although
there were parental challenges to the implementation of the 1988 legislation in various parts of the country, none of them had any significant
impact on what schools as a whole did (Hull 1996). However, the first
part of Hart's comment proved accurate in a way that he almost certainly
had not anticipated. The provisions of the 1988 Act did not reflect the
views of the very community that was expected to implement them; moreover
the wider population, unsurprisingly in view of the religious landscape
described in Chapter 1, was at best indifferent to the values that lay behind
the provisions with some sections of it being increasingly hostile to them
(Hull 1996).[29] The result was legislation that now all sides largely agree has
failed.

When the 1988 legislation had first been passed, Harte had written that the
legislation 'provides an opportunity to reassert the Christian heritage of the
nation's schools. Whether this opportunity is taken will show whether . . .
that heritage is still the bedrock of the nation' (Harte 1987–89, p 52). In fact
the 'opportunity' was not taken. The law has failed to 'Christianise' religious
education and collective worship in a way that a minority had wished;
something that was probably almost inevitable in the context of the dominant
secular, liberal approaches described in Chapters 1 and 2 of this book.
Beckford's conclusion is that:

> [t]he result [of the legislation] is a polarisation of extreme opinions over
> the appropriate place and character of religion in state schools . . . As
> in most boundary disputes, however, the majority of the population
> remains indifferent towards, or ignorant of, the issues which seem to
> concern only people with extreme views.
>
> (Beckford 1990, p 34)

---

29 Some studies note the opposition of children themselves to the legislation. Thus, for example,
Gill observes that '[i]n the secondary school, most teachers share with their students an
implicit understanding that the choice of commitment that has been made already, will be
pursued within the faith community, and is a personal matter' and that '[t]he comments made
by pupils beyond the age of about ten years demonstrate little sympathy for the provision of
collective worship in schools' (Gill 2004, pp 193 and 194).

Faith schools[30]

As we saw above, schools that were set up by particular faiths are an important part of the history of educational systems in Great Britain. They are also
an important part of the contemporary educational systems, illustrating
some of the possible accommodations that the liberal State can make for
religious groups.[31]

Independent faith schools

Any religious group can choose to set up an independent school in Great
Britain.[32] Even if that school purports to offer the educational provision that
is necessary for a parent to ensure that their child is receiving full-time education under s 7 of the Education Act 1996, the legal controls over that school
are comparatively limited.[33] Such schools must be registered and are subjected to inspection under the Education Act 2005.[34] However, they are not
required to teach the national curriculum, do not have to comply with the
1988 Act provisions as regards religious education or collective worship, and

---

30 For the purposes of this section I will define 'faith schools' as both those schools that are set
up with a religious ethos by faith communities on an independent basis and those schools
that both have some form of religious ethos and also receive some degree of direct State
funding.

31 They are important in a pragmatic as well as an ideological sense. As we saw in Chapter 1,
they continue to be a significant part of the education systems in Great Britain. In England in
2004 there were 1,175,520 FTEs in State-maintained faith primary schools; 9,090 FTEs were
in non-Christian schools (Statistics of Education 2004, p 48). In the same year there were
511,860 FTEs in State-maintained secondary schools of which 6,430 FTEs were in non-
Christian schools (Statistics of Education 2004, p 48). The State provided some degree of
direct support for 6,311 faith primary schools of which 32 were not Christian and 589 faith
secondary schools of which 8 were not Christian (Statistics of Education 2004, p 47). In
addition to this there are many schools in the independent sector that are faith-based.

32 Religious groups may also choose to educate their children at home in order to see that their
children's education conforms with the religious ethos of the faith group (see, for example,
Christadelphian home schooling at www.christadelphianschooling.co.uk/). On the phenomenon of home schooling generally, see the special issue of the Peabody Journal of Education
edited by McDowell and Day (McDowell and Day 2000).

33 The 1996 Act applies to England and Wales. In Scotland, the relevant provision is s 30(1) of
the Education (Scotland) Act 1980. For a detailed examination of the legal controls in
England and Wales, see, Parker-Jenkins 2005.

34 Part 1 Chapter 1 of the 2005 Act applies to England while Part 1 Chapter 3 applies to Wales.
Schools in Scotland are subject to inspection under s 66 of the Education (Scotland) Act
1980 and have to be registered under s 98A of the same Act. In England and Wales most
schools are inspected by Ofsted. However, some schools are inspected by the Independent
Schools Inspectorate and others by the School Inspection Service. On Ofsted generally, see,
Matthews and Smith 1995 and Cullingford 1999. On Ofsted in relation to spiritual development, see, White 1994. For a radical critique of Ofsted, see, Fielding 2001. On the Scottish
system of school inspection, see, McGlynn and Stalker 1995.

do not have to provide the sex education that, subject to a parental opt-out, is compulsory in State-funded schools in England and Wales under s 403(1) of the Education Act 1996. Nevertheless, there are some controls over the content of education in independent schools. Thus, for example, in England, the Education (Independent School Standards) (England) Regulations 2003/1910 says, at Schedule 1 paragraph 1(2)(a), that pupils must have 'experience in linguistic, mathematical, scientific, technological, human and social, physical and aesthetic and creative education', something that will cause difficulties for some faith schools.

The opening of the Talmud Torah Machzikei Hadass School, a Jewish school in London, illustrates the degree to which the law relating to independent schools works so as to accommodate the wishes of particular faith communities. Following the opening of the school and its initial inspection the school received an adverse report from Her Majesty's Inspectorate of Education, both because of its poor physical facilities and also because of the syllabus that it used for its pupils.[35] This syllabus was said to be too restrictive, not preparing the pupils for participation in the wider world that lay outside the particular Jewish community from which they came. On the basis of the report the Secretary of State sought to deregister the school. In response to this the school launched an action for judicial review. In his judgment in *R v The Secretary of State for Education and Science ex parte Talmud Torah Machzikei Hadass School Trust*, *The Times* 12th April 1985, Woolf J, as he then was, accepted that a syllabus would:

> be suitable if it primarily equips a child for life within the community of which he is a member rather than the way of life in the country as a whole, as long as it does not foreclose the child's option in later years to adopt some other form of life if he wishes to do so.[36]

He also observed that:

> the Secretary of State is entitled to regard a particular form of education as being too narrow but the requirements he lays down must not go beyond that which is necessary in his opinion to make the education suitable and he should be sensitive to the traditions of the minority sect and only interfere with them so far as this is necessary to make the school suitable.

This ruling gives considerable latitude to schools. Nevertheless, the freedom that the schools have in practice should not be exaggerated. Schools that cater

---

35 See, further, Bradney 1987, pp 417–419.
36 A copy of the full transcript of this judgment is available on the LexisNexis database.

mainly for Brethren children have been said by Ofsted to provide a good standard of education, even though Brethren practise a way of life that does not permit interaction with outsiders and, for example, eschews the use of information technology.[37] However, these schools teach in English and their pupils take public examinations such as GCSEs and the BTec.[38] In contrast, those Talmud Torah schools that are for the ultra-orthodox Jewish communities, and which teach only partially in English, devote extensive amounts of the school day to the religious rather than the secular curriculum and usually do not prepare their pupils for public examinations, are regularly criticised for these practices in Ofsted reports.[39] Thus, for example, the 2007 Ofsted report on the Talmud Torah Machzikei Hadass School accepted that 'pupils are well prepared for life in their community' but criticised the school because '[p]upils do not have sufficient knowledge of British institutions and services'. However, since the secular curriculum in these schools does provide basic teaching in literacy and numeracy and since, as the 2007 report on the Talmud Torah Yeter Lev school notes, 'the pupils and their families do not mix socially in the neighbourhood or use any of the traditional local facilities that are available', it is not entirely clear how these schools can be said to fail to meet the standards laid down in *R v The Secretary of State for Education and Science ex parte Talmud Torah Machzikei Hadass School Trust.*[40] Since the Education (Independent School Standards) (England) Regulations 2003/1910 makes no specific mention of the amount of time that is to be devoted to any particular subject, it is questionable whether Ofsted criticisms are justified in law.

Independent faith schools vary considerably in their educational provision. There are even significant differences among schools that take the same faith stance.[41] However, it is clear that some faith schools, because of their religious ethos, provide an education that restricts some of the opportunities that are

---

37 Times Educational Supplement, 12th August 2005.
38 Reports on these schools from the School Inspection Service can be found on the School Inspection Service website at www.schoolinspectionservice.co.uk/.
39 These reports are available on the Ofsted website at www.Ofsted.gov.uk/reports/.
40 The *Annual Report of Her Majesty's Chief Inspector of Schools: Standards and Quality in Education 2001/02* made a general criticism of a 'minority' of faith schools for allocating insufficient time to the secular curriculum (Ofsted 2003, para 445). For those who believe in, for example, a 'God centred education, with Christian values', and who have set up their school on this basis, this division between secular and religious education is, at best, problematic (Walford 1995, p 44).
41 Thus, for example, Getters Talmud Torah School, inspected in 2008, which provides education for children from orthodox Jewish families, 'does not teach information and communication technology, as to do so would not be in accord with its religious ethos'. However, the Torah Vodnas School, also inspected in 2008, which provides education for children from ultra-orthodox Jewish families, is described as providing 'a trolley' of laptops for its pupils.

available to their pupils.[42] Thus, for example, those schools that do not provide training in information technology make it more difficult for their pupils
to access a source of information that is increasingly central to the way in
which much of modern society functions.[43] In doing this the schools neither
respect nor seek to facilitate the development of their pupils' autonomy. For
some commentators this is a compelling argument for not permitting the
operation of some or all faith schools (see, for example, Brighouse 1998 and
Marples 2005).[44]

Faith schools and autonomy

Upon the face of it the liberal argument for not allowing schools to educate
children in such a way as to fail to develop their autonomy seems fairly clear.
As we saw in Chapter 2 autonomy and independence of judgement is basic to
the liberal conception of how individuals should live in society. Individuals
may choose to give up this independence in pursuit of their conception of the
good life, but they may not have it taken away from them. Some faith schools
and some parents who send their children to some faith schools are denying
their children's autonomy. Thus, for example, Sebba and Shiffer, writing
of the ultra-orthodox Jewish community in Israel, observe that '[t]he community does not adhere to any form of liberal principles . . . the concept of
individual rights is alien [to this form of Judaism], as is the concept of individual autonomy' (Sebba and Shiffer 1998, pp 183–184).[45] It therefore seems
to follow that ultra-orthodox Jewish schools are treating children in a manner
that the liberal State cannot permit. However, against this are a number of
different pragmatic and philosophical arguments.

First there is the fact that the British State has historically ceded to parents
a large degree of control over their children's lives. In this context it is not just
some faith schools that fail to accept and nurture children's autonomy; this is
also true for the way in which some and perhaps large numbers of parents
bring up their children.[46] In doing so, they break no law. The State lays down

---

42 In embedding them more firmly within their faith community this restriction is also an
     advantage. 'Faith schools can be defended in terms of the contribution they make to the sense
     of belonging and security that human beings rightly value. But those qualities are achieved at
     a price, the loss of some individual autonomy' (Burtonwood 2003, p 423).
43 See, for example, Johnston and Webber 2003.
44 Much of the writing in this area is directed to the more limited question of whether or not the
     State should fund schools that do not develop their pupils' autonomy.
45 For an examination of an ultra-orthodox Jewish community in Great Britain, see, Valins
     2003.
46 Indeed Silk et al. argue that parenting styles are more complex than there being a simple
     continuum between psychological control and autonomy granting (Silk et al. 2003). This puts
     in doubt the possibility of making any simple judgement about whether a parent or a school
     follows liberal precepts in the way that they deal with their children.

certain minimum standards with regard to the physical care of children (Lowe and Douglas 2007, p 380). It says relatively little about other matters. This, in part, reflects what Eekelaar calls 'the respect for the privileged sphere of parent-child relationship' (Eekelaar 2006, p 95).[47] This 'privileged sphere' is itself the product of both pragmatic and philosophical considerations. The State does not possess the resources to monitor closely the parenting of large numbers of children. Equally, such intrusive action would put in question the ability of individuals and communities to pursue their own notions of the good life.[48] The existence of faith schools that parents can educate their children in is, in part, a product of this 'privileged sphere of parent-child relationship'.

A second reason for defending the position of faith schools that do not seek to develop their pupils' autonomy lies in the complexities of the relationship between the education that a school provides and the nature of a child's autonomy. While the faith schools discussed above do not develop or even necessarily believe in their pupils' autonomy, the children are nonetheless autonomous.[49] Some will demonstrate that autonomy by leaving the community from which they come. What is at issue here is the degree to which the schools contribute to the development or expression of that autonomy. While it is possible to argue that the State can permit parental indifference to the autonomy of children in the privacy of family life, but must insist on that autonomy being acknowledged in the public life of schools, this can only be done at the potential cost of a high degree of dissonance between what the child experiences at home and at school.[50] More than this, were such a policy to be pursued successfully, since parents can withdraw their children from schools and educate them at home, close monitoring of the approach of faith schools to autonomy would also have to involve the close monitoring of those parents who educate their children at

47 In a similar fashion, Douglas describes 'the liberal view that the family and its members who comprise it should be free from arbitrary State interference' (Douglas 2001, p 77). Eekelaar's 'privileged sphere' reflects the public/private divide in liberalism whereby, among other things, 'families are (in theory) permitted to separate themselves into more-or-less homogeneous groups based on common interests and commitments' (Levinson 1997, p 337).

48 'Liberals who oppose faith schools run the risk of imposing a neocolonial educational regime that will threaten the sense of security of minority religious communities, push them onto the defensive, and consequently exacerbate the breakdown of social cohesion' (Wright 2003, p 152).

49 Autonomy is an existentialist truth about human nature no matter what the circumstances of our individual existence. 'Should I die in misery and squalor, heeded by no-one, of no material consequence to the world, I should be no less human . . . My radical autonomy on the other hand (my being an end in myself) is necessary (necessary in the strict sense) to my conception of myself as a human' (Detmold 1989, p 116).

50 On the complexities of the relationship between home and school, see, Vincent and Tomlinson 1997.

home.[51] However, as well as these pragmatic arguments for accepting the existence of faith schools that do not set out to develop their pupils' autonomy, there are also conceptual arguments.

Ultra-orthodox Jewish schools will serve as an illustration for a more general argument. As seen above, ultra-orthodox Jewish schools do not set out to develop their pupils' autonomy.[52] However, this is not to say that the education they provide does not in fact, to some degree, facilitate the development of that autonomy. As many writers have observed, ultra-orthodox Jewish communities are quintessential learning communities, the 'scholar's society' (Longman 2002, p 241).[53] Thus, Valins, citing Heilman, writes that:

> [a]mong haredim [ultra-orthodox Jews], education was everything. It was the essence of what they believed was demanded of them as Jews. To this end, they created a network of schools from youth to age and, wherever possible, evaded the harmful influence of secular education.
>
> (Valins 2000, p 580)[54]

How that attitude to learning manifests itself varies from ultra-orthodox community to community. Stadler, for example, observes that:

> [i]n Lithuania [one of the early sources of ultra-orthodox Judaism] . . . only a handful of prodigies, who were members of a select elite, dedicated their lives to studious activities. In present day Israel, all male Haredis [ultra-orthodox Jews] are obliged to devote most of their lives to the yeshiva . . .
>
> (Stadler 2002, p 459)[55]

---

51 In the context of the US, Carper argues that home schooling has been closely associated with faith groups (Carper 2000). In Great Britain a number of faith schools have been set up specifically for Brethren children who had previously been educated at home (see, for example, the 2007 inspection report for the Sceptre School at www.schoolinspectionservice.co.uk/).

52 The view that Jewish education should emphasise the differentness of Jews is not limited to the ultra-orthodox community (see, for example, Scholefield 2004 and Resnick 1996). The attitude towards the autonomy of pupils is, however, in the context of Jewish education, specific to such schools.

53 Education is central to Judaism in general. See, for example, Cohen's comment that '[t]he pursuit of knowledge has always formed a cardinal ideal in Jewish life (Cohen 1950, p 51) or Kaplan's suggestion that 'Judaism is a composite of three elements: education, worship, and philanthropy' (Kaplan 1991, p 21). However, the significance of education in ultra-orthodox Judaism takes on a particular force.

54 Valins also notes the importance of education to the ultra-orthodox community in preserving its cohesion. '[T]he institutionalisation of the religion . . . depends on socialising individuals in the orthodox system of life . . . arguably of prime importance is the education of children in the "ways of righteousness" ' (Valins 2000, p 580).

55 See, also, Berman 2000, p 908.

Nevertheless, to whatever degree it is followed, the education in ultra-orthodox Talmud Torah schools, as can be seen from the Ofsted reports referred to above, is invariably a predominantly text-based education in the interpretation of the sacred works of Judaism. It is this focus that, whatever the intentions of the schools concerned, can promote the autonomy of pupils. Goody argues that:

> the normative implications of the text often provide a yardstick for the difference between reality and potentiality, between what is and what should be, between existence and Utopia.
>
> (Goody 1986, p 20)

Further, he argues that:

> [t]he potentialities for change are especially apparent with longer texts because writing is obviously easier to review than speech, so that implicit contradictions are made explicit and hence readily resolved leading to cumulative advances in knowledge and procedures, though such advances give rise in turn to puzzles of different kinds. All this is part of the reflexive potentialities of writing which affects notions of consciousness on both levels, making the implicit explicit and rendering the result more available to reflexive inspection, to external argument and to further elaboration.
>
> (Goody 1986, p 174)

Part of the importance of education for ultra-orthodox Jewish communities lies in it preserving the cohesion of the communities. '[T]he institutionalisation of the religion ... depends on socialising individuals in the orthodox system of life ... arguably of prime importance is the education of children in the "ways of righteousness" ' (Valins 2000, p 580). However, for the pupils the education can also serve another purpose. The education provides a very detailed Talmudic knowledge combined with a limited and sometimes inaccurate secular knowledge (Valins 2000, p 581). Given Goody's arguments above, it would seem that this close study of Jewish texts will provide a vehicle for acquiring the powers of introspection, reflection and argument that are central to facilitating individual autonomy.[56]

---

56 The argument in relation to education for girls in ultra-orthodox Judaism is less strong, given the more limited nature of study. However, even here, El-Or argues that in ultra-orthodox education for girls, '[t]he linkage between literacy and women in haredi society is a paradoxical one; women are educated to maintain their ignorance ... The purpose of educating haredi women is to give them bodies of knowledge that will help them discern a single voice in the cacophony of modern society ... [H]owever, the very act of gathering for study, even under these conditions, enables them to listen to a whole range of voices – even if they themselves continue to hum the desired tune' (El-Or 1994, p 135). Longman similarly reports a partially positive impact of ultra-orthodox Jewish religious education (Longman 2002, p 244).

Showing that a school does not seek to develop the autonomy of a child does not provide a sufficient case for saying that the liberal State should not permit the education that the school provides counting as satisfying the general duty to provide a child with an education.[57] Much more detailed work needs to be done to show that what the school provides is such as not to allow the child's development of its autonomy at even a minimal level. The arguments above would suggest that, notwithstanding consistent criticism in Ofsted reports, it would be difficult to do this in the case of ultra-orthodox Jewish schools. This is not to say that this cannot be done in other cases. Faith schools cannot be defended within the context of a liberal State, merely on the grounds that they are faith schools. The physical facilities that they have, the qualifications of their teachers and even their educational philosophy may mean that they are unacceptable to the liberal State.[58] However in a liberal State, given the latitude given to the parenting of children and given the need to allow the pursuit of competing notions of the good, accepting that a particular faith school is not providing an appropriate form of education is something that should not be done lightly.

Faith schools and social cohesion

A second argument against faith schools that has come to the fore in recent years is the charge that faith schools do not promote social cohesion and, indeed, that their very existence may militate against such cohesion.[59] This is illustrated by the Cantle Report's comment that '[i]n terms of community cohesion … a significant problem is posed by existing and future mono-cultural schools' (Cantle 2001, p 33).[60]

A starting point for the role of faith schools in relation to social cohesion in society must be a consideration of what is meant by social cohesion in the context of the observations about the fractured nature of society in contemporary Great Britain in Chapter 1. On one level faith schools and the faith communities they reflect are indeed examples of division – one instance among many of the diversity of ways of living that are found in a

---

57 What a parent provides by way of supplementary or additional education will always be a quite separate issue.
58 See, for example, Küçükcan's comments on the Ikra School (Küçükcan 1998, p 40).
59 Short suggests that while the debate about faith schools was one about notions of autonomy and parental choice, it is now about divisiveness (Short 2002, p 559).
60 The Cantle Committee was set up, following riots in a number of northern cities, by the Home Secretary 'to consider and examine how national policies might be used to promote better community cohesion, based upon shared values and a celebration of diversity' (Cantle 2001, Foreword). The Ousley Report, that followed riots in Bradford, made a similar suggestion (Ousley 2001, p 6).

multicultural, multiethnic society that hovers on the edge of cosmopolitanism. As such the schools are not a problem; rather they are an example of the cultural wealth of present-day British society. Insofar as arguments about social cohesion are a proxy for a call for a return to cultural homogeneity (a homogeneity that may in fact have no place in history) they represent a rejection of liberalism. A social cohesion that insists on common British values is difficult to equate with liberal theory that encourages each person and each community to pursue their own notion of the good. 'Social cohesion' seen in this way is not a good in a liberal society. However, the concept of social cohesion can take on a much more limited form, indicating no more than the minimal conditions that are needed to allow those who pursue different notions of the good to coexist and interact to the degree that they wish for such interaction. Faith schools can still be seen as being a threat to social cohesion, even when the concept is being used in this more limited sense.

Short notes a range of different propositions that can be used in arguing that faith schools decrease social cohesion (Short 2002, pp 560–565). All are to some degree empirical propositions about either what faith schools actually do in their teaching or what will result in pupil attitudes because of what schools do. As we have noted above, faith schools, even schools from the same faith, have variant forms. Equally, the research into practices in faith schools is limited.[61] Assessing the accuracy of the empirical propositions described by Short is thus a perilous matter. For example, one argument about faith schools and social cohesion is that faith schools focus on their faith and therefore do not give their pupils the diversity of knowledge about other faiths that they need to live tolerantly with those other faiths (Short 2002, pp 562–563). One part of this proposition is the claim, largely unsubstantiated, that either knowledge or contact is a *sine qua non* for living with other faiths. However, more fundamental to the proposition is the claim that faith schools do not teach their pupils about other faiths. This claim may be true for some schools, but is certainly false for others (Short 2003, pp 133–139). This fact leads to the conclusion that 'the divisive nature of faith schools in some areas [or of some kinds, if indeed they are divisive,] is not an argument against faith schools *in general*' (Pring 2005, p 54). As in the case of arguments about pupil autonomy, careful arguments about particular schools have to be made to justify the suggestion that faith schools should not be accepted because of the threat that they pose to social cohesion. To date, these careful arguments have not been made and, indeed, in most if not all

---

61 'The assumption appears to be that research into faith-based schooling is a somewhat exotic minority activity primarily of interest to those in the various faith communities but hardly (post-Enlightenment) a major concern for mainstream educational research and discourse' (Grace 2003, p 150).

cases it would seem that the research does not exist to substantiate such claims.[62]

State funding for faith schools

To accept the legitimacy of faith schools is one thing; to go beyond that and offer direct State support for such schools, as happens in Great Britain, is another. To do this appears to involve the State in supporting and fostering particular views of the good life and thus fail in its duty of neutrality; liberal States may, perhaps should, tolerate faith schools, but should they do any more than that? The issue of State support for faith schools thus merits particular attention.

As we saw at the beginning of this chapter the offer of State funding for faith schools can be seen in part as a pragmatic rather than a principled response on the part of the State. It was the churches that took the initiative in setting up schools for the mass of the population. Later, as the churches grew less able to bear the financial burden of such an undertaking, the State took over much of the financial responsibility because it needed the network of schools that had been created to supplement State schools and thus provide an effective system of national education. Having entered into financial arrangements with Christian and Jewish schools, the State was then in a poor position to reject the claims of other religious groups who wanted support for their schools.[63] We therefore find, towards the end of the twentieth century, an eventual extension of financial support to a range of schools from other faiths, including both Muslim schools and Sikh schools as well as schools from more diverse forms of Christianity.[64] However, the provision of State aid for faith schools cannot be seen simply as a pragmatic matter. In part,

---

62 Thus, for example, Burtonwood argues against Short's position, viewing the fact that some Muslim schools wish to employ only teachers who 'model the Islamic moral code in all aspects of their lives' as a threat to social cohesion (Burtonwood 2003, pp. 419–420). I would argue that such a suggestion lacks credible empirical evidence of what impact such employment practices have on social cohesion. (There are quite separate rights-based arguments about the legitimacy of such employment practices.) The article that Burtonwood cites in support of his position specifically addresses the question of how Muslim schools do educate their pupils about the wider society around them (Hewer 2001, pp 524–525).

63 For a brief history of the State's financial support for faith schools, see, Jackson 2004, pp 39–43.

64 This alteration in practice is important in principle, changing what had largely been support for Christian schools (and even then Christian schools from a very restricted range of Christianity) to multi-faith support for faith schools. However, the importance of this change in principle should not distract attention from its practical consequences. In numerical terms, very few other schools have received financial support and, taken together, they constitute only a very small fraction of those schools receiving State support, most of whom continue to be either Church of England or Roman Catholic schools (Statistics of Education 2004, p 48).

providing State funding for faith schools has been a signal of State approval of such schools.[65] It is the legitimacy of this signal which is in question.

The argument for the liberal State, funding schooling in general, can be made in two ways. First, one can argue that the right to education is basic to the structure of liberal society alongside other rights such as freedom of speech or liberty. Secondly, one can argue that education is a public good benefiting both the individual who receives it and the wider society (De Jong and Snik 2002, p 573). Using either one of these arguments or a combination of both it seems clear that a liberal State must ensure that its citizens have access to an adequate educational system. If the liberal State provides schooling, it cannot be perfectionist in character, seeking to put forward a particular view of the good life. However, even if the State succeeds in providing for schooling, 'the state should not decide in which primary culture the child should be initiated' (De Jong and Snik 2002, p 583).[66] Parents thus have a right to send their children to faith schools that meet the minimal criteria set out in the sections above. However, if State support is not available for such schools, faith communities, particularly smaller and more fragile faith communities, may not be able to fund such schools or may only be able to fund them to a level that makes them objectively inferior in terms of facilities to State-supported schools.[67] Therefore, to the degree that the liberal State has a duty to not just tolerate its citizens' view of the good life, but also to facilitate them in achieving this end, State support for faith schools should be available.

A combination of history and principle suggests that there is an inevitability of State funding for faith schools in Great Britain.

> The realities of British educational history, together with the dilemmas posed by some of the reasons for supporting or rejecting faith based education, suggest that a pragmatic policy of compromise is most appropriate.
>
> (Jackson 2003, p 98)

What is important in the twenty-first century is that that funding should reflect the religious landscape of Great Britain as it is, not as it once was in the nineteenth century.

---

65 The Labour Government's White Paper, 'Schools – Achieving Success', with its explicit support for the place of faith schools in the education systems and their call for an extension of that role, emphasises this point (Schools – Achieving Success 2001, para 5.30).

66 Whether, in practice, any school can ever succeed in not favouring one view of the good life to any extent (or not disfavouring some views of the good life) is open to question.

67 As we have seen historically in the British case financial problems on the part of faith communities have resulted in State support. This being so, it is difficult to resist the argument that the financial problems of newer faith communities should not also result in State support.

Chapter 7

Law and religion: a new concordat?

Introduction

In this final chapter I want to try to bring together some of the themes that have developed in the previous chapters of this book.

Burtonwood, citing Walzer, writes that 'liberals and members of trad-itional religious communities are basically unhappy with each other – and yet they must find a way to live together' (Burtonwood 2003, p 423). This comment accurately summarises the situation in contemporary Great Britain. At root, those who adhere to institutionalised religion, whatever form it takes, base their lives on completely separate premises to those premises that form the foundation of the lives of the great mass of the population. Thus, for example, Joly writes that 'the greatest concern for the Muslims settled in Great Britain is . . . the *de facto* agnosticism and secularism which prevail' (Joly 1995, p 12). What divides the two groups is not so much the possibility of something existing beyond the normally understood natural world. We have seen that individual religiosity is part of the lives of many people in Great Britain who do not adhere to institutionalised religions. Instead, the divide is about the significance of anything beyond the natural world for people's quotidian lives and the importance and value of the structures of authority in institutionalised religions that purport to explain that which lies beyond the natural world. What counts most for those who belong to faith communities is, for the majority of the population, either false or, on a day-to-day basis, irrelevant.[1] This is true for both the beliefs of the faith com-munities and the way those beliefs are arrived at and managed. The society of strangers and provisional, revocable beliefs that we saw in Chapter 1 has little sympathy with the strong communities and foundational certainties that

---

1 These divisions are different. Those who deny the validity of the very premises of religion usually accept that, at some level, the matter is significant. For the majority, however, it is simply that the issues that lie at the heart of institutionalised religion are simply of no interest on a quotidian basis.

characterise institutionalised religion. Yet, the liberal, secular society must still grapple with faith communities for two reasons. First, as a matter of fact, they are still there. They form only part of that which now constitutes British society and they may well be a lot less significant than they think they are, but nevertheless they are there. Secondly, liberalism makes promises about how it allows people to live out their own pursuit of what they see as being the good life and faith communities are one place in which those promises are tested. The question for this book has been how well are those promises met in the State legal systems that are found in Great Britain.

The evidence in this book thus far is that there are both relatively successful examples of attempts by the State to accommodate believers and also examples of complete failure.

Respect for religion in law

Unsurprisingly, the historical expression of the relationship between State and religion – establishment – has not proved to be an appropriate mechanism for the twenty-first century State. Establishment is gradually losing its hold in Great Britain. During the short period of writing this book there has been a further slight weakening of establishment in England with the abolition of the law of blasphemy and the decision that the Prime Minister should no longer have any choice in the appointment of bishops of the Church of England. Establishment in Scotland was already weaker than in England, and devolution, which has brought with it greater opportunities for Scotland to express itself through separate political structures, may, perhaps paradoxically, further weaken establishment. Prior to devolution the Church of Scotland alongside things such as the separate Scottish legal system was one way in which a separate Scottish identity could find expression. Now, the Scottish government and the Scottish parliament with their legislative powers offer a more effective mechanism for expressing that identity. In any event, the very notion of establishment fails to reflect the present nature of British society. This is so, partially, because the respect for authority structures that it entails is widely rejected within society. How can a bishop of the Church of England speak out on behalf of those who reject religions and regard their own religiosity, if they have any, as a minor matter? More importantly, why should the fact that they are a bishop, make it more likely that they be heard? As we have seen, in fact, arguments in the public arena are now usually couched in rational terms and religious arguments have little persuasive force for the majority of citizens. Moreover, while some faiths, other than those that are established, still argue for establishment because they are aware of the political weakness of religions, the picture is patchy with some faiths themselves rejecting the notion of establishment (see, for example, Rosser-Owen 1997 and Kulananda 1997).

If the failure of establishment is not surprising, the failure of the Racial and Religious Hatred Act 2006 to address in an appropriate fashion the relationship between religion and law may seem more surprising, given the fact that it is recent legislation introduced by Government as a manifesto commitment. Charles Clarke, the then Home Secretary, said in the second reading debate in the House of Commons that the legislation was:

> about the nasty and extreme behaviour that drives people to hate others and sometimes . . . to turn that hatred against people and property. It is about behaviour that destroys individuals' lives and sets one community against another.
>
> (Hansard, House of Commons, vol 435 col 668, 21st June 2005)

The slow passage of the legislation – it being the third attempt to introduce such an offence – and the amendments that the Government were forced to accept showed, however, that the Government had completely underestimated the importance placed on issues of freedom of speech in a liberal society. More particularly, while the first drafts of the legislation seemed to suggest that religion was to have a special place for protection alongside race, the legislation that was finally implemented, with its freedom of speech provision, appeared to reject the notion that religion was to be treated with especial respect, simply because it was religion. Religion received no special rights in relation to the way that it was to be dealt with in public discourse.[2] As we saw in Chapter 4, the ambit of any new offence in the resultant legislation is now entirely unclear. The symbolic impact of the legislation is lost in the confusion of what it might mean. However, the Act is important in one respect. It does represent an attempt to come to terms with the complexities of the position of faith groups and their members in contemporary secular British society. The fact that that attempt is so unsatisfactory underscores how complex that position is.

Both the concept of establishment and the original provisions of what eventually became the Racial and Religious Hatred Act 2006, carry with them implications that there should be a particular respect for religion – that religion has a value that is not to be seen in other things. Establishment privileges a particular religion, seeing an especial good in that religion. Even if the established religion chooses to speak out on behalf of religions as a whole, that notion of privileging religion is still retained.[3] Similarly, the idea of incitement to religious hatred sees religious hatred as having some special

---

2 The Government did, however, use existence of the 2006 Act as part of its justification for introducing an amendment to the Criminal Justice and Immigration Bill, which abolished the common law offence of blasphemy (Maria Eagle, Hansard, House of Commons, vol 475 col 639, 6th May 2008).

3 Thus, for example, the only sectional representation that there is in the Houses of Parliament is on behalf of one religion.

status separate from hatred per se.[4] People more deserve to be protected from religious hatred than they do from most other forms of hatred; religion is different.[5] Contemporary Great Britain, however, does not, either on a communal basis or on an individual basis, in fact, have that respect for religion. Insofar as Great Britain is a secular society, it has rejected religion, either on the ground that religious beliefs are false or on the grounds that religiosity is a personal matter and not something properly dealt with on a communal or institutional basis. Insofar as Great Britain is a liberal society it does not believe in making the decisions about the merits of different forms of the good life, which would be inherent in a decision to accord respect to either religions in general or some religions in particular. Both secular society and liberal society permit and even encourage religious choices to be made by individuals, but it is the making of the choice that is respected, not the choice itself. Both establishment and the 2006 Act fail because they attempt to give religion a status that it simply does not have and cannot have in the present-day conditions of British society.

In a similar fashion to the 2006 Act the religious education and collective worship provisions of the Education Reform Act 1988 involved according a particular respect to religion, in this instance, just the Christian religion, and, because of that, they failed in their implementation. Here, the respect accorded to religion is even plainer than that found in either the case of establishment or the 2006 Act. The intentions of the Act were not simply educational. The historical dominance of Christianity in England and Wales was to be acknowledged in religious education, but there was also a require-ment that the Christian God be worshipped. It is difficult to see how greater respect could be accorded to a religion than legally to require worship of its God.[6] However, in practice, we have seen that in the main, the provisions of the 1988 Act have failed to be fully implemented. The respect that the statute accords to Christianity is not found in the population at large. It is not just the teaching profession that regards the provisions with suspicion. There has been no evidence of widespread enthusiasm for them among parents or indeed pupils either.

The examples above suggest that, in contemporary Great Britain, when the law attempts to value religion on its own terms, the law fails. Laws that, in some way or another, accept the truth claims of religions have proved to

---

4 A status that it shares with racial hatred and hatred on grounds of sexual orientation. For an argument against the attribution of such a special status, see, Jacoby 2002.

5 The schizophrenia of the 2006 Act of course means that this special respect accorded to religion is then denied by the freedom of speech provisions that are also contained in the legislation.

6 There are, of course, various opt-out provisions in the legislation, allowing individuals or groups to withdraw from both worship and education. Nevertheless, the rule introduced by the legislation is education in, and worship of, Christianity. Withdrawal is the exceptional case.

be unacceptable to the population at large. Because of this they do not provide a good model for finding a way to accommodate the needs of religious
believers.

Respecting choice and the *Begum* case

Both the law that relates to families and the law of education showed
much more successful accommodations made by State law to the particular
needs of faith communities. Two things distinguish the accommodations in
these areas of law from the legal incidents of establishment, the provisions of the Education Reform Act 1988 and the offence of inciting
religious hatred. The first is the fact that those accommodations that were
successful made no judgement about the truth of the religions that were
accommodated. The second is the voluntary character of the accommodation. Establishment of the Church of Scotland and the Church of England
is to a large extent imposed on society.[7] Insofar as any new offence is
committed by the Racial and Religious Hatred Act 2006, it carries with it
the full weight of the criminal law; obedience to it is mandatory. The
Education Reform Act 1988 was seen by its supporters as reforming legislation that would force a change in the educational orthodoxy of the day.
However, the accommodations in the areas of the law relating to families
and the law of education do not have this obligatory character. People
may, for example, choose to marry in a range of religious venues, but they
do not have to. Parents may send their children to faith schools or not, as
they so wish. The rights that people have are limited and in Chapters
5 and 6 I argued that they are more limited than they should be. Nevertheless, notwithstanding their limitations, these accommodations are an example of a way of allowing members of faith communities to live both within
their faith and while still respecting the wider legal system. Permitting
choice offers a way forward for the State legal systems' interactions with
religions.

The case of Shabina Begum (*R (on the application of Begum) v
Headteacher and Governors of Denbigh High School* [2006] UKHL 15) seems
to be an unpropitious way to discuss the way in which the British State legal
systems can accommodate religious diversity by allowing choice wherever
possible. In this case Begum failed in her attempt to make Denbigh High

---

7 As we saw in Chapter 3, whether a church is established or not is, in the final analysis, a
statement about its place in the political structure of the State. Legal incidents, like for
example the place of bishops in the House of Lords, stem from establishment but do not, even
when considered as a whole, make for establishment. If the Church of England is wholly
ignored in practice and regarded by everyone outside the Church as being an irrelevance,
it ceases to be established, whatever legal incidents remain. Nonetheless, there remains an
element of imposition in those legal incidents.

School allow her to wear the jilbab as part of her school uniform. Her right to make this particular choice was denied; yet, notwithstanding the fact that Begum lost her case, an acknowledgement of the importance of choice lies at the centre of the House of Lords ruling in this case.

Denbigh High School is a school with a very high percentage of Muslim pupils. The school had a school uniform whose purpose was, inter alia, to create 'communal identity' (para 6). That uniform was arrived at after a period of consultation. Those who were consulted included the Imams of three local mosques (para 7). The uniform had a number of variations, including the shalwar kameeze. Those consulted accepted that the shalwar kameeze conformed with Muslim notions of modesty in dress. Shabina Begum lived outside the school's catchment area (para 9). She nevertheless decided to apply to attend the school, knowing of its uniform requirements. Having become a pupil of the school she at first wore the shalwar kameeze, but later decided that it did not conform with Muslim standards of modesty and instead wanted to wear the jilbab.[8] The jilbab did not conform with the school's requirements as to the wearing of a uniform. When Begum notified the school of her decision they both attempted to negotiate with her and carried out further consultations with Islamic authorities in order to make sure that, in the opinion of those authorities, the shalwar kameeze conformed with Muslim standards of modesty (para 13). Having received an affirmative answer the school insisted on Begum wearing the shalwar kameeze. Instead, she elected to not attend school. She sought judicial review in an attempt to make the school change its policy on uniforms, citing her European Convention right to freedom of religion.

The importance of permitting choice forms an important element of the House of Lords ruling in the *Begum* case. First, the school had given an element of choice in the standards for its uniform by allowing the wearing of the shalwar kameeze. The school had consulted Muslims about the appropriateness of its uniform and did so again when faced with Begum's demand to wear the jilbab. Begum had chosen to go to a school that did not allow her to wear the jilbab. There were other schools that she could attend that would have allowed her to wear the jilbab and she had been told about them.[9] A school that had a policy of making its pupils wear a uniform because it wanted to promote a sense of community could not allow individuals to not conform with that policy without doing damage to the rationale for the

8 Tarlo argues, on the basis of her observations, that Begum's brother, who was her legal guardian, was influenced by a Muslim group, Hizb ut-Tahir, and that the case was 'a convenient avenue for [Hizb ut-Tahir] . . . to push its sartorial agenda indirectly' (Tarlo 2005, p 14). Even if this is so, the House of Lords in fact dealt with the case on the basis that Begum's objections were personal and genuine (para 21).

9 Lord Bingham makes explicit reference to this fact in his judgment, as does Lord Hoffmann (paras 25 and 50).

policy. The school's response to Begum's position was, in the words of Lord Scott, 'a thoughtful and proportionate response to reconciling the complexities of the situation' (para 98). Most Muslims at Denbigh High School could choose a uniform that they would find acceptable and Begum could choose to wear the jilbab, albeit at another school.[10]

The *Begum* case illustrates many of the appropriate ways of dealing with issues of religion. First, the school took religion seriously. Secondly, the school consulted widely in order to see what the religious needs of its pupils actually were. Thirdly, the matter was dealt with on an individual basis as well as on a communal scale. Finally, there was an attempt to arrive at an individual accommodation.[11] The questions of the merits of Begum's religious belief, or the beliefs of other pupils at the school, were never raised. What was at issue was simply the question of whether the school could accommodate what she wanted to do – because of her beliefs – into the normal practices of the school, practices that were themselves a result of detailed consideration of what it was appropriate for the school to do. The *Begum* case is, in many ways, similar to more longstanding accommodations to religion that are to be found in a variety of areas of law. It shows that a liberal, secular society can go some way to recognising the particular needs of religious believers.

The Employment Equality (Religion and Belief) Regulations 2003

Like the Racial and Religious Hatred Act 2006 the Employment Equality (Religion and Belief) Regulations 2003 (SI 2003:1660) are a contemporary attempt to recognise and deal with the problems of religious adherents in

---

10 There are certain parallels between this case and cases in countries such as France and Turkey where there is a State ban on wearing religious dress in educational institutions. However, the fact that decisions about religious dress are a matter for individual schools in Great Britain and the further fact that different schools make different decisions mean that these parallels are limited. For the House of Lords the fact that the decision was solely about what one school had done was an important matter. At the beginning of his judgment, Lord Bingham observed that '[t]he House is not, and could not be, invited to rule whether Islamic dress, or any feature of Islamic dress, should or should not be permitted in the schools of this country. That would be a most inappropriate question for the House in its judicial capacity' (para 2). For an examination of the different approaches in different jurisdictions, see, Langlaude 2006. For an argument that the reasons for the decision in the *Begum* case are not dissimilar to the reasons that the French State has for its total ban on religious dress in schools, see, Gies 2006.

11 Although the school decided that allowing the wearing of the jilbab was too radical a departure from its uniform to be acceptable, it had previously accepted a request to allow the wearing of headscarves, specifying both the material to be used and their colour (para 7).

modern-day society.[12] Unlike the 2006 Act, whose antecedents lie almost completely in domestic policy concerns, the background for the 2003 Regulations is broader and lies partly in European Union policy on equality and nondiscrimination (Vickers 2008, pp 1–2).[13] The Regulations cover both the decision to employ someone and decisions made about someone during the course of employment (Vickers 2008, p 153). The scheme that the Regulations create is complex. However, the core provision of the Regulations is that, under Regulation 6, it is unlawful for an employer to discriminate against a person in employment on grounds of religion or belief. Under Regulation 3(1), discrimination on grounds of religion or belief is defined as being where:

(1) For the purposes of these Regulations, a person ('A') discriminates against another person ('B') if –
(a) on the grounds of the religion or belief of B or of any other person except A (whether or not it is also A's religion or belief) A treats B less favourably than he treats or would treat other persons; or
(b) A applies to B a provision, criterion or practice which he applies or would apply equally to persons not of the same religion or belief as B, but –
(i) which puts or would put persons of the same religion or belief as B at a particular disadvantage when compared with other persons,
(ii) which puts B at that disadvantage. . . .[14]

However, as with other legislation with respect to nondiscrimination, discrimination on grounds of religion or belief is not made unlawful per se. Regulation 7(2) provides an exception for religious discrimination where religion or belief is a genuine occupational qualification. Equally, unlawful discrimination under Regulation 3(1)(b) is only found where, under Regulation 3(b)(iii), an employer 'cannot show [the discrimination] to be a proportionate means of achieving a legitimate aim'. While these provisions are in keeping with previous discrimination legislation, Regulation 7(3) is rather different. Regulation 7(3) applies to those employers who have a 'religious ethos'. In such cases that ethos has to be taken into account when deciding whether or not a religious belief is a genuine occupational

---

12 The original 2003 Regulations were amended by the Equality Act 2006. These regulations are not the first attempt to legislate with respect to religion in the field of employment in Great Britain. However, previous attempts were either limited to particular areas of employment or the impact on religion was a secondary consequence of broader legislation in the area of employment (see, further, Bradney 1993, ch 8).
13 For an analysis of European Union in this area see Bell 2002.
14 There is also a range of other specific or general exceptions to the legislation. See Regulation 7 and Regulations 24 to 26.

qualification. This Regulation follows on from general European Union policy about giving specific exemptions to religious organisations (Bell 2002, pp 117–118). Like Regulation 7(2), Regulation 7(3) not only requires there to be a genuine occupational qualification for the exception to take hold, but also requires it to be 'proportionate' to apply that requirement. However, the existence of Regulation 7(3) alongside Regulation 7(2) suggests a 'less rigorous approach' in deciding upon whether or not there really is a genuine requirement for an occupational qualification (Vickers 2008, p 136).

There is, as yet, relatively little case law in relation to the 2003 Regulations. Assessing their impact is therefore difficult.[15] However, the two key areas for analysis seem likely to be the approach that courts and tribunals take to interpreting what constitutes religious belief and how they approach notions of genuine occupational qualification, and proportionately. In the past, in other contexts, the courts have defined the nature of religious belief relatively narrowly. Thus, for example, for Eliot J, a belief in corporal punishment was not a religious belief. A belief in the efficacy of corporal punishment was not a religious belief:

> even if the reason for holding that belief is that it is supported by a religious text. It is not one of the articles of faith. It may be accurate to say that someone has a religious conviction that everything in the Bible is true, but it would surely be odd to describe, say, a belief in angels as a religious conviction or as itself constituting an article of religious faith. It is a belief which is in accordance with the religious faith, but it does not embody or define the belief or conviction itself.
>
> (*The Queen on the Application of Williamson v Secretary of State for Education and Employment* [2002] 1 FLR 493 at p 503)

A conservative approach to the definition of religion and religious belief such as this would considerably restrict the effectiveness of the legislation. Sandberg, however, notes one tribunal decision – *Hussain and Bhuller Bros* – applying the Regulations, which explicitly holds that there is a need for a liberal interpretation of religion and religious belief and which goes on to accept that the need to stay at home 'for bereavement purposes' formed part of the claimant's religion (Sandberg 2007, p 88).

The 2003 Regulations make no judgment, explicitly or implicitly, about the value of religion. The claimant may be, in the words of Sir John Romilly in the well-known case on religious charitable trusts, *Thornton v Howe*, 'foolish [and] ignorant' and their beliefs may be 'very foolish'.[16] Neither of these things will have any bearing on the validity of the claim. They simply provide

15 For discussion of such case law as there is, see, Sandberg 2007 and Vickers 2008.
16 *Thornton v Howe* (1862) 31 Beav 14 at p 18 and p 19.

a scheme whereby individuals can make choices about the way in which they pursue their lives that will reflect their religious convictions. The choices are not unlimited. As in Begum's case (above) the choices that an employee wants to make may not be able to be accommodated by the employer. A work practice that disadvantages a believer may nevertheless be a work practice that the employer can show to 'be a proportionate means of achieving a legitimate aim'. However, as happened in Begum's case, the employer will need to think about religious needs if they are to defend their position. If they fail to do so then they are likely to lose in litigation (Sandberg 2007, pp 90–91). In this sense the legislation conforms to the liberal notion of encouraging the individual to pursue what they see as being the good in their lives, insofar as they can do so without impinging on others' pursuit of the good.[17]

Conclusion

The past few years have seen much greater attempts to accommodate the needs of religious believers than was so several decades ago. While some of these attempts may have been little more than political window-dressing, it remains the case that there has been a significant attempt to grapple with the implications of the presence of religious communities in contemporary Great Britain. If it is true, as this book contends, that those attempts that have operated at the level of facilitating individual choice have been the most effective legislative provisions, then the questions of who chooses, how they choose and when they choose become of primary significance. Children, women and young men can be particularly vulnerable, especially in communities that traditionally have little access to wealth or education. Existentially, such people remain in a position to make choices. In practice, they will also in fact make choices and among the range of genuine choices made will be decisions to renounce the ability to make individual choice. However, the fact that individual choice can sometimes be constrained in an unacceptable manner by communities, families or other individuals, also needs to be remembered. Thus it becomes important for the law not only to provide for choice but also, insofar as it can, to provide for free choice and the ability to change choices.

In providing for choice the State increases the competition for loyalty. In

17 The argument here is not that attempts to accommodate religion have to be made on the individual level if they are to be successful. Special dispensations made towards Sikhs in a variety of ways are all general in some sense (even if individual in the sense that Sikhs may use, not must use them). The Human Rights Act 1998 gives a right to freedom of religion (although again that right need not be enforced if the individual does not wish to do so). However, laws that allow for individual choices seem to be more likely to be successful than laws that make general, obligatory statements.

that, there is a loss for the State itself. A State that contains a cosmopolitan society and encourages diversity can no longer assume the old attachments that it once did. People have multiple and changing identities. Patriotism no longer seems straightforward as an idea nor necessarily commendable. Great Britain – composed of England, Wales and Scotland – is itself part of the larger United Kingdom that is, in turn, part of the even greater European Union. This creates multiple commitments. There are also loyalties based on similarities of class, ethnicity, political ethos or religion. Each compete with each other and institutions within those competitions must be alive to the possibility of exit by their members. Religions seem to be among the more vulnerable groups within these competitions. There is no guarantee that any individual religion will survive and there is every likelihood, on the basis of the figures in Chapter 1, that in the case of contemporary Great Britain, some will not. Nevertheless, promoting and protecting choice for believers, including the right to change one's choices, will do as much as the law can do to honour the promises that a liberal State makes in the context of a secular society.

Bibliography

Addison, N (2007) *Religious Discrimination and Hatred Law*, Routledge-Cavendish: London

Ahdar, R (2001) *Worlds Colliding: Conservative Christians and the Law*, Ashgate: Aldershot

Ahdar, R and Leigh, I (2004) 'Is Establishment Consistent with Religious Freedom?' in Vol 49 No 3 *McGill Law Journal*, pp 635–681

Ahdar, R and Leigh, I (2005) *Religious Freedom in the Liberal State*, Oxford University Press: Oxford

Ahmed, A (2003) *Islam Under Siege*, Polity Press: Cambridge

Akhtar, S (1989) *Be careful with Muhammad!: The Salman Rushdie Affair*, Bellew Publishing: London

Alderman, G (1989) *London Jewry and London Politics: 1889–1986*, Routledge: London

Alderman, G (1992) *Modern British Jewry*, Clarendon Press: Oxford

Ali, M (2005) 'Do We Need Laws on Hatred?' in Appignanesi, L (ed) *Free Expression is No Offence*, Penguin Books: London

Allen, C and Nielsen, J (2002) *Summary Report on Islamophobia in the EU after 11 September 2001*, European Monitoring Centre on Racism and Xenophobia

Allott, A (1980) *The Limits of Law*, Butterworths: London

Alves, C (1991) 'Just a Matter of Words? The Religious Education debate in the House of Lords' in Vol 13 No 3 *British Journal of Religious Education*, pp 168–174

Amirallay, O and Mallas (1994) 'Night' in *For Rushdie: Essays by Arab and Muslim Writers in Defense of Free Speech*, George Braziller: New York

Anderson, N (1982) 'The Marriage with a Deceased Wife's Sister Bill' Controversy: Incest Anxiety and the Defense of Family Purity in Victorian England' in Vol XXI No 2 *The Journal of British Studies*, pp 67–86

Ansari, H (2004) 'The Legal Status of Muslims in the UK' in Aluffi Beck-Peccoz, R and Zincone, G (eds) *The Legal Treatment of Islamic Minorities in Europe*, Peeters: Leuven

Appiah, K (1994) 'Identity, Authenticity, Survival: Multicultural Societies and Social Reproduction' in Gutmann, A (ed) *Multiculturalism: Examining the Politics of Recognition*, Princeton University Press: Princeton

Appiah, K (2006) *Cosmopolitanism: Ethics in a World of Strangers*, WW Norton & Company: New York

Appignanesi, L and Maitland, S (eds) (1989) *The Rushdie File*, Fourth Estate Ltd: London

Asad, T (2003) *Formations of the Secular: Christianity, Islam, Modernity*, Stanford University Press: Stanford

Aspinall, P (2000) 'Should a Question on "Religion" be Asked in the 2001 British Census? A Public Policy Case in Favour' in Vol 34 No 5 *Social Policy and Administration*, pp 544–600

Auld, R (2001) *A Review of the Criminal Courts of England and Wales*, The Stationery Office: London

Badawi, Z (1981) *Islam in Britain*, Ta Ha Press: London

Badawi, Z (1995) 'Muslim Justice in a Secular Society' in King, M (ed) *God's Law Versus State Law*, Grey Seal: London

Bailey, V and McCabe, S (1979) 'Reforming the Law of Incest' in *Criminal Law Review*, pp 749–764

Barnes, P (2006) 'The Misrepresentation of Religion in Modern British (Religious) Education' in Vol 54 No 4 *British Journal of Religious Education*, pp 395–411

Barry, B (2001) *Culture and Equality: An Egalitarian Critique of Multiculturalism*, Polity Press: Cambridge

Bartholomew, G (1952) 'Private Interpersonal Law' in Vol 1 No 3 *International and Comparative Law Quarterly*, pp 325–344

Bartholomew, G (1961) 'Application of Jewish Law in England' in Vol 3 No 1 *University of Malaya Law Review*, pp 83–111

Batteson, C (1999) 'The 1944 Education Act Reconsidered' in Vol 51 No 1 *Educational Review*, pp 5–15

Bauman, Z (1991) *Modernity and Ambivalence*, Polity Press: Cambridge

Bauman, Z (2003) *Liquid Love*, Polity Press: Cambridge

Bauman, Z (2005) *Liquid Life*, Polity Press: Cambridge

BBC (2002) *80 years of religious broadcasting on the BBC*, www.bbc.co.uk/pressoffice/pressreleases/

Beck, U (2006) *Cosmopolitan Vision*, Polity Press: Cambridge

Beckford, J (1990) 'The Politics of Defining religion' in Platvoet, J and Molendijk, A (eds) *The Pragmatics of Defining Religion: Contexts, Concepts and Contests*, Brill: Leiden

Beckford, J and Gilliat, S (1998) *Religion in Prison: Equal Rites in a Multi-Faith Society*, Cambridge University Press: Cambridge

Bell, G (1935) *Randall Davidson: Archbishop of Canterbury: Volume II*, Oxford University Press: London

Bell, M (2002) *Anti-Discrimination Law and the European Union*, Oxford University Press: Oxford

Berkovits, B (1990) '*Get* and *Talaq* in English Law: Reflections on Law and Policy' in Mallat, C and Connors, J (eds) *Islamic Family Law*, Graham and Trotman: London

Berman, E (2000) 'Sect Subsidy, and Sacrifice: An Economist's View of Ultra-Orthodox Jews' in Vol 115 No 3 *Quarterly Journal of Economics*, pp 905–953

Bhatti, G (2004) *Behzti*, Oberon Books Ltd: London

Bidwell, S (1976) *Red, White and Black*, Gordon and Cremonesi: London

Bittles, A (2001) 'Consanguinity and its relevance to clinical genetics' in Vol 60 No 2 *Clinical Genetics*, pp 89–98

Bocking, B (1995) 'Fundamental Rites? Religion, State, Education and the Invention of Sacred Heritage in post-Christian Britain and pre-War Japan' in Vol 25 No 3 *Religion*, pp 227–247

Bogdanor, V (1995) *The Monarchy and the Constitution*, Clarendon Press: Oxford

Boyd, M (2004) *Dispute Resolution in Family Law: Protecting Choice, Promoting Inclusion*, Ministry of the Attorney-General: Toronto

Bradley, D (2003) 'Comparative Law, Family Law and Common law' in Vol 23 No 1 *Oxford Journal of Legal Studies*, pp 127–146

Bradney, A (1984) 'Arranged Marriages and Duress' in *Journal of Social Welfare Law*, pp 278–281

Bradney, A (1987) 'Separate Schools, Ethnic Minorities and the Law' in Vol XIII No 3 *New Community*, pp 412–420

Bradney, A (1993) *Religions, Rights and Laws*, Leicester University Press: Leicester

Bradney, A (1996) 'Christian Worship?' in Vol 8 No 2 *Education and the Law*, pp 127–136

Bradney, A (2000) 'Faced by Faith' in Oliver, P, Scott, S and Tadros, V (eds) *Faith in Law: Essays in Legal Theory*, Hart Publishing: Oxford

Bradney, A (2006) ' "It's About Power": Law in the Fictional Setting of a Quaker Meeting and in the Everyday Reality of "Buffy the Vampire Slayer" ' in Vol 8 *Issues in Legal Scholarship* (www.bepress.com/ils/iss8/art2)

Bradney, A (forthcoming) 'Some Sceptical Thoughts About the Academic Analysis of Law and Religion' in Doe, N and Sandburg, R (eds) *Law and Religion: New Horizons*, Brill: Leiden

Bradney, A and Cownie, F (2000) *Living Without Law: An ethnography of Quaker decision-making, dispute avoidance and dispute resolution*, Ashgate: Aldershot

Bridge, C (2002) 'Religion, Culture and the Body of the Child' in Bainham, A, Sclater, S and Richards, M *Body Lore and Lores*, Hart Publishing: Oxford

Brierley, P (1991) *'Christian' England: What the English Church Census Reveals*, MARC Europe: London

Brighouse, H (1998) 'Civic Education and Liberal Legitimacy' in Vol 108 No 4 *Ethics*, pp 719–745

Brown, C (2001) *The Death of Christian Britain*, Routledge: London

Brown, R (1993–1995) 'What of the Church in Wales?' in Vol 3 *Ecclesiastical Law Journal*, pp 20–29

Bruce, S (1995) *Religion in Modern Britain*, Oxford University Press: Oxford

Bruce, S (2001) 'Christianity in Great Britain, RIP' in Vol 62 No 2 *Sociology of Religion*, pp 191–203

Bruce, S (2002) 'Praying Alone? Church-Going in Britain and the Putnam Thesis' in Vol 17 No 3 *Journal of Contemporary Religion*, pp 317–328

Bursell, R (2007) 'Turbulent Priests: Clerical Misconduct Under the Clergy Discipline Measure 2003' in Vol 9 No 3 *Ecclesiastical Law Journal*, pp 250–263

Burtonwood, N (2003) 'Social Cohesion, Autonomy and the Liberal Defence of Faith Schools' in Vol 37 No 3 *Journal of Philosophy of Education*, pp 415–425

Bush, J (1990–1991) ' "Include Me Out": Some Lessons of Religious Toleration in Britain' in Vol 10 Nos 3–4 *Cardozo Law Review*, pp 881–923

Cairncross, J (1974) *After Polygamy Was Made a Sin: The Social History of Christian Polygamy*, Routledge and Kegan Paul: London

Canovan, M (1990) 'On Being Economical with the Truth: Some Liberal Reflections' in Vol 38 No 1 *Political Studies*, pp 5–19

Cantaur, R and Ebor, S (2007) *Crown Appointments in the Church of England: A Consultation Paper from the Archbishops*, Church House: London

Cantle Committee (2001) *Community Cohesion: A Report of the Independent Review Team*, Home Office: London

Carey, G (2005) *Know the Truth*, Harper Perennial: London

Carper, J (2000) 'Pluralism to Establishment to Dissent: The Religious and Educational Context of Home Schooling' in Vol 75 No 1/2 *Peabody Journal of Education*, pp 8–19

Carroll, L (1997) 'Muslim Women and "Islamic Divorce" in England' in Vol 17 No 1 *Journal of Muslim Minority Affairs*, pp 97–115

Cashmore, E (1979) *Rastaman: The Rastafarian Movement in England*, George Allen and Unwin: London

Chadwick, O (1966) *The Victorian Church: Part One*, Adam and Charles Black: London

Chadwick Commission (1970) *Church and State: Report of the Archbishop's Commission*, Church Information Office: London

Chambers, I (1994) *Migrancy, Culture, Identity*, Routledge: London

Chambers, P (2005) *Religion, Secularization and Social Change in Wales*, University of Wales Press: Cardiff

Chambers, P (2006) 'Secularisation, Wales, and Islam' in Vol 21 No 3 *Journal of Contemporary Religion*, pp 325–340

Chandler, A (1993) 'The Church of England and the Obliteration Bombing of Germany in the Second World War' in Vol CVII No CCCCXXIX *English Historical Review*, pp 920–946

Cheetham, R (2000) 'Collective Worship: A Window into Contemporary Understandings of the Nature of Religious Belief?' in Vol 22 No 2 *British Journal of Religious Education*, pp 71–81

Church of Scotland (nd) www.churchofscotland.org.uk/organisation/orgqueen.htm

Cohen, I (1950) *Contemporary Jewry: A Survey of Social, Cultural, Economic and Political Conditions*, Methuen: London

Cohen, S (1971) 'Hate Propaganda – The Amendments to the Criminal Code' in Vol 17 No 4 *McGill Law Journal*, pp 740–791

Cole, W and Sambhi, P (1978) *The Sikhs*, Routledge and Kegan Paul: London

Collins, L (ed) (2006) *Dicey, Morris and Collins on The Conflict of Laws*, Sweet and Maxwell: London

Commission on British Muslims and Islamophobia (1997) *Islamophobia: a challenge for us all*, The Runnymede Trust: London

Commission on British Muslims and Islamophobia (2004) *Islamophobia: issues, challenges and action: A Report by the Commission on British Muslims and Islamophobia*, Trentham Books: Stoke on Trent

Copley, T (1997) *Teaching Religion: Fifty years of religious education in England and Wales*, University of Exeter Press: Exeter

Cooper, Lord (1991) 'The Scottish Legal Tradition' in Meston, M, Sellar, W and Cooper, Lord *The Scottish Legal Tradition*, The Saltire Society and The Stair Society: Edinburgh

Council of the European Union (2007) *Press Release: 8364/07 (Presse 77)*, Council of the European Union: Brussels

Cox, E (1983) *Problems and Possibilities for Religious Education*, Hodder and Stoughton: London

Cox, J (1982) *The English Churches in a Secular Society: Lambeth, 1870–1930*, Oxford University Press: Oxford

Cranmer, F. (2003) 'Regulation Within the Religious Society of Friends' in Vol 7 No 2 *Ecclesiastical Law Journal* pp 176–194

Cranston, M (1987) 'John Locke and the Case for Toleration' in Mendus, S and Edwards, D (eds) *On Toleration*, Clarendon Press: Oxford

Cretney, S (1974) *Principles of Family Law*, Sweet and Maxwell: London

Cretney, S (2003) *Family Law in the Twentieth Century: A History*, Oxford University Press: Oxford

Cretney, S, Masson, J and Bailey-Harris, R (2002) *Principles of Family Law*, Sweet and Maxwell: London

Cross-Party Working Party on Religious Hatred (2002) *Tackling Religious Hatred*, Scottish Executive: Edinburgh

Cruickshank, M (1963) *Church and State in English Education*, Macmillan: London

Cullingford, C (ed) (1999) *An Inspector calls: Ofsted and its effect on school standards*, Kogan Page Limited: London

Cumper, P (2000) 'Religious Organisations and the Human Rights Act 1998' in Edge, P and Harvey, G (eds) *Law and Religion in Contemporary Society: Communities, Individualism and the State*, Ashgate: Aldershot

Cumper, P (2006) 'Outlawing incitement to religious hatred – a British perspective' in Vol 1 No 3 *Religion and Human Rights: An International Journal*, pp 249–268

Dandelion, P (1996) *A Sociological Analysis of the Theology of Quakers: The Silent Revolution*, Edwin Mellen Press: Lewiston

Dainow, J (1940) 'Limitations on Testamentary Freedom in England' in Vol 25 No 3 *Cornell Law Quarterly*, pp 337–360

Dane, P (2001) 'The Intersecting Worlds of Religious and Secular Marriage' in O'Dair, R and Lewis, A (eds) *Law and Religion*, Oxford University Press: Oxford

Davie, G (1994) *Religion in Britain Since 1945*, Basil Blackwell: Oxford

Davie, G (2002) 'Praying Alone? Church-Going in Britain and Social Capital: A Reply to Steve Bruce' in Vol 17 No 3 *Journal of Contemporary Religion*, pp 329–334

Davies, A (2000) *The Quakers in English Society: 1655–1725*, Oxford University Press: Oxford

Davies, D, Watkins, C and Winter, M (1991) *Church and Religion in Rural England*, T & T Clark: Edinburgh

Davies, R (1976) 'Church and State' in Vol 7 *Cambrian Law Review*, pp 11–30

De Jong, J and Snik, G (2002) 'Why Should States Fund Denominational Schools?' in Vol 36 No 4 *Journal of Philosophy of Education*, pp 573–587

Derrett, J (1968) *Religion, Law and the State in India*, Faber and Faber: London

Detmold, M (1989) *Courts and Administrators*, Weidenfeld and Nicholson: London

Devlin, Patrick (1965) *The Enforcement of Morals*, Oxford University Press: Oxford

Diduck, A and Kaganas, F (2006) *Family Law, Gender and the State: Text, Cases and Materials*, Hart Publishing: Oxford

Dobe, K and Chhokar, S (2000) 'Muslims, Ethnicity and the Law' in Vol 4 *International Journal of Discrimination and the Law*, pp 369–386

Dobson, A (2006) 'Thick Cosmopolitanism' in Vol 54 No 1 *Political Studies*, pp 185–215

Doe, N (1996) *The Legal Framework of the Church of England: A Critical Study in a Comparative Context*, Clarendon Press: Oxford

Doe, N (1998) *Canon Law in the Anglican Community*, Clarendon Press: Oxford

Doe, N (2004) 'The Church in Wales and the State: A Juridical Perspective' in Vol 2 No 1 *Journal of Anglican Studies*, pp 99–124

D'Onofrio, E (2005) 'Child Brides, Inegalitarianism, and the Fundamentalist Polygamous Family in the United States' in Vol 19 No 3 *International Journal of Law, Policy and the Family*, pp 373–394

Douglas, G (2001) *An Introduction to Family Law*, Oxford University Press: Oxford

Dundas, P (1992) *The Jains*, Routledge: London

Eberle, C (2002) *Religious Conviction in Liberal Politics*, Cambridge University Press: Cambridge

Edgar, D (2006) 'Shouting fire: art, religion and the right to be offended' in Vol 48 No 2 *Race and Class*, pp 61–76

Edge, P (2002) *Legal Responses to Religious Differences*, Kluwer Law International: The Hague

Edwards, C (2007) *Death in Ancient Rome*, Yale University Press: New Haven

Eekelaar, J (2006) *Family Law and Personal Life*, Oxford University Press: Oxford

Eekelaar, J and Clive, E with Clarke, K and Raikes, S (1977) *Custody After Divorce*, Oxford Centre for Socio-Legal Studies: Oxford

Elliott, K (2004) 'Between two worlds: the Catholic educational dilemma in 1944' in Vol 33 No 6 *History of Education*, pp 661–682

El-Or, T (1994) *Educated and Ignorant: Ultraorthodox Jewish Women and their World* Lynne Reinnar Publishers: Boulder, Colorado

Emon, A (2006) 'Conceiving Islamic Law in a Pluralist Society: History, Politics and Multicultural Jurisprudence' in No 2 *Singapore Journal of Legal Studies*, pp 331–355

Evans, M (1997) *Religious Liberty and International Law in Europe*, Cambridge University Press: Cambridge

Farhi, M (2005) 'God Save Us from Religion!' in Appignanesi, L (ed) *Free Expression is No Offence*, Penguin Books Ltd: London

Feinberg, J (1985) *The Moral Limits of the Criminal Law: Volume Two: Offense to Others*, Oxford University Press: Oxford

Festenstein, M (1999) 'Toleration and Deliberative Politics' in Horton, J and Mendus, S (eds) *Toleration, Identity and Difference*, Palgrave Macmillan: London

Field, C (2007) 'Render Unto Caesar? The Politics of Church of England Clergy since 1980' in Vol 5 No 1 *Journal of Anglican Studies*, pp 89–108

Fielding, M (2001) 'OFSTED, Inspection and the Betrayal of Democracy' in Vol 35 No 4 *Journal of Philosophy of Education*, pp 695–709

Findlay, M (1999) 'Mysan Isaac Berger' in Vol 143 No 7 *Solicitors Journal*, p 172

Fitzmaurice, D (1993) 'Liberal Neutrality, Traditional Minorities and Education' in Horton J (ed) *Liberalism, Multiculturalism and Toleration*, Macmillan: Basingstoke

Fleming, J (2003) 'Eyes open to religion' in Vol 100 No 2 *Law Society Gazette*, pp 24–27

Focus on Ethnicity and Religion: 2006 edition (2006) Palgrave Macmillan: Basingstoke

Freeman, M (1995) 'Marriage and Divorce in England' in Vol 29 No 3 *Family Law Quarterly*, pp 549–566

Freeman, M (2001) 'Is the Jewish *Get* Any Business of the State' in O'Dair, R and Lewis, A (eds) *Law and Religion*, Oxford University Press: Oxford

Frimer, D (1990) 'Israel Civil Courts and Rabbinical Courts Under One Roof' (in response to Prof P Shifman) in Vol 24 Nos 3 and 4 *Israel Law Review*, pp 553–559

Galanter M and Jayanath K (2000) 'Personal Law and Human Rights in India and Israel' in Vol 34 No 1 *Israel Law Review*, pp 101–133

Gardner, P (1984) *The Lost Elementary Schools of Victorian England*, Routledge, London

Giddens, A (1990) *The Consequences of Modernity*, Stanford University Press: Stanford

Giddens, A (1991) *Modernity and Self-Identity*, Polity Press: Cambridge

Gies, L (2006) 'What Not to Wear: Islamic Dress and School Uniforms' in Vol 14 No 3 *Feminist Legal Studies*, pp 377–389

Gill, J (2004) 'The act of collective worship: pupils' perspectives' in Vol 26 No 2 *British Journal of Religious Education*, pp 185–196

Gill, Lord (2000) 'Racism and Xenophobia: A Brief Note on the Scottish Experience' in Vol 22 No 1 *Liverpool Law Review*, pp 39–46

Gill, R (1992) 'Secularization and Census Data' in Bruce, S (ed) *Religion and Modernization: Sociologists and Historians Debate the Secularization Thesis*, Clarendon Press: Oxford

Gill, R (2002) 'A Response to Steve Bruce's "Praying Alone" ' in Vol 17 No 3 *Journal of Contemporary Religion*, pp 335–338

Gillat-Ray, S (1998) 'Multiculturalism and Identity: Their relationship for British Muslims' in Vol 18 No 2 *Journal of Muslim Minority Affairs*, pp 347–355

Glaeser, E (2005) 'The Political Economy of Hatred' in Vol 120 No 1 *Quarterly Journal of Economy*, pp 45–86

Glendon, M (1977) *State, Law and Family: Family Law in transition in the United States and Western Europe*, North-Holland Publishing Co: Amsterdam

Goodall, K (2007) 'Incitement to Religious Hatred: All Talk and No Substance?' in Vol 70 No 1 *Modern Law Review*, pp 89–113

Goody, J (1986) *The logic of writing and the organization of society*, Cambridge University Press: Cambridge

Grace, G (2003) 'Educational Studies and Faith-Based Schooling: Moving From Prejudice to Evidence-Based Argument' in Vol 51 No 2 *British Journal of Educational Studies*, pp 149–167

Grainger, H (2006) *Trade Union Membership 2005*, Department of Trade and Industry: London

Gray, I (1999) 'Religious Observance in Schools: A Scottish Perspective' in Vol 22 No 1 *British Journal of Religious Education*, pp 35–45

Grimley, M (2004) *Citizenship, Community, and the Church of England: Liberal Anglican Theories of the State between the Wars*, Clarendon Press: Oxford

Habermas, J (1994) 'Struggles for Recognition in the Democratice Constitutional State' in Gutmann, A (ed) *Multiculturalism: Examining the Politics of Recognition*, Princeton University Press: Princeton

Halifax, Marquess of (1969) *Complete Works*, Penguin Books: Harmondsworth

Hall, P (1999) 'Social Capital in Britain' in Vol 29 No 3 *British Journal of Politics*, pp 417–461

Hamilton C (1995) *Family, Law and Religion*, Sweet and Maxwell: London

Hampsher-Monk, I (1999) 'Toleration, the Moral Will and the Justification of

Liberalism' in Horton, J and Mendus, S (eds) *Toleration, Identity and Difference*, Palgrave Macmillan: London

Hanbury, H (1954) 'Introduction' in Crowther, C *Religious Trusts*, George Ronald: Oxford

Hannerz, U (2007) 'Foreign Correspondents and Varieties of Cosmopolitanism' in Vol 33 No 2 *Journal of Ethnic and Migration Studies*, pp 299–311

Harris, N (1993a) 'Local Complaints Procedures under the Education Reform Act 1988' in *Journal of Social Welfare and Family Law*, pp 19–39

Harris N (1993b) 'Complaints about schooling: limitations of the Education Reform Act 1988' in Vol 5 No 2 *Education and the Law*, pp 65–71

Hart, C (1993) 'Legislation and religious education' in Vol 5 No 1 *Education and the Law*, pp 7–17

Harte, J (1987–1989) 'The Religious Dimension of the Education Reform Act 1988' in Vol 1 No 5 *Ecclesiastical Law Journal*, pp 32–52

Hassouneh-Phillips, D (2001) 'Polygamy and Wife Abuse: A Qualitative Study of Muslim Women in America' in Vol 22 No 8 *Health Care for Women International*, pp 735–748

Hastings, A (1986) *A History of English Christianity: 1920–1985*, William Collins: London

Hastings, A (1997) 'The Case for Retaining Establishment' in Modood, T (ed) *Church, State and Religious Minorities*, Policy Studies Institute: London

Hayward, M (2006) 'Curriculum Christianity' in Vol 28 No 2 *British Journal of Religious Education*, pp 153–171

Henriques, H (1909) *Jewish Marriages and the English Law*, Jewish Historical Society: Oxford

Hensher, P (2005) 'Free Speech Responsibly' in Appignanesi, L (ed) *Free Expression is No Offence*, Penguin Books: London

Heubel, E (1965) 'Church and State in England: The Price of Establishment' in Vol 18 No 3 *Western Political Quarterly*, pp 646–655

Hewer, C (2001) 'Schools for Muslims' in Vol 27 No 4 *Oxford Review of Education*, pp 515–527

Hill, M (2001) *Ecclesiastical Law*, Oxford University Press: Oxford

Holdsworth, W (1920) 'The State and Religious Nonconformity: An Historical Retrospect' in Vol 36 No 4 *Law Quarterly Review*, pp 339–358

Holdsworth, W (1938) *A History of English Law: Volume X*, Methuen: London

Holdsworth, W (1965) *A History of English Law: Volume XV*, Methuen: London

Honiq, B (1999) ' "Culture Made Me Do It" ' in Cohen, J, Howard, M and Nussbaum, M (eds) *Is Multiculturalism Bad for Women?* Princeton University Press, Princeton

Hooker, M (1975) *Legal Pluralism: An Introduction to Colonial and Neo-Colonial Laws*, Clarendon Press: Oxford

Hooker, M (1976) *The Personal Laws of Malaysia*, Oxford University Press: Kuala Lumpur

Horton, J (1993) 'Liberalism, Multiculturalism and Toleration' in Horton, J (ed) *Liberalism, Multiculturalism and Toleration*, Macmillan: London

Howard, E (2005) 'Anti-Race Discrimination Measures in Europe: An Attack on Two Fronts' in Vol 11 No 4 *European Law Journal*, pp 468–486

Hull, J (1989a) 'School Worship and the 1988 Education Reform Act' in Vol 11 No 3 *British Journal of Religious Education*, pp 119–125

Hull, J (1989b) *The Act Unpacked*, University of Birmingham School of Education: Birmingham

Hull, J (1995) 'The theology of the Department of Education' in Vol 47 No 3 *Educational Review*, pp 243–254

Hull, J (1996) 'A Critique of Christian Religionism in Recent British Education' in Astley, J and Francis, L (eds) *Christian Theology and Religious Education: Connects and Contradictions*, SPCK: London www.johnhull.biz

Hull, J (2003) 'The Blessings of Secularity: Religious Education in England and Wales' in Vol 51 No 3 *Journal of Religious Education*, pp 51–58 www.johnhull.biz

Hunt, K (2003) 'The Spirituality of Non-Churchgoers' in Davie, G, Heelas, P and Woodhead, L (eds) *Predicting Religion: Christian, Secular and Alternative Futures*, Ashgate: Aldershot

Idriss, M (2002) 'Religion and the Anti-Terrorism, Crime and Security Act 2001' in *Criminal Law Review*, pp 890–911

Ignatieff, M (2005) 'Respect and the Rules of the Road' in Appignanesi, L (ed) *Free Expression is No Offence*, Penguin Books: London

Illes, A (2007) 'The Clergy Discipline Measure Act 2003: A Canter Through its Provisions and Procedures' in Vol 9 No 1 *Ecclesiastical Law Journal*, pp 10–23

Impartiality Review (2004) www.bbcgovernorsarchive.co.uk/docs/reviews/religion_impartiality.html

Isaac, J (1990) 'The New Right and the Moral Society' in Vol 43 No 2 *Parliamentary Affairs*, pp 209–226

Jackson, R (2004) *Rethinking Religious Education and Plurality: Issues in diversity and pedagogy*, RoutledgeFalmer: Abingdon

Jackson, T (2003) 'Should the State Fund Faith Based Schools?' in Vol 25 No 2 *British Journal of Religious Education*, pp 89–102

Jacobson, J (1998) *Islam in Transition: Religion and Identity Among British Pakistani Youth*, Routledge: London

Jacoby, J (2002) 'Punish Crime, Not Thought Crime' in Ignanski, P (ed) *The Hate Debate*, Profile Books: London

Jeremy, A (2007) 'Practical Implications of the Racial and Religious Hatred Act 2006' in Vol 9 No 2 *Ecclesiastical Law Journal*, pp 187–201

Johnston, B and Webber, S (2003) 'Information Literacy in Higher Education: a review and a case study' in Vol 28 No 3 *Studies in Higher Education*, pp 335–352

Joly, D (1995) *Britannia's Crescent: Making a Place for Muslims in British Society*, Avebury: Aldershot

Jones, P (1989) 'The ideal of the neutral state' in Goodin, R and Reeve, A (eds) *Liberal Neutrality*, Routledge: London

Jones, P (1994) 'The Satanic Verses and the Politics of Identity' in Fletcher, D (ed) *Reading Rushdie: Perspectives on the fiction of Salman Rushdie*, Rodopi: Amsterdam

Kamali, M (1997) *Freedom of Expression in Islam*, Islamic Texts Society: Cambridge

Kaplan, M (1991) *The Making of the Jewish Middle Class: Women, Family, and Identity, in Imperial Germany*, Oxford University Press: Oxford

Katz, D (1982) *Philo-Semitism and the Readmission of the Jews to England*, Clarendon Press: Oxford

Keiner, J (1996) 'Opening up Jewish Education to Inspection: the Impact of the OFSTED Inspection System in England' in Vol 4 No 5 *Education Policy Analysis Archives*, http://epaa.asu.edu/epaa/v4n5.html

Kellas, J (1989) *The Scottish Political System*, Cambridge University Press: Cambridge

Kelly, R (2005) *The Racial and Religious Hatred Bill: Research paper 05/48*, House of Commons: London

Kerrigan, H and Addison, N (2005) *The Impact on Scotland of the Racial and Religious Hatred Bill*, www.christianscotland.org/religioushatred/kerrigan &addison_opinion.pdf

Khaliq (2001–2002) 'The Accommodation and Regulation of Islam and Muslim Practices in English Law' in Vol 6 No 4 *Ecclesiastical Law Journal*, pp 332–351

Khanum, S (2001) 'The household patterns of a "Bangladeshi village" in England' in Vol 27 No 3 *Journal of Ethnic and Migration Studies*, pp 489–504

King Murray, R (1958) 'The Church of Scotland' in *Public Law*, pp 155–162

Kiralfy, A (1957) 'Matrimonial Disputes and their Procedure' in Graveson, R and Crane, F (eds) *A Century of Family Law: 1857–1957*, Sweet and Maxwell: London

Kirby, D (1995) 'Responses Within the Anglican Church to Nuclear Weapons: 1945–1961' in Vol 37 No 3 *Journal of Church and State*, pp 599–622

Kirsh, H (1971) 'Conflict Resolution and the Legal Culture: A Study of the Rabbinical Court' in Vol 9 No 2 *Osgoode Hall Law Journal*, pp 335–357

Knott, K (1986) *Religion and Identity, and the Study of Ethnic Minority Religions in Britain*, University of Leeds Community Religions Project: Leeds

Knott, K and Khokher, S (1993) 'Religious and ethnic identity among young women in Bradford' in Vol 19 No 4 *New Community*, pp 593–610

Küçükcan, T (1998) 'Community, Identity and Institutionalization of Islamic Education: The Case of Ikra Primary School' in Vol 28 No 1 *British Journal of Religious Education*, pp 32–43

Küçükcan, T (1999) *Politics of Ethnicity, Identity and Religion: Turkish Muslims in Britain*, Ashgate: Aldershot

Kulananda, D (1997) 'A Buddhist Perspective' in Modood, T (ed) *Church, State and Religious Minorities*, Policy Studies Institute: London

Kumar, K (1978) *Prophecy and Progress: The Sociology of Industrial and Post-Industrial Society*, Penguin Books: Harmondsworth

Kunzru, H (2005) 'Respecting Authority, Taking Offence' in Appignanesi, L (ed) *Free Expression is No Offence*, Penguin Books: London

Kuper, A (2002) 'Incest, Cousin Marriage, and the Origin of the Human Sciences in Nineteenth Century England' in Vol 174 No 1 *Past and Present*, pp 158–183

Kutwala, S (2006) 'Faith in Democracy: The Legitimate Role of Religion' in Vol 12 No 4 *Public Policy Research*, pp 246–251

Labour Party (2005) *Labour party Manifesto 2005: Britain forward not back*, Labour Party: London

Laidlaw, J (1995) *Riches and Renunciation: Religion, Economy and Society among the Jains*, Clarendon Press: Oxford

Langlaude, S (2006) 'Indoctrination, secularism, religious liberty, and the ECHR' in Vol 55 No 4 *International and Comparative Law Quarterly*, pp 929–944

Laughlin, R (1988) 'Accounting in its Social Context: An Analysis of the Accounting Systems of the Church of England' in Vol 1 No 2 *Accounting, Audit and Accountability Journal*, pp 19–42

Laundy, P (1958) 'Parliament and the Church' in Vol XII No 3 *Parliamentary Affairs*, pp 445–460

Law Commission (1982) *Polygamous Marriages: Capacity to Contract a Polygamous Marriage and the Concept of the Potentially Polygamous Marriage: Working Paper No 83*, Her Majesty's Stationery Office: London

Law Commission (1985) *Criminal Law: Offences Against Religion and Public Worship: Law Commission Report No 145*, Her Majesty's Stationery Office: London

Leigh, I (2004) 'By Law Established? The Crown, constitutional reform and the Church of England' in *Public Law*, pp 266–273

Lemmings, D (1996) 'Marriage and the Law in the Eighteenth Century: Lord Hardwicke's Marriage Act of 1753' in Vol 39 No 2 *The Historical Journal*, pp 339–360

Leopold, P (1977) 'Incitement to Hatred – The History of a Controversial Offence' in *Public Law*, pp 389–405

Levinson, M (1997) 'Liberalism versus Democracy? Schooling Private Citizens in the Public Square' in Vol 27 No 3 *British Journal of Political Science*, pp 333–360

Levy, L (1995) *Blasphemy: Verbal Offense Against the Sacred, from Moses to Salman Rushdie*, University of North Carolina Press: Chapel Hill

Longman, C (2002) 'Empowering and engendering "religion". A critical perspective on ethnographic holism' in Vol 10 No 2 *Social Anthropology*, pp 239–248

Louden, L (2004) 'The conscience clause in religious education and collective worship' in Vol 26 No 3 *British Journal of Religious Education*, pp 273–289

Lowe, N and Douglas, G (2007) *Bromley's Family Law*, Oxford University Press: Oxford

Lukes, S (1991) *Moral Conflicts and Politics*, Clarendon Press: Oxford

Lyotard, J (1984) *The Postmodern Condition: A Report on Knowledge*, Manchester University Press: Manchester

MacDonald, Z (2002) 'Official Crime Statistics: Their Use and Interpretation' in Vol 112 No 2 *The Economic Journal*, pp F85–F106

Machin, G (2000) 'Parliament, the Church of England, and the Prayer Book Crisis, 1927–8', in Parry, J and Taylor, S (eds) *Parliament and the Church, 1529–1960*, Edinburgh University Press: Edinburgh

Machin, S (2003) 'Trade Union decline, new workplaces and new workers' in Gospel, H and Wood, S (eds) *Representing Workers: Union Recognition and Membership in Britain*, Routledge: London

Macklem, T (2000) 'Reason and Religion' in Oliver, P, Douglas Scott, S and Tadros, V (eds) *Faith in Law: Essays in Legal Theory*, Hart Publishing: Oxford

Madeley, J (2003) 'European Liberal Democracy and the Principle of State Religious Neutrality' in Vol 26 No 1 *West European Politics*, pp 1–22

Maer, L (2007) *Prime Ministerial involvement in ecclesiastical appointments*, House of Commons Library: London

Major, J (1999) *The Autobiography*, HarperCollins Publishers: London

Malik, M (2000) 'Faith and the State of Jurisprudence' in Oliver, P, Scott, S and Tadros, V (eds) *Faith in Law: Essays in Legal Theory*, Hart Publishing: Oxford

Marples, R (2005) 'Against faith schools: a philosophical argument for children's rights' in Vol 10 No 2 *International Journal of Children's Spirituality*, pp 133–147

Marriage, divorce and adoption statistics (2007) Office for National Statistics: London

Marshall-Taylor, G (2002) 'Religious Education and Collective Worship' in Broadbent, L and Brown, A (eds) *Issues in religious education*, RoutledgeFalmer: New York

Martin, D (2005) *Secularization: Towards a Revised General Theory*, Ashgate: Aldershot

Martino, T (2007) 'In conversation with Professor Eric Barendt: hatred, ridicule, contempt and plain bigotry' in Vol 18 No 2 *Entertainment Law Review*, pp 48–55

Matthews, P and Smith, G (1995) 'OFSTED: Inspecting schools and improvement through inspection' in Vol 25 No 1 *Cambridge Journal of Education*, pp 23–34

McClean, D (2003/2004) 'The Changing Legal Framework of the Church of England' in Vol 7 No 3 *Ecclesiastical Law Journal*, pp 292–303

McDowell, S and Day, B (2000) 'Special Issue' in Vol 75 No 1/2 *Peabody Journal of Education*

McGlynn, A and Stalker, H (1995) 'Recent developments in the Scottish process of school inspection' in Vol 25 No 1 *Cambridge Journal of Education*, pp 13–22

Medhurst, K (1991) 'Reflections on the Church of England and Politics at a moment of Transition' in Vol 44 No 2 *Parliamentary Affairs*, pp 240–261

Medhurst, K (1999) 'The Church of England: A Progress Report' in Vol 52 No 2 *Parliamentary Affairs*, pp 275–290

Menski, W (1987) 'Legal Pluralism in the Hindu marriage' in Burghart, R (ed) *Hinduism in Great Britain: The Perpetuation of Religion in an Alien Cultural Milieu*, Tavistock Publications: London

Menski, W (1993) 'Asians in Britain and the Question of Adaption to a New Legal Order: Asian Laws in Britain?' in Israel, M and Wagle, N (eds) *Ethnicity, Identity, Migration: The South Asian Context*, Centre for South Asian Studies, University of Toronto: Toronto

Menski, W (2000) *Comparative law in a global context: The legal systems of Asia and Africa*, Platinum Publishing: London

Menski, W (2003) *Hindu Law: Beyond Tradition and Modernity*, Oxford University Press: Oxford

Michaelson, M (1987) 'Domestic Hinduism in a Gujarati trading caste' in Burghart, R (ed) *Hinduism in Great Britain*, Tavistock Publications: London

Mill, J (1972) 'On Liberty' in Acton, H (ed) *Utilitarianism, Liberty, Representative Government*, JM Dent and Sons: London

Minkenberg, M (2003) 'The Policy Impact of Church-State Relations: Family Policy and Abortion in Britain, France, and Germany' in Vol 26 No 1 *West European Politics*, pp 195–237

Mitchell, C (2004) 'Is Northern Ireland Abnormal?: An Extension of the Sociological Debate on Religion in Northern Ireland' in Vol 38 No 2 *Sociology*, pp 237–254

Mitchell, J (1971) *Women's Estate*, Penguin Books: Harmondsworth

Modood, T (1993) 'Muslims, Incitement to Hatred and the Law' in J Horton (ed) *Liberalism, Multiculturalism and Toleration*, Macmillan Press: London

Modood, T (1994) 'Establishment, Multiculturalism and British Citizenship' in Vol 65 No 1 *Political Quarterly*, pp 53–73

Modood, T (2005) *Multicultural politics: Racism, Ethnicity and Muslims in Britain*, Edinburgh University Press: Edinburgh

Montaigne, M. de (1869) *Essays*

Montgomery, J (2000) 'Healthcare Law for a Multi-Faith Society' in Murphy, J (ed) *Ethnic Minorities, their Families and the Law*, Hart Publishing: Oxford

Mookherjee, M (2007) 'Permitting Dishonour: Culture, Gender and Freedom of Expression' in Vol 13 No 1 *Res Publica*, pp 29–52

Moore, E (1967) *An Introduction to English Canon Law*, Clarendon Press: Oxford

Moore, S (1978) *Law as Process*, Routledge and Kegan Paul: London

Moran, L (1996) *The Homosexual(ity) of Law*, Routledge: London

Mortensen, R (1998–99) 'A Christian State? A Comment' in Vol 13 No 2 *Journal of Law and Religion*, pp 509–515

Mortensen, R (2000) 'Art, Expression and the Offended Believer' in Ahdar, R (ed) *Law and Religion*, Ashgate: Aldershot

Munby, Mr Justice (2005) 'Families old and new – the family and Article 8' in Vol 17 No 4 *Child and Family Law Quarterly*, pp 487–509

Munroe, C (1996–1997) 'Does Scotland have an Established Church?' in Vol 4 *Ecclesiastical Law Journal*, pp 639–645

Murad, K (1986) *Muslim Youth in the West: Towards a New Education Strategy*, The Islamic Foundation: Leicester

Murphy, J (1971) *Church, State, and Schools in Britain, 1800–1970*, Routledge and Kegan Paul: London

Nash, D (1999) *Blasphemy in Modern Britain: 1789 to the Present Day*, Ashgate: Aldershot

Nash, D and Bakalis, C (2007) 'Incitement to Religious Hatred and the "Symbolic": How Will the Racial and Religious Hatred Act 2006 Work?' in Vol 28 No 3 *Liverpool Law Review*, pp 349–375

National Statistics Online (2007) *Religion in Britain*, www.statistics.gov.uk/cci/nugget.asp?id=293

Nazir-Ali, M (1997) 'A Spiritual and Moral Framework for Society' in Modood, T (ed) *Church, State and Religious Minorities*, Policy Studies Institute: London

Nicholls, D (1990) 'Politics and the Church of England' in Vol 61 No 2 *The Political Quarterly*, pp 132–142

Nicholson, P (1985) 'Toleration as a moral ideal' in Horton, J and Mendus, S (eds) *Aspects of Toleration: Philosophical Studies*, Methuen: London

Norman, E (1976) *Church and Society in England 1770–1970: A Historical Study*, Clarendon Press: Oxford

North, P and Fawcett, J (1999) *Cheshire and North's Private International Law*, Oxford University Press: Oxford

Nozick, R (1974) *Anarchy, State, and Utopia*, Basil Blackwell: Oxford

O'Beirne, M (2004) *Religion in England and Wales: Findings from the 2001 Home Office Citizenship Survey; Home Office Research Study 274*, Home Office Research and Development and Statistics Directorate: London

O'Brien, D and Carter V (2002–2003) 'Chant Down Babylon: Freedom of Religion and the Rastafarian Challenge to Majoritarianism' in Vol 18 No 1 *Journal of Law and Religion*, pp 219–248

Ofcom (2005) *Religious Programmes and the Broadcasting Code*, Ofcom: London

Ofcom (2007) *Public Service Broadcasting: Annual report 2007*, Ofcom: London

Ogilvie, M (1990) 'What is a Church by Law Established?' in Vol 28 No 1 *Osgoode Hall Law Journal*, pp 179–235

Okin, S (1999) 'Is Multiculturalism Bad for Women?' in Cohen, J, Howard, M and Nussbaum, M (eds) *Is Multiculturalism Bad for Women?* Princeton University Press: Princeton

Olivier, J (2007) 'The Legal Protection of Believers and Beliefs in the United Kingdom' in Vol 9 No 1 *Ecclesiastical Law Journal*, pp 66–86

Omariba, D and Boyle, M (2007) 'Family Structure and Child Mortality in Sub-Saharan Africa: Cross-National Effects of Polygyny' in Vol 62 No 2 *Journal of Marriage and Family*, pp 528–543

Ousley, H (2001) *Community Pride Not Prejudice: Making Diversity Work in Bradford*, Bradford Vision: Bradford

Outhwaite, R (1995) *Clandestine Marriage in England, 1500–1850*, The Hambledon Press: London

Parekh, B (2006) *Rethinking Multiculturalism: Cultural Diversity and Political Theory*, Macmillan: Basingstoke

Parker-Junkins, M (2005) 'The legal framework for faith-based schools and the rights of the child' in Gradner, G, Cairns, J and Lawton, D (eds) *Faith Based Schools: Consensus or Conflict?*, Routledge: London

Paton, H (1948) *The Moral Law: Kant's Groundwork of the Metaphysic of Morals*, Hutchinson: London

Patrick Glenn, H (2004) *Legal Traditions of the World*, Oxford University Press: Oxford

Pearce, A (2001) 'Religious Denomination or Public Religion? The Legal Status of the Church of England' in O'Dair, R and Lewis, A (eds) *Law and Religion*, Oxford University Press: Oxford

Pearl, D and Menski, W (1998) *Muslim Family Law*, Sweet and Maxwell: London

Peletz, M (2002) *Islamic Modern: Religious Courts and Cultural Politics in Malaysia*, Princeton University Press: Princeton

Pinhas, S (1990) 'Family Law in Israel: The Struggle Between Religious and Secular Law' in Vol 24 Nos 3 and 4 *Israel Law Review*, pp 537–552

Post, R (1988) 'Cultural Heterogeneity and Law: Pornography, Blasphemy and the First Amendment' in Vol 76 No 2 *California Law Review*, pp 297–335

Poulter, S (1986) *Ethnic Minorities and the Law*, Butterworths: London

Poulter, S (1990) 'The Claim to a Separate Islamic System of Personal Law for British Muslims' in Mallat, C and Connors, J (eds) *Islamic Family Law*, Graham and Trotman: London

Poulter, S (1998) *Ethnicity, Law and Human Rights: The English Experience*, Clarendon Press: Oxford

Pring, R (2005) 'Faith schools: can they be justified?' in Gardner, R, Cairns, J and Lawton, D (eds) *Faith Schools: Consensus or Conflict?*, Routledge: London

Proctor, J (1983) 'The Church of Scotland and the Struggle for a Scottish Assembly' in Vol 25 No 3 *Journal of Church and State*, pp 523–543

Putnam, R (2000) *Bowling Alone: The Collapse and Revival of American Community*, Simon and Schuster: New York

Qualifications and Curriculum Authority (2004) *The non-statutory national framework for religious education*, Qualifications and Curriculum Authority: London

Quinton, A (1978) *The Politics of Imperfection: The religious and secular traditions of conservative thought in England from Hooker to Oakeshott*, Faber and Faber: London

Qureshi, S and Khan, J (1989) *The Politics of the Satanic Verses: Unmasking Western Attitudes*, Muslim Community Studies Institute: Leicester

Rabbinical Courts (1970) 'Rabbinical Courts: Modern Day Solomons' in Vol 6 No 1 *Columbia Journal of Law and Social Problems*, pp 49–75

Raphael, D (1988) 'The intolerable' in Mendus, S (ed) *Justifying Toleration: Conceptual and Historical Perspectives*, Cambridge University Press: Cambridge

Rawls, J (1988) 'The Priority of the Rights and Ideas of the Good' in Vol 17 No 4 *Philosophy and Public Affairs*, pp 251–276

Raz, J (1986) *The Morality of Freedom*, Clarendon Press: Oxford

Raz, J (1988) 'Autonomy, toleration, and the harm principle' in Mendus, S (ed) *Justifying Toleration: Conceptual and Historical Perspectives*, Cambridge University Press: Cambridge

Raz, J (1994) 'Multiculturalism: A Liberal Perspective' in Raz, J *Ethics in the Public Domain: Essays on the Morality of Law and Politics*, Clarendon Press: Oxford

Read, Fr G (1990–1992) 'The Catholic Tribunal System in the British Isles' in Vol 2 No 4 *Ecclesiastical Law Journal*, pp 213–221

Religious Education Council (2007) *A National Strategy for Religious Education: Proposals by the Religious Education Council of England and Wales*, Religious Education Council for England and Wales: London

Resnick, D (1996) 'Jewish multicultural education: A minority view' in Vol 91 No 2 *Religious Education*, pp 209–221

Review of Public Order (1985) Cmnd 9510

Rivers, J (2000) 'From Toleration to Pluralism: Religious Liberty and Religious Establishment under the United Kingdom's Human Rights Act' in Ahdar, R (ed) *Law and Religion*, Ashgate: Aldershot

Rivers, J (2001) 'Religious Liberty as a Collective Right' in O'Dair, R and Lewis, A (eds) *Law and Religion*, Oxford University Press: Oxford

Robilliard, S (1981) 'Offences Against Religion and Worship' in Vol 44 No 5 *Modern Law Review*, pp 556–563

Rockefeller, S (1994) 'Comment' in Gutmann, A (ed) *Multiculturalism: Examining the Politics of Recognition*, Princeton University Press, Princeton

Rodes Jr, R (1977) *Ecclesiastical Administration in Medieval England*, University of Notre Dame Press: Notre Dame

Rodes Jr, R (1990–1991) 'Pluralist Establishment: Reflections on the English Experience' in Vol 10 Nos 3–4 *Cardozo Law Review*, pp 867–880

Rose, D (2006) 'Recent trends in religious education in England: a survey of reactions of Standing Advisory Committees for Religious Education towards increasing centralising influences since 1988' in Vol 28 No 2 *British Journal of Religious Education*, pp 185–199

Rosser-Owen, D (1997) 'A Muslim Perspective' in Modood, T (ed) *Church, State and Religious Minorities*, Policy Studies Institute: London

Rushdie, S (1983) 'The Indian Writer in England' in Butcher, M (ed) *The Eye of the Beholder*, Commonwealth Institute: London

Rushdie, S (1991) ' "Errata": Or, Unreliable Narration in Midnight's Children' in Rushdie, S *Imaginary Homelands*, Granta Books: London

Rushdie, S (1991b) 'In Good Faith' in Rushdie, S *Imaginary Homelands*, Granta Books: London

Sacks, J (1990) 'The Environment of Faith' in 15th November 1990 *The Listener*

Sadurski, W (1990) *Moral Pluralism and Legal Neutrality*, Kluwer Academic Publishers: Dordrecht

Sandburg, R (2007) 'Flags, Beards and Pilgrimages: A Review of the Early Cases on Religious Discrimination' in Vol 9 No1 *Ecclesiastical Law Journal*, pp 87–100

Sartre, J (nd) *Being and Nothingness*, Philosophical Library: New York

Saunders, D (1997) *Anti lawyers: Religion and the critics of law and state*, Routledge: London

Scarman, Lord (1987) 'Toleration and the Law' in Mendus, S and Edwards, D (eds) *On Toleration*, Clarendon Press: Oxford

Scherpe, J (2006) 'Should There be Degrees in Prohibited Degrees?' in Vol 65 No 1 *Cambridge Law Journal*, pp 32–35

Scholefield, L (2004) 'Bagels, schnitzel and McDonald's – "fuzzy frontiers" of Jewish identity in an English Jewish secondary school' in Vol 26 No 3 *British Journal of Religious Education*, pp 237–248

Schools – Achieving Success (2001) Cm 5320, The Stationery Office: London

Schuz, R (1996) 'Divorce and Ethnic Minorities' in Freeman, M (ed) *Divorce: Where Next?*, Dartmouth: Aldershot

Sebba, L and Shiffer, V (1998) 'Tradition and the Right to Education: The Case of the Ultra-Orthodox Community in Israel' in Douglas, G and Sebba, L (eds) *Children's Rights and Traditional Values*, Dartmouth: Aldershot

Seldon, A (2004) *Blair*, Simon & Schuster UK: London

Select Committee on Religious Offences (2003) *Report on Religious Offences in England and Wales*, HL Paper 95-I, 95-II, 95-III The Stationery Office: London

Self, A and Zealey, L (2007) *Social Trends: No 37*, Palgrave Macmillan: London

Sennett, R (1998) *The Corrosion of Character*, WW Norton: New York

Sezgin, Y (2004) 'Theorizing Formal Pluralism: Qualification of Legal Pluralism for Spatio-temporal Analysis' in Vol 50 *Journal of Legal Pluralism and Unofficial Law*, pp 101–108

Shachar, A (2001) *Multicultural Jurisdictions: Cultural Differences and Women's Rights*, Cambridge University Press: Cambridge

Shah, P (2005) *Legal Pluralism in Conflict: Coping with Cultural Diversity in Law*, Glasshouse Press: London

Sherin, C, Barlow, R, Wallington, T, Meadway, S and Waterworth, W (2002) *Williams on Wills*, Butterworths: London

Shiloh, I (1970) 'Marriage and Divorce in Israel' in Vol 4 No 4 *Israel Law Review*, pp 479–498

Short, G (2002) 'Faith-Based Schools: A Threat to Social Cohesion?' in Vol 36 No 4 *Journal of Philosophy of Education*, pp 559–572

Short, G (2003) 'Faith Schools and Social Cohesion: Opening Up the Debate' in Vol 25 No 2 *British Journal of Religious Education*, pp 129–141

Silk, J, Morris, A, Kanaya, T, Steinberg, L (2003) 'Psychological Control and Autonomy Granting: Opposite Ends of a Continuum or Distinct Constructs?' in Vol 13 No 1 *Journal of Research on Adolescence*, pp 113–128

Simon, B (1986) 'The 1944 Education Act: A Conservative measure?' in Vol 15 No 1 *History of Education*, pp 31–43

Skinner, G (1990) 'Religion, Culture and Education' in Pumfrey, P and Varma, G (eds) *Race Relations and Urban Education*, The Falmer Press: Basingstoke

Slaughter, M (1993) 'The Salman Rushdie Affair: Apostasy, Honor and Freedom of Speech' in Vol 79 No 1 *Virginia Law Review*, pp 153–204

Smart, N (1969) *The Religious Experience of Mankind*, Charles Scribner's Sons: New York

Smith, C (2003) 'The Place of Representatives of Religion in the Reformed Second Chamber' in *Public Law*, pp 674–696

Social Trends 1996 (1996) Her Majesty's Stationery Office: London

Social Trends 2006 (2006) Palgrave Macmillan: London

Stadler, N (2002) 'Is Profane Work an Obstacle to Salvation? The Case of Ultra Orthodox (Haredi) Jews in Contemporary Israel' in Vol 63 No 4 *Sociology of Religion*, pp 455–474

Stark, R (1999) 'Secularization: RIP' in Vol 60 No 3 *Sociology of Religion* pp 249–273

Statistics for Mission 2005 (2007) www.cofe.anglican.org

Statistics of Education: Schools in England: 2004 edition (2004) Her Majesty's Stationery Office: London

Stekel, W (1953) *Disorders of the Instincts and the Emotions: The Psychology of Hatred and Cruelty: Volume One*, Vision Press: London

Stone, L (1990) *The Road to Divorce*, Oxford University Press: Oxford

Stone, O (1960) 'The Last of the "In-Laws" ' in Vol 23 No 5 *Modern Law Review*, pp 538–540

Stoper, G (2003) 'Countenancing the oppression of women: How liberals tolerate religious and cultural practices that discriminate against women' in Vol 12 No 1 *Columbia Journal of Gender and Law*, pp 154–221

Swann Committee (1985) *Education for All: Report of the Committee of Inquiry into the Education of Children from Ethnic Minority Groups*, Cmnd 9453, Her Majesty's Stationery Office: London

Swatos, Jr, W and Christian, O (1999) 'Secularization Theory: the Course of a Concept' in Vol 60 No 3 *Sociology of Religion*, pp 209–228

Tamanaha, B (2001) *A General Jurisprudence of Law and Society*, Oxford University Press: Oxford

Tarlo, E (2005) 'Reconsidering stereotypes: Anthropological reflections on the *jilbab* controversy' in Vol 21 No 6 *Anthropology Today*, pp 13–17

Taylor, C (1994) 'The Politics of Recognition' in Gutmann, A (ed) *Multiculturalism: Examining the Politics of Recognition*, Princeton University Press: Princeton

Taylor, C (2007) *A Secular Age*, The Belknap Press of Harvard University Press: Cambridge, Massachusetts

Taylor, D (1987) 'The Community of the Many Names of God: A Saivite ashram in rural Wales' in Burghart, R (ed) *Hinduism in Great Britain: The Perpetuation of Religion in an Alien Cultural Milieu*, Tavistock Publications: London

Taylor, M (1989) *Religious Education Values and Worship: LEA Advisers' Perspectives on the Implementation of the Education Reform Act 1988*, National Foundation for Educational Research: Slough

Taylor, P (2005) *Freedom of Religion: UN and European Human Rights Law and Practice*, Cambridge University Press: Cambridge

Taylor, S (2003) 'Disestablished Establishment: High and Earthed Establishment in the Church in Wales' in Vol 18 No 2 *Journal of Contemporary Religion*, pp 227–240

Taylor, T (1957) 'Church and State in Scotland' in *Juridical Review*, pp 121–137

Thatcher, M (1993) *The Downing Street Years*, HarperCollins Publishers: London

Thompson, P (2004) *Whatever Happened to Religious Education*, The Lutterworth Press: Cambridge

Tonnies, F (1955) *Community and Association*, Routledge and Kegan Paul: London

Torke, J (1995–1996) 'The English Religious Establishment' in Vol 12 No 2 *Journal of Law and Religion*, pp 399–445

Unsworth, C (1995) 'Blasphemy, Cultural Divergence and Legal Relativism' in Vol 58 No 4 *Modern Law Review*, pp 658–677

Valins, O (2000) 'Institutionalised religion: sacred texts and Jewish spatial practice' in Vol 31 No 4 *Geoforum*, pp 575–586

Valins, O (2003) 'Stubborn identities and the construction of socio-spatial boundaries: ultra-orthodox Jews living in contemporary Britain' in Vol 28 No 3 *Transactions of the Institute of British Geographers*, pp 158–175

Vandeveer, D (1979) 'Coercive Restraint of Offensive Actions' in Vol 8 No 2 *Philosophy and Public Affairs*, pp 175–193

Vickers, L (2008) *Religious Freedom, Religious Discrimination and the Workplace*, Hart Publishing: Oxford

Vincent, C and Tomlinson, S (1997) 'Home-school relationships: "The swarming of disciplinary mechanisms"?' in Vol 23 No 3 *British Journal of Educational Research*, pp 361–378

Vitta, E (1970) 'The Conflict of Personal Laws' in Vol 5 No 1 *Israel Law Review*, pp 170–202

Voas, D (2006) 'Religious Decline in Scotland: New Evidence on Timing and Spatial Patterns' in Vol 45 No 1 *Journal for the Scientific Study of Religion*, pp 107–118

Voas, D (2007) 'Does religion belong in population studies?' in Vol 39 No 5 *Environment and Planning A*, pp 1166–1180

Voas, D and Crockett, A (2005) 'Religion in Britain: Neither Believing nor Belonging' in Vol 39 No 1 *Sociology*, pp 11–28

Wakeham, Lord (2000) *A House for the Future*, Cm 4534

Waldron, J (1988) 'Locke: toleration and the rationality of persecution' in Mendus, S (ed) *Justifying Toleration: Conceptual and Historical Perspectives*, Cambridge University Press: Cambridge

Waldron, J (1989) 'Legislation and moral neutrality' in Goodin, R and Reeve, A (eds) *Liberal Neutrality*, Routledge: London

Waldron, J (1993) 'Rushdie and Religion' in Waldron, J *Liberal Rights: Collected Papers 1981–1991*, Cambridge University Press: Cambridge

Waldron, J (2003) 'Toleration and Reasonableness' in McKinnon, C and Castiglione, D (eds) *The culture of toleration in diverse societies: Reasonable tolerance*, Manchester University Press: Manchester

Walford, G (1995) *Educational Politics: Pressure groups and faith-based schools*, Avebury: Aldershot

Walker, D (1983) *Principles of Scottish Private Law: Volume IV*, Clarendon Press: Oxford

Wallace, R (1981) 'The Origins and Authorship of the 1944 Education Act' in Vol 10 No 4 *History of Education*, pp 283–290

Warnock, M (1987) 'The Limits of Toleration' in Mendus, S and Edwards, D (eds) *On Toleration*, Clarendon Press: Oxford

Watkin, T (1990–1992) 'Vestiges of Establishment: The Ecclesiastical and Canon Law of the Church in Wales' in Vol 2 *Ecclesiastical Law Journal*, pp 110–119

Watson, J (2001) 'OFSTED's Spiritual Dimension: an analytical audit of inspection reports' in Vol 31 No 2 *Cambridge Journal of Education*, pp 205–219

Weale, A (1985) 'Toleration, individual differences and respect for persons' in Horton, J and Mendus, S (eds) *Aspects of Toleration: Philosophical Studies*, Methuen: London

Webster, R (1990) *A Brief History of Blasphemy: Liberalism, Censorship and 'The Satanic Verses'*, The Orwell Press: Southwold

Weinberg, M (1976) 'The Law of Testimonial Oaths and Affirmations' in Vol 3 No 1 *Monash University Law Review*, pp 25–40

Weller, P (ed) (2001) *Religions in the UK: 2001–03*, University of Derby: Derby

Weller, P (2004) 'Identity, Politics, and the Future(s) of Religion in the UK: The Case of The Religion Questions in the 2001 Decennial Census' in Vol 19 No 1 *Journal of Contemporary Religion*, pp 3–21

Welsh, M and Smith, A (1995) 'Cystic Fibrosis' in Vol 273 No 6 *Scientific American*, pp 52–60

Werbner, P (2005) 'Islamophobia: incitement to religious hatred – legislating for a new fear?' in Vol 21 No 1 *Anthropology Today*, pp 5–9

White, C (1998) 'Law, Policing and the Criminal Justice System' in Hainsworth, P (ed) *Divided Society: Ethnic Minorities and Racism in Northern Ireland*, Pluto Press: London

White, J (1994) 'Instead of OFSTED: A Critical Discussion of OFSTED on "Spiritual, Moral, Social and Cultural Development" ' in Vol 24 No 3 *Cambridge Journal of Education*, pp 369–378

White, J (2004) 'Should religious education be a compulsory school subject?' in Vol 26 No 2 *British Journal of Religious Education*, pp 151–144

Williams, D (1967) *Keeping the Peace*, Hutchinson: London

Williams, R (2008a) *The James Callaghan Memorial Lecture: Religious Hatred and Religious Offence*, www.archbishopofcanterbury.org/1301

Williams, R (2008b) *Civil and Religious Law in England: a Religious Perspective*, www.archbishopofcanterbury.org/1575

Wilson, B (1982) *Religion in Sociological Perspective*, Oxford University Press: Oxford

Wilson, B (1988) 'Religion in the Modern World' in Sutherland, S and Clarke, P (eds) *The Study of Religions: Traditional and New Religion*, Routledge: London

Wolf, S (1994) 'Comment' in Gutmann, A (ed) *Multiculturalism: Examining the Politics of Recognition*, Princeton University Press: Princeton

Wright, A (2003) 'Freedom, Equality, Fraternity? Towards a Liberal Defence of Faith Schools' in Vol 25 No 2 *British Journal of Religious Education*, pp 142–152

Yanay, N (2002) 'Understanding Collective Hatred' in Vol 2 No 1 *Analyses of Social Issues and Public Policy*, pp 53–60

Yilmaz, I (2001) 'Law as Chameleon' in Vol 21 No 2 *Journal of Muslim Minority Affairs*, pp 297–308

Yilmaz, I (2002) 'The challenge of post-modern legality and Muslim legal pluralism in England' in Vol 28 No 2 *Journal of Ethnic and Migration Studies*, pp 343–354

Yilmaz, I (2005) *Muslim Laws, Politics and Society in Modern Nation States: Dynamic Legal Pluralisms in England, Turkey and Pakistan*, Ashgate: Aldershot

Yip, A (2003) 'The Self as the Basis of Religious Faith: Spirituality of Gay, Lesbian and Bisexual Christians' in Davie, G, Heelas, P and Woodhead, L (eds) *Predicting Religion: Christian, Secular and Alternative Futures*, Ashgate: Aldershot

Young, H (1991) *One of Us*, Macmillan London: London

Yousif, A (2000) 'Islam, Minorities and Religious Freedom: A Challenge to Modern Theory of Pluralism' in Vol 20 No 1 *Journal of Muslim Minority Affairs*, pp 29–41

Index